The Owner-Managed Business

The Owner-Managed Business

Austin Moore Solicitor

Butterworths
London, Edinburgh and Dublin
1998

United Kingdom	Butterworths, a Division of Reed Elsevier (UK) Ltd, Halsbury House, 35 Chancery Lane, LONDON WC2A 1EL and 4 Hill Street, EDINBURGH EH2 3JZ
Australia	Butterworths, SYDNEY, ADELAIDE, BRISBANE, CANBERRA, MELBOURNE and PERTH
Canada	Butterworths Canada Ltd, TORONTO and VANCOUVER
Ireland	Butterworth (Ireland) Ltd, DUBLIN
Malaysia	Malayan Law Journal Sdn Bhd, KUALA LUMPUR
New Zealand	Butterworths of New Zealand Ltd, WELLINGTON and AUCKLAND
Singapore	Reed Elsevier (Singapore) Pte Ltd, SINGAPORE
South Africa	Butterworths Publishers (Pty) Ltd, DURBAN
USA	Michie, CHARLOTTESVILLE, Virginia

A CIP Catalogue record for this book is available from the British Library.

ISBN 0 406 89596 1

Typeset by M Rules, London
Printed and bound in Great Britain by Mackays of Chatham plc, Chatham, Kent

Preface

The choice of title to this book was not immediately obvious. The objective in writing it was to draw together a number of issues and regulatory requirements facing new and emerging businesses regarding their structure and administration. I was not attracted to titles such as 'Business Start-up' or 'Business Formation', because they might indicate that the book was limited to the initial steps and to very modest businesses. The fact is that the majority of businesses satisfy the very basic criterion to be an owner-managed business, namely that they are managed by their owners. This includes some very substantial companies and includes family companies, management buyout vehicles and 'partnership companies'.

So how do I justify a separate text on owner-managed businesses? The principal legislation governing limited companies, being the Companies Act 1985, would apply equally to an owner-managed business as to the subsidiary of a multinational. The standard works on company law provide perfectly adequate commentary on the legislation and case law. I think it is, however, fair to say that there is more concentration on issues facing large groups and public companies and the division of powers and responsibilities of directors and shareholders, rather than particular problems facing companies where the directors and shareholders are one and the same. The same comment could be made concerning the established works on company and commercial law precedents. It is easier to find a suggested form of shareholders' agreement of a very substantial length which is more in the nature of a joint venture agreement than to find a simple agreement which might be easier to use (and easier for the client to grapple with) in relation to a management buyout vehicle.

I would like to play a very small part in encouraging legal agreements to be simpler and more concise. The volume and complexity of English law continues to increase and commercial clients become more sophisticated and demanding. This makes it increasingly difficult to remain concise without being imprecise or ambiguous. Clients want their agreements to be tailored to particular situations rather than 'standard'. The only way the busy practitioner is going to achieve that is to have straightforward and relatively short precedents at his or her disposal which can be adapted and tailored to each case. This book aims to provide the practitioner with such precedents.

This book is primarily aimed at legal practitioners although it will also be of use to accountants and business people who are involved in advising owner-managed businesses. The book could be read as an introductory text by a lawyer with limited experience of the topics covered. It is, however, intended to be of use to established practitioners of corporate and commercial law and as a fresh approach to the legal issues viewed specifically from the owner-manager's perspective. The book should be used in conjunction with statutory and case materials and more detailed reference works on company law in appropriate cases. It is intended that this book should assist in indentifying key issues so the practitioner is at least on the right track. The writer would be pleased to think that this book remained by the practitioner's side for regular reference rather than lying on a library shelf.

I would like to thank my colleagues Mark Rutherford and Gavin White for their assistance in compiling this book and special thanks to Melanie Roper for her exceptional word processing skills.

Austin Moore

Contents

Table of statutes

References in this Table to *Statutes* are to Halsbury's Statutes of England showing the volume and page at which the annotated text of the Act will be found.
References in **bold** type indicate where the section of an Act is set out in part or in full.

Table of statutory instruments

Part I

Commentary

1 Introduction

Scope

1.1 The term 'owner-managed business' or OMB refers to any business where the individuals who have day-to-day management responsibilities for the operations of the business are also its proprietors. It thus covers virtually all sole traders and partnerships. Whilst statistics cannot be exact on this, it is thought to cover the majority of limited companies in the United Kingdom. It is also thought that the majority of the workforce in the United Kingdom is employed by OMBs.

1.2 Whilst the expression may have only gained popularity in recent years, the concept of an owner-manager is as old as commerce itself. However, certain institutions in the banking and accounting worlds use the OMB label in relation to a specific sector of their market. Since it is a matter of choice (and to an extent 'marketing'), individual institutions may have different parameters for the OMB category (just as a 'small business' means something totally different to a high street accounting firm and to one of the international firms). Whilst rather subjective, the attributes the writer would expect from a business with the OMB label would include:

(a) hard working managers with a stake in the business;
(b) probably undergoing relatively rapid growth or expansion;
(c) expecting to undergo significant changes in the short to medium term, either through acquisition, sale or introduction of additional capital;
(d) a special reason why they are successful, whether in terms of product, expertise, service or other competitive advantage.

1.3 It is important to appreciate that this book only assumes that the OMB is *controlled* by its management and not necessarily that it is *owned outright*. It is in fact a key feature of this sector that it may have or be considering outside investment in the form of venture capital, development capital or other outside investors. In fact, much of the corporate legal work for OMBs relates to that relationship with outside investors.

Why write this book?

1.4 There is no separate body of law relevant to OMBs and there is certainly no attempt to portray the subject matter of this book as a separate legal specialism. The first justification for a book on this subject is that the Companies Act 1985 and related legislation assumes that the owners (shareholders) will be different persons from the managers (directors). Thus the relationship between owner-managers is unlikely to be adequately reflected by relying on the general law. Secondly, the OMB sector of the market for legal services tends to require a particular approach. Clients are likely to be busy, demanding and cost conscious particularly in the 'start up' phase. They are therefore liable to require a direct and pragmatic approach. These factors point to the difficulty of passing the client round a number of lawyers specialising in particular fields of corporate and commercial law. At the risk of gross generalisation, the likelihood is that the OMB client will latch upon a commercially minded lawyer and consult him or her on a variety of issues on a regular basis. This would be a challenge in itself, given the increasing complexity of commercial law, but this book aims to cover a number of relevant fields in a 'package'.

Growth potential

1.5 Not all OMBs are aiming to attract new capital or develop in any way other than through steady organic growth. However, one of the key attractions of taking on small- to medium-sized clients is the prospect of some of them developing into large clients in years to come. Client loyalty is no longer guaranteed but it can be earned. Amongst the ways a lawyer can assure his future with a developing client are the following:

(a) obviously, giving good advice;
(b) becoming immersed in the client's affairs and thereby gaining a commercial understanding of the business;
(c) amassing knowledge of past dealings which may even surpass the client's memory of them;
(d) personal bonding with key individuals, having been through 'thick and thin'.

1.6 A developing client may possess little or no experience of corporate and financial matters. There is no situation where a corporate/commercial lawyer plays a more important part. Good decisions and bad decisions made now can have a long lasting effect. From the point of view of documentation, the complexity of the terms may be equal to that of transactions of ten times the value and it is thus not possible to compromise on advice on documents just because values are low. Firstly, those amounts are liable to be very important to the persons concerned. Secondly, the level of financial tolerance involved in these transactions is liable to be very small. Thirdly, a shareholders agreement (for example) for a start up company may end up being construed by a court in future years when the company is very valuable indeed.

The challenge for lawyers

1.7 Having created a stereotypical picture of an OMB client, the challenge for the lawyer is to deliver legal services which are clear, concise, commonsensical and cost conscious. Table 1 sets out a checklist of basic information to be gleaned in respect of a new OMB client. Not all of this information could (or should) be obtained at the first meeting and some of it may be totally irrelevant in a given case. The purpose of considering this checklist is to encourage understanding of the client. This should enable the lawyer to gain one of the most vital attributes in respect of client dealings, namely empathy.

TABLE 1: CHECKLIST ON ACTING FOR OMB CLIENT

1. Names and home addresses of the managers, dates of birth, job descriptions and special responsibilities.
2. Why did they instruct you and (if relevant) who was involved in that decision? Who if anyone does not know that you are instructed?
3. In the case of a company, full details of share capital and shareholders.
4. Are there any shareholder agreements or (where relevant) written or oral understandings between the parties about their relationships?
5. Details of any service agreements and remuneration packages (where appropriate to ask).
6. Details of any previous or existing legal advisers and of the relationship with such advisers.
7. Details of accountants and other relevant advisers and bankers, how they view those relationships and how those relationships came about. Whether you may speak to those other advisers.
8. In due course and over time, details of personal interests and aspirations, family and leisure interests.
9. Is there is a business plan which is up to date? Can or should you read it. When will you be able to meet other members of the management team, visit their premises and have a brief explanation of their business operations?
10. Obtaining an understanding about costs. Do they want you to work on an estimate or a quotation or within a budget? Do they want regular advice on the amount of charges and perhaps even to be billed monthly?
11. Are there other lawyers within the practice they should meet?
12. Do they have adequate details of you, such as direct and mobile telephone numbers, where appropriate home telephone number, name of your secretary and (where relevant) other lawyers involved in the matter.
13. Should they receive a brochure and/or details of other legal services provided by the firm?
14. Where should an engagement letter be sent?

2 Choice of business medium

Available choices

2.1 The basic choice of medium is between carrying on a business personally whether as a sole trader or in partnership or carrying on a business through a limited company. There are other choices, such as an unlimited company or a limited partnership but these are of restricted application and so are not dealt with in this book. The purpose of this section is to examine the distinctions between these media and factors which might influence the OMB to choose one or the other.

2.2 Where the business is carried on by a sole trader or a partnership, the essential characteristic is that the individual (or each of the individual partners) carries on the business in his or her own right, contracting personally with customers and suppliers. It thus follows that the individual attracts personal liability in respect of all of the obligations of the business and that such liability is unlimited as against third parties. A partnership is not recognised as a distinct legal entity under English law and so it is the individuals themselves who are carrying on a partnership business. Even a so-called 'silent partner' normally shares joint liability with fellow partners.

2.3 Where a limited company is formed, the company is a separate legal entity with an existence independent of its owners. It thus follows that the company contracts with customers and suppliers, engages employees and normally owns the assets used in the business. Save where the owner-managers give personal guarantees or are liable under a statute or the general law in respect of their actions as officers of the company, they will not have personal liability for the debts and obligations of the company. It is far more possible for an individual wishing to invest in a limited company to play no active part in management without the same degree of responsibility as a partner would have.

2.4 The factors influencing a choice between carrying on business through a limited company and carrying on business as a sole trader or partner can be divided into the following four features for each medium:

(a) the relative ease of creation;
(b) the manner of operation;
(c) the relative ease of disposal;
(d) taxation considerations.

Relative ease of creation

2.5 Two factors may be influential: speed and cost. The extent to which legal or other formalities are involved will have a direct bearing on these key factors. There are no formalities necessarily involved prior to the establishment of a sole trader or partnership business. The relation of partners subsists from the moment the statutory definition in the Partnership Act 1890, s 1 is met. The business is established de facto from the moment trading commences. Although all types of business need to comply with the various legal requirements of revenue and other governmental authorities, in the case of a sole trader or partnership business such compliance is in no way a prerequisite to the legal establishment of the business. As a result of this, a partnership or sole trader business may be established with little time delay and at little or no cost.

2.6 To trade through a company necessitates the formation of a limited company. The proprietors will not enjoy the benefits of the company's separate legal existence until a certificate of incorporation has been issued, denoting that the company has entered into legal existence. The formation of a new company entails an application in statutory form to the Registrar of Companies and the payment of a registration fee (as to which see section 3). Because of these procedural formalities there is prima facie a greater cost and time involved in forming a company. These apparent disadvantages can be substantially reduced by the use of 'off-the-shelf' companies, ie companies previously established by company formation agents and stock piled available for immediate use. The essential requirement is that these companies have not previously traded, a certificate to that effect being commonly supplied to the purchaser.

2.7 However, due to the many vagaries of partnership law and company law the legal adviser in each case may well recommend that the participators in the business clearly define their respective roles and responsibilities through a contract between them: a partnership agreement or, in the case of a limited company, a shareholders' agreement. Whilst prima facie the creation of a partnership appears to have advantages both in terms of time-scale and costs, the use of ready-made companies can redress any timing difficulties and the advisability of a formal agreement will, in the majority of cases, serve to substantially diminish, if not eradicate entirely, any differential on the costs of establishment.

2.8 As a result the differences are unlikely of themselves to be a significant factor in the majority of cases in the decision-making process.

Manner of operation

2.9 At the heart of the distinction between the sole trader/partnership business and the limited company is the relationship which subsists between owners and the company. As previously stated, the limited company, once incorporated, is a separate legal entity with an existence independent of its proprietors. As a result the limited company may own property, enter into its own contracts and incur its own debts. The company may sue or be sued in its corporate name.

2.10 It is the company which carries on the business. The shareholders of the limited company are not generally liable for the debts or other commitments of the company. They benefit from limited liability. If the shares are issued 'fully paid', then in the event of the company incurring liabilities which exceed available assets, resulting in the failure and liquidation of the company, the members cannot be called to contribute further to meet the shortfall to creditors. The value of their investment is lost but the personal estates of the members are not further jeopardised by the business failure. By contrast, a sole trader or partnership does not have a legal existence independent of the individuals. Accordingly, the individual sole trader or partners are liable to the full extent of their personal estates to meet business liabilities incurred. This legal distinction, the ability of the owner of a company to be at 'one step removed' from the trading business, constitutes a significant advantage to the owner in conducting business through a limited company.

2.11 However, as this concept of limited liability places a significant limitation on the remedies available to creditors of a failing business it is hardly surprising that practical measures have been developed for the benefit of creditors which serve to undermine (in part) the apparent advantages of a limited liability company. It is common for certain categories of creditor, when dealing with a limited company, to seek from the proprietors personal guarantees of the company's liabilities. Such guarantees are commonly insisted upon by the major voluntary creditors, such as the company's bankers, finance companies (in respect of operational leases) and the landlord of leasehold premises occupied by the company. Newly established businesses may be unable to establish credit lines for the acquisition of goods and services from suppliers without the furnishment by the owners of personal guarantees, although this practice is far from common-place. Involuntary creditors of a company, such as HM Customs and Excise (in respect of VAT) and the Inland Revenue (in respect of taxation, particularly employees' income tax collected under the PAYE system), do not have the option of insisting upon the provision of personal guarantees.

2.12 Because of the likelihood that trade credit lines will be available in the absence of personal guarantees, and the position of revenue creditors already referred to, there are still advantages to the owner in establishing a limited company. Further, customers of the business (particularly consumers) are unlikely to insist upon personal guarantees in respect of supplies made. Resultant claims covering matters such as defective goods would be a matter for the company alone. These advantages must, however, be weighed against other factors considered below. The legal adviser may be able to assist the sole trader or partnership in minimising the exposure to business creditors of personal assets. For instance, the extent to which potential liabilities may be the subject of insurance cover at commercially acceptable rates should be examined.

2.13 The sole trader has the sole right and responsibility for the management and conduct of his business. He may engage staff to assist but ultimately the responsibilities vest in him alone. Similarly, in the case of a partnership, it is a fundamental right of each partner, in the absence of any agreement to the contrary between the partners, to be involved in the management of the partnership business. This contrasts with a limited company where the functions of the owners (shareholders) and the managers (directors) are clearly distinct even in the case of an OMB. The separation of functions is most commonly regulated by the company's articles of association but this distinction is also recognised, even reinforced, by statute.

2.14 Further, as the roles of owner and manager are in a limited company generally distinct, an individual may be removed from office as manager whilst continuing to enjoy the benefits of ownership. In the case of OMBs, this statement must be made subject to the rights of shareholders to remain involved in management by reason of any agreement or arrangement made or to be implied between them to the effect that the company's affairs would be conducted as a quasi-partnership. This may entitle them, inter alia, to petition for relief under the Companies Act 1985, s 459 (as to which see section 4.40). In the case of a partnership in the absence of an agreement to the contrary, under the terms of the Partnership Act 1890 each partner is allowed to participate in management however unsuitable they may be. There are only limited grounds for removing rights of management and even then such change cannot be brought about, under the terms of the Act, without a dissolution of the partnership.

2.15 In the case of OMBs the respective management roles to be performed by individual partners or directors/shareholders (including any limitation on the implied powers and authorities) are matters usually regulated by agreement between the owners. The differences between the two alternative business media are thus likely to be of lesser importance.

Agency

2.16 The laws of agency are applicable both to partnerships and limited companies. A limited company has no physical as opposed to legal personality and therefore depends entirely upon agents, typically the directors and other persons appointed to specific executive positions, to conduct its business. The members, qua members, having no management role, do not have the power to act as agent. This distinction is liable to be of minimal importance in the case of an OMB since the shareholders will almost certainly be directors.

Raising capital

2.17 It is in the area of the raising of finance that the advantages of a corporate structure are most readily seen. A limited company, unlike a sole trader or partnership, is able to offer security in the form of a floating charge over its assets. This form of charge is commonly comprised within the standard security documents known as debentures taken by clearing banks and other lending institutions. An individual may not grant this form of security. Such a charge, if granted by an individual in respect of personal chattels, would constitute a registrable bill of sale under the Bills of Sale Acts. Accordingly, the scope for raising bank finance secured upon the assets of the business is substantially reduced. Depending upon the nature of the business, it is highly likely that the majority (in value terms) of business assets of a new or emerging business are of a classification that can be made the subject of a floating charge only, not a fixed charge. Examples of such assets are stocks and work in progress and loose plant and equipment.

2.18 Similarly, the scope for introducing equity capital is limited in the case of a partnership. Given the risks of unlimited liability under constraints of the partnership capital structure, institutional equity capital commonly provided by venture capitalists may not be as readily available for non-corporate businesses. This type of investment is characterised by the creation of special rights to participate in income coupled with special negative control rights in relation to fundamental matters concerning the business. Such requirements lend themselves most naturally to the corporate structure with the possibility of creation of tailor-made classes of shares embodying the special rights.

Reporting requirements

2.19 Even accepting the practical constraints, there is a clear advantage to the proprietors of a limited company in obtaining the benefit of limited liability. It may be said that the quid pro quo for this and other advantages of a corporate structure is the increased level of statutory compliance. The principle statutory source is the Companies Act 1985 (as amended) which prescribes a multitude of regulatory and reporting obligations which are reinforced by a system of criminal sanctions (principally financial penalties) which may be levied against defaulting companies and their officers.

2.20 The main areas in which a company's reporting obligations are greater than that of a partnership or sole trader are in the areas of public access to financial and other information concerning the company. Information is made available to the public either through the system of filing and returns which companies are obliged to make under the Companies Act or through the provision of information to individual members of the public on application. In addition to the information made available to members of the public by either means, shareholders have enhanced entitlement to receive information as of right or to be furnished with information upon request. Information to which members of the public may obtain access (CA 1985, s 709), via company search agents or credit reference agencies, most commonly includes:

(a) details of company officers;
(b) annual accounts and directors' statement;
(c) documentation relating to the establishment of the company, first appointed officers and memorandum and articles (these documents to be updated from time to time);
(d) an annual return lodged with the annual accounts providing up-dated information on changes in company officers and shareholders;
(e) the charges register giving details of debentures, mortgages and other registerable charges.

2.21 The financial accounts of a limited company, unlike a normal trading partnership or sole trader, are required to be the subject of an independent audit except in the case of companies with a turnover less than £350,000. For further detail of the exemption from audit for such companies, see the Companies Act 1985 (Audit Exemption) (Amendment) Regulations 1997, SI 1997/936, which came into force on 15 April 1997 and apply to a small company's accounts in respect of any financial year ending two months or more after that date.

2.22 Notwithstanding the available exemptions for small companies in respect of the content of annual accounts (and, where relevant, the audit of those accounts) which must be made available, these accounting obligations have the effect of:

(a) increasing the level of regulatory control over the conduct of a company's business with a consequent increase in management time necessarily spent to ensure compliance;
(b) raising the costs of compliance, auditors and other fees;
(c) the diminution in privacy of the business affairs of the proprietors concerning the structure, financing and performance of the business. This information is made generally available to competitors and others.

2.23 Whilst annual accounts and taxation returns must be made to the Inland Revenue by sole traders and partnerships there is not the same on-going reporting obligation. This is essentially a private matter between the business and the relevant authorities.

Ease of disposal

2.24 A sole trader is obviously free from any constraints upon his ability to dispose of his business, subject only to his being able to find a purchaser. Similarly, shares in a limited company are freely transferable subject, as is most commonly the case, to any restrictions in the company's memorandum and articles. A partnership share may be assigned, although this will confer on the assignee financial entitlements only, not a right of participation (see the Partnership Act 1890, s 31). Assignment may be prohibited under the terms of a partnership agreement. A decision to introduce a new partner requires unanimity (PA 1890, s 24).

2.25 There are, therefore, prima facie significant drawbacks in a partnership structure, certainly in partnerships regulated by the implied terms contained in the Partnership Act 1890, when compared with a limited company. What must be borne in mind is the equalising influence of a company's articles of association which, in the case of a private company, may place restrictions upon the transfer of shares akin to those facing a partnership. There is also the practical limitation facing an individual who wishes to dispose of a minority shareholding in a limited company. There may be insurmountable difficulties facing the investor wishing to realise the investment in finding a buyer himself willing to accept shares subject to restrictions on subsequent disposal and without the right to participate in management.

2.26 In both partnership or limited company structures particularly in the case of OMBs the individual participator must consider the possibility of their being 'locked in' to their investment with the only possibility of an exit route being a dissolution of the partnership or liquidation of the company (with possible adverse commercial and taxation ramifications). With a partnership at will there is at least the possibility of a guaranteed exit route by giving notice of a dissolution (however unpalatable the consequences). With a limited company there are very limited grounds for securing an exit in the absence of agreement between all (or at least 75% by voting rights of) participators to procure winding up or sale of the company. Due to the practical problems associated with realisation of investment it is advisable for these matters to be formally regulated under a shareholders' agreement or partnership agreement.

Taxation considerations

2.27 The different taxation treatment of sole traders and partnerships on the one hand and limited companies on the other hand is liable to be a serious consideration in deciding on which business medium to choose and indeed for a sole trader or partnership which is subsequently considering the incorporation of his business. It is particularly important to bear in mind that the separate legal personality of a limited company means that the company is liable to corporation tax on its income profits and capital gains and in addition the individual owner-managers will be subject to taxation on amounts they receive from the company whether by way of remuneration for services, income or capital distributions or indeed on the sale of their shares.

2.28 The paragraphs below are intended to highlight the differences between the different business media by way of overview and for detailed consideration of these terms, it will be necessary to consult the standard texts on taxation. Note also that the rates, limits and figures set out below are based on those applying for the tax year 1997/98 and those details will be subject to regular change.

2.29 A company whose profits for an accounting period do not exceed the upper relevant maximum amount (£1,500,000 for the tax year 1997/98) may benefit from the small companies' rate of corporation tax. Where profits do not exceed the lower relevant maximum amount (£300,000 for tax year 1997/98), they are taxed at the small companies' rate (21% for tax year 1997/98). Where profits fall between the lower and upper amounts, tapering relief applies. Profits are charged to tax at the full corporation tax rate and then a deduction is made, the amount of which is determined by reference to a statutory formula (applying a marginal rate being 33.5% for tax year 1997/98). The effect is to provide a smooth graduation in the average rate of corporation tax from 21% to 31%.

2.30 A sole trader is subject to tax at 40% where income from all sources exceeds £30,145 (taking into account the trader's personal allowance of £4,045 for tax year 1997/98). A company with profits not exceeding £300,000 pays corporation tax at the small companies' rate of 21% as noted above.

2.31 A perceived benefit here is a reduction from 40% to 21% in the tax borne by the profits. This benefit is partly illusory, because it is a benefit only if profits are retained in the company. A distribution of profits by the company gives rise to a tax liability in the hands of the recipient. In the case of dividends, for example, there may be double taxation. Where a company disposes of an asset it is liable to corporation tax on the chargeable gain arising. The company may pass that profit to the shareholder by way of dividend. Dividends are not deductible when calculating the company's liability to corporation tax.

Dividends are then taxed in the hands of the recipient, although he should have the advantage of the associated tax credit. At best, therefore, a distribution of profits by a company is tax neutral but could, in some situations, be positively disadvantageous (see paragraph below).

2.32 A partner or sole trader is charged to tax whether or not he extracts profits. On distributing profits, a company must pay advance corporation tax ('ACT') at the rate of one-quarter of the amount distributed. However, a recipient of a dividend who is an individual is treated as receiving a cash dividend plus a tax credit equal to the amount of ACT paid so that the ACT represents 20% of the gross amount received and satisfies his lower or basic-rate liability on the dividend. From April 1999 the tax credit regime is to change for individual shareholders. The rate of tax credit will be halved to 10% and tax credits will no longer be payable to shareholders with no tax liability.

2.33 Appropriations by partners or a sole trader are ignored when calculating taxable profits. A company's taxable profits are calculated by reference to profits as shown in the accounts. Salaries paid to employees are tax deductible (although taxable in the hands of the recipient).

2.34 Interest paid by an unincorporated business is only deductible for tax purposes if it is incurred wholly and exclusively for the purposes of the trade, and for certain qualifying purposes, eg for the purchase of land. Broadly, all interest paid by a company is deductible whether for investment purposes or not.

2.35 Tax on the profits of an unincorporated business is payable in two equal instalments; the first on 1 January in the year of assessment and the second on 1 July next. Corporation tax is payable nine months and one day after the end of a company's accounting period if an interest charge is to be avoided.

2.36 Losses of an incorporated business can be set against other income of a partner or sole trader. Losses of a company are available only to relieve profits of the company and not of its shareholders.

2.37 A sole trader or partner will pay Class 2 National Insurance Contributions of £6.15 per week plus Class 4 NIC at 6% on profits or gains between £7,010 and £24,180 per annum. Class 1 NICs are payable by both an employer-company and employees on the amount of salary paid. An employee's maximum contribution is £2,160 per annum. An employer's maximum annual contribution is on a sliding scale up to 10% of earnings paid with no maximum.

2.38 For partners or sole traders, a tax deduction is given for contributions to personal pension schemes by reference to earned income only. Both a company and an employee may contribute to either an exempt approved scheme or a personal pension scheme and the company's contributions are a deduction against profits.

2.39 The withdrawal of business goods for private use by partners or traders prevents a tax deduction of the cost or, alternatively, it is treated as an appropriation at market value of goods. A tax deduction is available to the company in most cases, but the employee will be assessed on the value of the goods as a benefit in kind. In addition, if the company is a close company (as defined for taxation purposes), there may be a deemed distribution to an employee-shareholder.

2.40 A share of profits due to a non-working spouse-partner is unlikely to be challenged by the Inland Revenue. Salary paid by a company to a non-working spouse or family member is not deductible.

2.41 Capital gains tax retirement relief is readily available for a partner or a sole trader. For a shareholder in a company, retirement relief restrictions might apply.

2.42 A share in a partnership normally qualifies for inheritance tax business property relief at 100%. Shareholdings in unquoted companies generally qualify for 100% relief but the provisions are somewhat more complex and a reduction in the level of the relief is perhaps more likely than in the case of the partnership shares. Different classes of shares can be used to reduce the value of the business in the hands of the shareholders for inheritance tax purposes. This is achieved, for example, by having one class of voting shares held by certain trusts or individuals, whilst non-voting shares which have preferential rights to income, or deferred rights, can be held by either party. In this way, the control premium element of any share valuation can be avoided, provided of course that the related property provisions do not apply.

2.43 In a partnership, where a car is used by a partner capital allowances are available only to the extent of business use. If, however, an employee or director of a company is provided with a car, capital allowances are available, but the employee or director is subject to scale charges which also apply for NIC Class 1A and VAT.

2.44 A close company is a company which is under the control of five or fewer participators, or of participators who are directors (without limitation on the number). A participator is a person who has shares or an interest in the capital or income of a company. Accordingly, most OMBs will be close companies. A company is also a close company if, on a winding up, more than half of its assets would be available to five or fewer participators, or to its directors (without limitation on the numbers).

2.45 If a company is a close company for tax purposes, three points need to be noted:

(a) If any loan is made to a participator or an associate of his by a close company, the company is required to notify the Inland Revenue and make a payment to them equal to advance corporation tax (although this payment is not advance corporation tax: in particular, the payment cannot be set against the company's mainstream corporation tax liability) (see ICTA 1988, s 419).
(b) The meaning of 'distribution' for tax purposes is extended for close company purposes to include expenditure incurred by the company in providing benefits in kind for participators or associates of participators and advance corporation tax must therefore be paid thereon (see ICTA 1988, s 418).

(c) Relief for the accruing discount element of a deep discount security issued by a close company, is, in some circumstances, only allowed on payment.

2.46 When a loan is subsequently repaid by a participator the tax is refunded on a claim being made. If a loan to a participator is released, then the tax paid becomes irrecoverable. The participator is treated for higher-rate purposes as receiving (in the tax year in which the release takes place) a sum equal to the amount released, grossed up at the lower rate of income tax (see ICTA 1988, s 421).

Disincorporation

2.47 Tax considerations on incorporation of a business are dealt with in section 3. Transferring the business of a company back into the hands of partners or a sole trader ('disincorporation') is generally not tax efficient. Capital gains will crystallise in the company on any disposal by the company of capital assets which have appreciated in value; balancing charges will be crystallised where the value of plant and machinery exceeds tax written down value for capital allowance purposes; stamp duty will be payable on the transfer of various assets; and losses which have accrued to the company will not be available to be passed to the partners or sole trader. To some extent, however, current year losses can be used against capital gains crystallised, and carried forward losses against any balancing charges. However, in the case of a successful business, its disincorporation will almost invariably be prohibited by the tax costs arising.

Franchising

2.48 Technically speaking franchising does not amount to an alternative business medium in that the franchisee will still carry on business as a sole trader, in partnership or through a limited company. The relationship with the franchisor is contractual, based on the franchise agreement which will invariably be prepared on behalf of the franchisor primarily to protect its interests. In brief outline, the contrasting factors of carrying on business through a franchise are as follows:

(a) the franchisee acquires some of the benefits of a business with an established goodwill in that it would enjoy the benefit of the trading name and reputation of the franchisor, although note that the goodwill must be capable of extending to the geographical location where the franchised business is to be established;
(b) the franchisee will also benefit from the established business systems and methods and know-how of the franchisor and from the provision of support in the establishment and operation of the business;
(c) as a result of the preceding two factors, the franchised business should be established in its own right more quickly and with less risk of failure although account must taken of fees and royalties payable to the franchisor out of trading income.

TABLE 2: COMPANY OR SOLE TRADER/PARTNERSHIP

Advantages of company

1. Limited liability for debts and liabilities (except where guaranteed or liability imposed by statute).
2. Ability to divorce management responsibilities from ownership.
3. Greater scope for bank borrowing, because of ability to grant floating charge over assets.
4. Easier mechanics for disposal of shares.
5. Lower rate of tax (usually) where profits are retained.
6. Less restriction on deductibility of interest.
7. Greater scope for tax avoidance in respect of disposal of shares.

Advantages of sole trader/partnership

1. Minimal formality (save that for partners, partnership agreement will be required).
2. Less regulation under statute, in particular as regards disclosure and audit of financial statements.
3. No double taxation or extraction of profits.
4. Freedom to set off losses against other income.
5. Generally lower national insurance contributions.
6. Less restriction on availability of retirement relief for capital gains tax purposes and business property relief for inheritance tax purposes.

3 Incorporation of an existing business

What is involved?

3.1 Incorporation of an existing business effectively comprises three elements:

(a) the formation of a new company (as to which see section 4);
(b) the purchase by the company of the business carried on by the sole proprietor or partners of the business;
(c) in the case of incorporation of a partnership, the ongoing relationship between the former partners as directors and shareholders of the company.

3.2 Reasons for incorporation are dealt with in section 2. The additional consequences of incorporating an existing business are dealt with below. Taxation is likely to be the major factor.

Formation issues

3.3 The procedure for formation of a company is dealt with in section 4. There is no substantive difference in the method of formation where the company is to be used as the vehicle for incorporation of an existing business. The parties may enter into a formation agreement which would provide for the company to be incorporated and purchase the business and also deals with the post-formation relationship of the parties. Given that 'off-the-shelf' companies can be obtained without any delay and the provisions for purchase of the business are best contained in a separate agreement anyway, it is submitted that there is little point in a formation agreement. Terms relating to the continuing relationship between the partners should be dealt with in a shareholders' agreement although that agreement may recite the circumstances in which it came about and should also (if this is the parties' intention) reflect the terms that previously applied between them as partners so far as possible.

Business sale

3.4 Document 1 in Part II comprises a precedent agreement for incorporation of a business. The principal differences between this precedent and a 'standard' business purchase agreement are as follows:

(a) the definition of the assets and rights to be transferred is wider in the case of the incorporation agreement, because the intention will invariably be to ensure that all assets and rights included in the business are included – note also that the inclusion of all assets (other than cash) is important for tax considerations as noted below;
(b) liabilities of the partnership other than in respect of taxation are to be assumed by the company, in contrast to the normal position on a business purchase where liabilities are not usually assumed: this obviously reflects the fact that the partners will wish all obligations to be discharged by the company;
(c) title covenants given by vendors are more likely to be restricted and no warranties are given by the vendors for obvious reasons;
(d) the consideration comprises the issue of shares in the company to the partners and the assumption of liabilities – note that this is not necessarily the case and cash consideration could be provided although this would have an effect on the taxation position of the vendors and on the solvency of the company.

3.5 As in the case of any business purchase, contracts with customers and suppliers may not be assignable without third-party consents and the parties should still apply for these or risk being in breach of contract. It is possible that consent to the assignment may only be obtained on terms that the vendors guarantee the obligations of the company. This should not be a problem, provided it is limited to existing obligations, since the vendors are already personally liable as the original contracting party. If there are assets held on hire purchase lease or other finance terms, the transfer to the company will almost certainly require consent from the relevant finance company. Often the parties will allow the finance agreement to continue in the names of the vendors although technically this will amount to a breach of the terms of the finance agreement in that the vendors will be parting with possession of the assets to the company.

3.6 The parties should pay particular attention to the need to obtain any licences or authorisations to carry on business, bearing in mind that the company is a separate legal person. Many regulatory licences are not transferable so that the company will have to apply for a new licence in its own name. Care should be taken to ensure that any such application is made in good time so that the company is able to carry on business lawfully from the date the business is incorporated.

3.7 Similar considerations to those referred to in paragraph 3.5 apply in respect of property leases in that landlords' consent to assignment will usually be required and allowing a company to occupy the premises will usually amount to a breach of covenant. Where freehold property is to be transferred to the company, not only stamp duty (referred to below) but also Land Registry fees will be incurred.

Employees

3.8 As noted in the precedent agreement, the Transfer of Undertakings (Protection of Employment) Regulations 1981 ('the Transfer Regulations') will apply to the transfer to the company so that contracts of employment will transfer to the company under reg 5. The obligation to consult with any recognised trade union or employee representatives will also apply notwithstanding the internal nature of the transfer. The requirements to inform and consult employees are contained in the Collective Redundancies and Transfer of Undertakings (Protection of Employment) (Amendment) Regulations 1995, SI 1995/2587. These regulations require the vendors to provide information to the relevant representatives on the following:

(a) the fact that the relevant transfer is to take place, when approximately it is to take place and the reasons for it;
(b) the legal, economic and social implications of the transfer for the affected employees;
(c) the measures which the vendors envisage will be taken in relation to the employees (if any).

In relation to an incorporation of an existing business, there will usually be no planned changes to employment terms so consultation should be somewhat of a formality. It would not be safe, however, to ignore the requirement to consult given that failure can result in an award of up to four weeks' pay to each affected employee if an application is made to the industrial tribunal. The information must be provided to representatives long enough before the transfer to enable consultations to take place.

3.9 It should not be forgotten that the transfer is subject to the provisions of the Transfer Regulations in all respects. It follows that the company will be exposed to risk in relation to any dismissals made at or about the time of incorporation. It is not uncommon for incorporation of an existing business to take place at the same time as a restructuring of the business. Any dismissal for a reason connected with the transfer of the business on incorporation will be automatically unfair unless the purchaser can show that the reason for the dismissal was an economic, technical or organisational reason entailing changes in the workforce (reg 8). Given that this exception is quite restricted and is restrictively interpreted, it will be well to avoid dismissals at about the time of the incorporation or indeed changes to terms of employment which could entitle the employees to treat themselves as constructively dismissed.

3.10 Whilst rights in respect of occupational pension schemes do not transfer to the purchaser pursuant to the Transfer Regulations, the parties will doubtless amend their pension arrangements to take into account the incorporation.

Practical issues

3.11 As stated above, rights and obligations in respect of contracts may not be transferable to the purchaser without the consent of third parties. In any event, incorporation can create confusion and concern amongst the customers of the business which would of course be detrimental. For both these reasons, the parties should plan ahead for the announcement of incorporation to customers and suppliers. The vendors will often write to customers 'informing' them that with effect from a certain day all existing orders and contracts will be transferred to the company and any future payments should be addressed to the company. This may annoy important customers if they take the point that the contracts are not transferable. In addition, many customers will be anxious about addressing payments which are legally due to the vendors to the company. Customers will want to be sure that they obtain a good discharge by any such payment and that it is not taken as an acceptance that the vendors are no longer liable. The preferred method would be to stipulate that existing contracts remain with the vendors (even though as a matter of practice they may be completed by the company on behalf of the vendors) and that existing debts should continue to be paid to the vendors. The vendors of the company can provide between them for such money to be held on trust by the vendors for the purchaser. A residual difficulty remains in that the vendors will probably not wish to issue any further VAT invoices after completion and yet, if there are uncompleted contracts at completion which are not assigned with consent to the purchaser, this would be technically correct. If it is possible under the terms of the contract or is otherwise agreed with the relevant customer, the work done to the date of transfer would be invoiced or indeed the whole contract could be billed in advance.

Company law formalities

3.12 Document 2 in Part II comprises a set of draft board minutes and notice of extraordinary general meeting relevant to the incorporation of an existing business. These forms are designed for use in conjunction with the precedent agreement. Apart from the formalities for the issue of new shares as consideration for the purchase, the key company law issue is the approval by the shareholders of the purchase for the purposes of s 320 of the Companies Act 1985. The business will certainly include a non-cash asset and will invariably be of the requisite value to bring about the requirement for shareholder approval of the purchase (on the assumption that the vendors will be directors of the company at the relevant time).

3.13 Since there will be a new issue of shares in consideration of the transfer of business assets, it will be necessary to file with the Registrar of Companies form 88(2) and form 88(3) within one month after completion. Since form 88(2) must be accompanied by duly stamped particulars of the transfer (and form 88(3) must itself be stamped), the ability to avoid stamp duty on the transfer will be restricted.

Taxation considerations

3.14 If a trader transfers the whole of his business to a company he ceases, for tax purposes, to carry on the trade. The closing year rules will apply for businesses commenced prior to 6 April 1994 and tax is assessed in the final tax year on the actual profits from 6 April until cessation. In the penultimate and prepenultimate tax years the normal preceding year basis applies, but if the aggregate profits or gains of the trade of those two years exceeds income assessed on a preceding year basis, the Inland Revenue must elect to tax them on an actual basis. For businesses commenced after 5 April 1994 (for which the preceding year basis will not have applied) the final year's tax will be assessed on all of the profits since the last accounting period (see ICTA 1988, s 63).

Capital allowances

3.15 The incorporation of a business may involve the transfer to the company of items of plant and machinery on which the trader has claimed capital allowances. The trader would have been entitled to claim a writing-down allowance of 25% per annum of the pool on a reducing balance basis for each chargeable period during which there is a balance of qualifying expenditure to write down and during the whole of which the trade was being carried on.

3.16 When there is a disposal of plant, the general rule is that the consideration received is deducted from the pool of qualifying expenditure. The remaining balance is reduced by the writing-down allowance at the year end. Such a procedure, however, applies only while the trade continues. When a business is incorporated, the trade for this purpose ceases to exist. In the final year of assessment of an unincorporated business, no writing-down allowance is given. Additions are added to the pool of qualifying expenditure and final disposal proceeds are deducted. If the proceeds exceed the pool of qualifying expenditure, a balancing charge arises. If the balance of qualifying expenditure exceeds the proceeds, a balancing allowance is given.

3.17 Where the transferee and transferor are 'connected' as they will be where the purchaser is controlled by the vendors, they may elect for plant to be transferred at its tax written down value (see Capital Allowances Act 1990, s 77). The effect is that the transferee takes over the capital allowance position of the transferor. A balancing charge on the transferor can therefore be avoided.

Loss relief

3.18 Trading losses of a sole trader or partner which remain unrelieved on incorporation may be carried forward and set against income received by the trader from the company, provided that:

(a) the consideration for the transfer of the business to the company comprises solely or mainly (which is regarded by the Inland Revenue as meaning 80%) of the allotment of shares;
(b) the shares remain beneficially owned by the former trader throughout the tax year for which relief is sought; and
(c) the company continues to carry on the business throughout that tax year (ICTA 1988, s 386).

Relief is given against dividends, directors' remuneration etc.

3.19 A loss incurred in the last 12 months before a trade is discontinued is a terminal loss. Terminal loss relief may be claimed against 'available income' of the three tax years before the tax year in which the trade or business ceases. The loss is set off against income of the latest year first.

Capital Gains Tax

3.20 The transfer of assets by a trader to a company constitutes numerous disposals of assets by the trader for capital gains tax purposes. Computations of gains and losses are required in respect of each disposal. The disposals to the company may give rise to a number of chargeable gains and allowable losses.

3.21 A former trader and a company which he controls are connected persons for capital gains tax purposes (TCGA 1992, s 286). Where a person who is making a disposal of an asset is connected with the person acquiring the asset, they are treated as being parties to a transaction otherwise than at arm's length (TCGA 1992, s 18). The disposal is deemed to have taken place at market value and a chargeable gain or allowable loss is calculated accordingly. Where an allowable loss accrues on a disposal between connected persons, it may only be set off against chargeable gains resulting from some other disposal to that person even when market value is substituted.

3.22 Four types of relief from capital gains tax may apply on the transfer of a business to a company. These are retirement relief, rollover relief on transfer of a business, holdover relief for gifts of business assets and reinvestment relief; these are dealt with in outline in turn below.

3.23 Retirement relief applies in relation to gains arising on a disposal of chargeable business assets (see TCGA 1992, ss 163, 164). The relief is available for a 'material disposal' of business assets by an individual who, at the time of making the disposal is either aged 50 or over, or has retired below the age of 55 because of ill-health. This would include disposal of his business on incorporation.

3.24 A disposal is a material disposal if the business was owned by the trader for at least one year ending with the date of disposal and, on or before the date on which the business ceased to be carried on, he had reached the age of 50 or retired because of ill-health below that age. Full relief is available only if all the conditions are satisfied throughout a ten year qualifying period. Relief also covers disposal of privately owned assets used for the purpose of the business.

3.25 Rollover relief on the transfer of a business pursuant to TCGA 1992, s 162 applies automatically if all the relevant conditions are met. The amount of the net chargeable gains realised on the disposal to a company of a business, together with the whole of the assets of that business, is deducted from the base cost of the shares acquired in that company by the former trader. The gains arising on disposal are, therefore, automatically deferred until a later disposal of shares by the former trader. Full relief is available only if the following conditions are met:

(a) the business must be transferred as a going concern;
(b) the whole of the assets (other than cash) must be transferred to the company; and
(c) the consideration for the transfer of the business must be wholly or partly the issue of shares in the company. If consideration consists of items other than shares, only part of the gains arising may be rolled over into the shares.

3.26 The main disadvantage with rollover relief is that the whole of the assets of the business must be transferred for the relief to apply. This may give rise to a double charge to tax. Any gain accruing on an asset held by the company is liable to two charges. First there is a charge on a disposal of the asset by the company. A second charge arises on a disposal by shareholders of shares, the increased value of which in part reflects the gain that has accrued to the company. This double charge can be avoided if assets are held outside the company. Although this is not possible with rollover relief, it is available with holdover relief.

3.27 Holdover relief under TCGA 1992, s 165 may also apply if a claim is made. The chargeable gain accruing on a disposal of any business asset which is transferred to a company is deducted from the company's cost of acquisition of the asset. The effect of this relief is that the charge to tax is deferred until the company disposes of the asset. The charge falls not on the individual but on the company.

3.28 Holdover relief applies on an asset-by-asset basis. This has two advantages. An asset which is pregnant with gains is transferred to and held by a company and its value is not reflected in the value of the shares. Secondly, some assets may be held by a former trader outside the company, thereby avoiding the double charge referred to above.

3.29 The following conditions must be met if holdover relief is to be available:

(a) the transferee company must be UK resident;
(b) the disposal by the trader must be otherwise than under a bargain at arm's length;
(c) the asset transferred must have been used for the purposes of the trader's business; and
(d) the claim for relief must be made jointly by the trader and the company.

3.30 There are various restrictions for non-business periods of use of an asset and non-business use of part of a building. As it is only the chargeable gain that is held over, any retirement relief is given before holdover relief and only the balance is held over to reduce the acquisition costs.

Reinvestment relief

3.31 Reinvestment Relief is available under TCGA 1992, s 164A where a chargeable asset is disposed of and a new qualifying investment is acquired within three years after or twelve months before the disposal. 'Qualifying investment' means eligible shares in a qualifying company. A 'qualifying company' is an unquoted company carrying on one or more qualifying trades. The relief is not automatic and must be claimed. If relief is granted, there is (broadly) a reduction of the disposal proceeds by the smaller of the gain accruing on the disposal or the consideration given for the acquisition of the qualifying investment, and a reduction in the acquisition cost of the new shares by a corresponding amount. Thus the charge to tax is deferred until disposal of the new shares. There are anti-avoidance provisions which may cause a charge to tax to arise earlier.

Stamp duty

3.32 Where there is a contract to transfer the assets of a business to a company, the agreement is stampable as a 'conveyance or transfer on sale' under the

Stamp Act 1891, s 59(1). The rate of duty is 1% where the consideration (including assumption of liabilities) exceeds £60,000 (below which no duty is payable provided a certificate of value is given); 1.5% where the consideration exceeds £250,000; and 2% where the consideration exceeds £500,000. Duty is payable on land and property of any description, including in this context stock, debts and goodwill, excluding any moveable chattels title to which passes by delivery. Where the business is transferred in consideration of the issue of shares or other stock or marketable securities by the company, the agreement is stampable on the value of the shares issued.

3.33 In order to calculate correctly the stamp duty payable on an agreement transferring a business a form Stamps 22 should be completed which shows the balance of the value of assets transferred to the consideration given in cash, shares, or by the assumption of liabilities.

If the consideration for the transfer of the business is the issue of shares by the company, a stamped copy of the contract must be filed at Companies House within one month of allotment of shares together with companies form 88(2). Failure to do so gives rise to a fine. If no written contract exists, written particulars must be supplied on companies form 88(3), which must also be duly stamped (Companies Act 1985, s 88(3)).

Value Added Tax

3.34 The sale of the assets of the business may constitute a supply for VAT purposes and if the transferor is a registrable person VAT may be chargeable. If the transferor is not registered, the transfer of business assets by him may require him to register because the value of the assets being transferred may take him over the registration threshold. However, if the transaction is the transfer of a business as a going concern, it is exempt from VAT under the Value Added Tax (Special Provisions) Order 1992, SI 1992/3129, art 5. As a result, VAT is not chargeable on the value of the assets transferred. For the transfer to be treated as a transfer of a business as a going concern, the effect of the transfer must be to put the transferee company in possession of a business which can be operated as such; the business transferred must be a going concern at the time of the transfer; the assets transferred must be intended for use by the company in carrying on the same kind of business; the transferee company must be registered for VAT or, at the time of the transfer, must become liable to be registered, or must be accepted for voluntary registration; there must be no significant break in the normal trading pattern of the business before or immediately after the transfer; and, if part only of the business is transferred, that part must be able to operate alone. Special rules apply in the case of the transfer of land with the business. Given the uncertainty as to the application of this test, it is possible to seek a ruling from the transferor's local VAT office.

TABLE 3: OUTLINE OF INCORPORATION

Step no	Event	Documents
1.	Structure of incorporation agreed and advice obtained on the availability of holdover relief under s 162 of the TCGA 1992.	Heads of terms
2.	Acquisition of Newco 'off the shelf' with appointment of partners as directors and transfer of subscriber share(s).	Forms 288a and share transfer(s)
3.	Application made to the landlord for consent to the assignment of leasehold premises to Newco.	Application letter setting out proposal in outline and giving details of Newco
4.	Consultation with employee representatives pursuant to the 1995 Regulations referred to in paragraph 6.4.	Letter outlining the transaction
5.	Making arrangements with partnership bankers to 'transfer' account into name of Newco with appropriate security.	Bank mandates, guarantees and debenture
6.	Partners and Newco enter into agreement for the transfer of the business of the partnership to Newco in consideration of the issue of new shares to the partners.	Draft agreement
7.	Newco issues the new consideration shares.	Papers for an extraordinary general meeting of Newco to increase authorised share capital and authorise the directors to allot shares together with minutes of board meeting at which shares allotted.
8.	Business purchase agreement and form 88(3) (particulars of a contract relating to shares allotted as fully or partly paid up otherwise than in cash) submitted to Inland Revenue for stamping.	Form stamp 22, form 88(3) and completed business transfer agreement
9.	Customers and suppliers notified of incorporation and requested to novate contracts and amend credit account details as appropriate.	Standard letters to customers and suppliers, novation agreements
10.	Completion of the assignment of leasehold premises.	Assignment, licence to assign
11.	Names of partners entered in the register of members in respect of new allotments and return of allotments filed with the Registrar of Companies within one month after allotment.	Register of members, form 88(2) (return of allotments) and form 88(3) (particulars of a contract relating to shares allotted as fully or partly paid up otherwise than in cash)

4 Corporate structure

Pre-incorporation contracts

4.1 A contract purportedly entered into by or on behalf of a company prior to its incorporation cannot be enforced against the company. Any person who purports to contract on behalf of a non-existing company will incur personal liability (Companies Act 1985, s 36C). A company cannot ratify a contract made on its behalf prior to its incorporation although it may enter into a new contract in similar terms following incorporation.

4.2 It follows that the promoters may wish to enter into a formation agreement which binds all of them to procure that a company shall enter into a new contract on incorporation to replace any agreement that the promoters may have entered into on its behalf prior to incorporation. Note that such a replacement contract may not absolve the personal responsibility of the promoters, for example in respect of rent payable under a lease entered into by the promoters and subsequently taken over by the company.

Formalities of registration

4.3 Table 4 sets out the necessary steps to register a new company. Note that this procedure can be carried out on a 'same day' basis by special application and on payment of an additional fee to Companies House.

Restrictions on company name

4.4 A private limited company must use the word 'limited' at the end of its company name, with limited exceptions unlikely to be relevant to an owner-managed business. These exceptions include a company limited by guarantee whose objects are to promote commerce, arts, science, education, religion, charity or any profession.

4.5 A name cannot be accepted for registration if it is the same as one already appearing on the index. For this purpose, certain minor differences are to be disregarded as listed in the Companies Act 1985 s 26(3). A company may be called upon within 12 months of registration to change its name if it is too

TABLE 4: CHECKLIST FOR INCORPORATION

1. Check availability of name with Companies House and that the proposed name does not require prior approval of the Secretary of State.
2. Consider whether the name or part of it may comprise a trade mark. Consider search at Trade Marks Registry. Also advise client of potential liability for passing off and ask them to confirm that there are no competing businesses with similar names of which they are aware.
3. Prepare forms of memorandum and articles of association and arrange for them to be signed by two subscribers or if relevant by the sole subscriber and for such signature(s) to be witnessed.
4. Lodge with Companies House the signed memorandum and articles, statutory declaration of compliance (form 12), the statement of first directors and secretary and situation of intended registered office (form 10) together with the registration fee.
5. Arrange for printing of memorandum and articles as registered.
6. Obtain statutory registers, share certificate forms, minute book and (if the company requires one) a seal.
7. Arrange appointment of first directors and the secretary and prepare minutes for first board meeting.
8. Arrange any additional share issues and file return of allotments, (form 88(2)).
9. If the company wishes to choose an accounting reference date other than the last day of the month in which the anniversary of its incorporation falls, file a notice to the Registrar (companies form 225).

similar to an existing entry on the index or is subsequently regarded as giving a misleading indication of its activities (Companies Act 1985, s 32). If so required to change its name, the company must do so or face a fine. It is possible to check the index of names to ensure that there is no company with an identical or very similar name but there is no facility for reserving a company name.

4.6 The Secretary of State has a discretion to prevent use of a name which would constitute a criminal offence or which in his opinion is offensive. Approval of the Secretary of State is required if a name is in his opinion likely to give the impression that the company is connected with HM government or with a local authority or it includes any words or expression included in the Company and Business Names Regulations 1981, SI 1981/1685 as amended, or the Business Names Act 1985. Details are set out in Table 8 (on page 59).

4.7 As noted in Table 4, registration of a company name does not give the company any protection in an action for passing off nor guarantees that the use of the name does not infringe a registered trade mark. Similar registered trade marks can be ascertained by a search of the Trade Marks Registry. It is more difficult to ascertain whether there is a risk of passing off. It is possible to search the register of business names maintained by the London Chamber of Commerce and Industry. Apart from that, the promoters of the company are perhaps the best sources of information on businesses in a similar line which may have confusingly similar names.

4.8 Registration will result in the issue by the Registrar of Companies of a certificate of incorporation. This is conclusive evidence that all the requirements of the Companies Act 1985 in respect of registration have been complied with. If the certificate is lost or destroyed, a copy may be obtained from the Registrar. Contrary to the belief of many company owners (whose reception areas suffer as a result), there is no need to display the certificate of incorporation.

Registered office

4.9 A company must at all times have a registered office in England and Wales for the company to be incorporated there. The registered office does not have to be a place from which the company's business is carried on. It forms the proper address for the service of all legal and formal communications. The registered office may be changed, usually by a resolution of the board of directors, but such a change does not take effect until notice of it has been given to the Registrar of Companies (using companies form 287) and the change has been registered by the Registrar (see Companies Act 1985, s 287(3)). Until the end of the period of 14 days beginning with the date on which the change is registered, a person may validly serve any document on the company at its previous registered office. This is to protect parties serving legal documents on the old registered office in reliance upon a search less than 14 days old.

4.10 A number of registers and documents must be kept at the registered office and, unless the directors decide otherwise, the accounting records of the company must also be kept there (Companies Act 1985, s 222(1)). In particular, the company's register of members must be kept at its registered office unless it is made up at another office of the company or at the company's registrars.

Shelf companies

4.11 For a modest fee, company formation agents can provide a new company 'off the shelf' for almost immediate use. These will have standard memorandum and articles of association. Some amendment may be appropriate (in particular to the objects clause) but this is unlikely to override the speed and ease of using a shelf company. Where new companies are often required, solicitors may themselves create shelf companies for use by their clients. This can be achieved quite easily and efficiently and it carries the advantage that relevant paperwork to appoint new directors and transfer initial shares can be signed 'in house'.

4.12 Two essential features for a shelf company are first that it has never carried on any business or incurred any liabilities and secondly that the date of incorporation is fairly recent (and certainly not old enough as to restrict the time to which the first accounts of the company are to be made up bearing in mind that the first accounting period cannot exceed the period of 18 months from incorporation).

4.13 The formation agent will usually require that a new director and secretary are appointed before the certificate of incorporation is released and the registered office is changed. The subscriber shares will only be transferred once signed forms 288(a) and form 287 are received by the agents. Incorporating companies 'in house' would avoid this delay.

4.14 The particulars relating to the shelf company will almost certainly require adaptation. This is achieved by holding a 'first board meeting' to deal with the appointment of new directors, change of registered office and the issue of additional shares. This will therefore usually involve the passing of resolutions by the shareholders either at a extraordinary shareholders' meeting held on short notice or by way of written resolutions pursuant to s 381A of the Companies Act 1985. Document 3 in Part II comprises a sample set of minutes for a first board meeting although obviously the needs of each individual situation may vary. Document 4 in Part II comprises forms for passing of shareholders' resolutions and some sample resolutions. Table 5 sets out a list of matters commonly required to be dealt with by way of resolutions of the shareholders.

TABLE 5: CHECKLIST OF CHANGES TO SHELF COMPANY

1. Change of objects of the company (even where the company has objects as a general commercial company). Banks lending money to the company may prefer specific objects. The company may need specific investment company articles for taxation reasons.
2. Increase in the authorised share capital of the company and possibly creation of separate classes of shares, in which case the articles of association will require alteration.
3. Changes to the articles of association to create restrictions on transfer of shares and pre-emption rights (usually missing from shelf company articles).
4. Change of the name of the company.
5. Giving of authority to the directors to allot shares pursuant to the Companies Act 1985, s 80 and disapplying the pre-emption provisions of the Companies Act 1985, s 89(1) so far as not already dealt with in the articles.
6. Approval for the purposes of the Companies Act 1985, s 320 regarding arrangements for the sale or acquisition between the company and directors of the company in relation to non-cash assets of the requisite values.

Memorandum of association

4.15 The memorandum of a private company limited by shares must state:

(a) the company's name;
(b) whether the registered office is to be situated in England and Wales or in Wales or in Scotland;
(c) the objects of the company;
(d) that the liability of the members is to be limited to the amount unpaid on the shares respectively held by them;

(e) the amount of capital with which the company proposes to be registered and its division into shares.

4.16 A formal treatise on the contents of the objects clause is beyond the scope of this book. Suffice it to say that protection for persons dealing with the company is now conferred by ss 35, 35A and 35B of the Companies Act 1985. Third parties dealing with the company, in particular banks providing loans, will, however, often wish to see specific objects and powers. The main points often raised by banks proposing to lend money to the company are as follows:

(a) that the main objects clause should reflect the actual or proposed activities of the company (as opposed, for example, to relying upon the main object being that of a 'general commercial company' in accordance with the Companies Act 1985, s 3A which on the strict wording of that section only applies in any event where it is the only object of the company);
(b) inclusion of specific objects relating to the giving of security and third-party guarantees (which are arguably not covered by the expression 'general commercial company', as referred to above, which implies that the company has power to do all such things as are incidental or conducive to the carrying on of any trade or business by it);
(c) inclusion of a specific power to give financial assistance for the purchase of the company's own shares (which is not a requirement of any of the exceptions from the prohibition of giving financial assistance contained in the Companies Act 1985, s 151, but is a 'preferred' inclusion in the eyes of many banking lawyers).

4.17 A sample memorandum is included as document 5 in Part II.

4.18 It is possible to alter the provisions in the memorandum relating to name, registered office, objects and capital, subject to the conditions set out in the Companies Act 1985. Note that technically the memorandum should be reprinted following each such alteration including changes to the amount of the authorised share capital of the company. The standard practice is to endorse reference to resolutions amending the capital.

Articles of association

4.19 Every company limited by shares must register articles of association which will from registration 'bind the company and its members to the same extent as if they respectively had been signed and sealed by each member and contained covenants on the part of each member to observe all the provisions of the articles' (Companies Act 1985, s 8(1)). The effect of these words is to create a contract between the company and each of the members but the court will not enforce a provision inserted in the articles for the benefit of a member otherwise than in his capacity as a member. Accordingly, a shareholders' agreement and/or employment agreements will usually supplement the articles in the case of an OMB. The articles should, however, set out the agreement between the members in regard to such matters as rights to appoint directors and the dividend, voting, and capital rights attaching to shares.

4.20 Most private companies will adopt articles which either comprise or are based closely upon Table A as contained in the Companies (Tables A-F) Regulations 1985, SI 1985/805 as amended ('Table A'). Table A applies to every company limited by shares registered after 1 July 1985 save in so far as its registered articles exclude or modify Table A. In the case of an owner-managed business, Table A is unlikely to reflect the intentions of an OMB client. This is partly because Table A, like most of the regime of the Companies Act 1985, assumes that the directors will constitute a separate body of persons from the shareholders in certain respects and that the share capital of the company would be held by a number of persons without creating a deadlock. Table 6 sets out a brief list of matters in respect of which Table A would commonly require amendment to make the articles suitable for an owner-managed business.

TABLE 6: TYPICAL REQUIREMENTS FOR OMB ARTICLES

1. Pre-emption provisions on the issue of additional shares, whether or not for cash consideration.
2. Pre-emption provisions on the transfer of shares (but note that where pre-emption provisions are included, there should not normally be any discretion on the part of the directors to refuse to register a transfer of shares other than in the limited circumstances provided in Table A).
3. Provision for the directors to have authority to allot shares pursuant to s 80 of the Companies Act 1985 (subject to pre-emption provisions as relevant).
4. Potentially, the right for owner-managers holding a given proportion of the share capital to appoint themselves or another as a director (and to re-appoint in case of removal).
5. Provision for notices of board meetings to be given whether or not directors are absent from the United Kingdom and provisions that board meetings can be held by telephone.
6. Removal on the restriction of a director from voting and counting in a quorum present at a board meeting in relation to any matter in which he has an interest, provided he has declared that interest to the meeting.
7. Exclusion of any chairman's casting vote.

4.21 Documents 6 and 7 in Part II comprise sample articles which may be an appropriate starting point for the articles of association of an owner-managed business. Document 6 comprises fairly 'standard' articles which are based upon Table A but with some alterations appropriate to an owner-managed business. Document 7 comprises articles for a company with separate classes of shares, being A shares and B shares, on the basis that those shares would have very simple class rights. This precedent is thus suitable for a situation where two individuals (or potentially two groups of individuals) are involved both as owners and managers and the company is effectively a 'partnership company'. The key provisions are as follows:

(a) the proportions of the A shares and B shares are preserved by providing that except by authorisation of a special resolution (for which purposes it is assumed the consent of holders of A shares and B shares will be required) new shares may only be issued in equal proportions (Article 4). Where existing holdings of A and B shares are not equal, it would usually be necessary to amend this provision to provide for new issues to be in proportion to such holdings;

(b) pre-emption provisions on transfer with priority to holders of the same class of shares (Article 6(7));
(c) provision for meetings to require one A shareholder and one B shareholder to be present in order for the meeting to be quorate (Articles 7 and 10);
(d) restrictions on an A shareholder voting for the removal of a director appointed by the B shareholders (and note it is possible to go further and say that no resolution can be passed without votes being passed by both A and B shareholders in respect of certain other restricted matters);
(e) the right for the A shareholders and the B shareholders respectively to appoint one or more directors (Article 12);
(f) similar provisions in respect of board meetings (Article 14) to the effect that no board resolution can be passed without the approval of directors appointed by both the A shareholders and the B shareholders.

4.22 Document 8 in Part II comprises a much simpler set of articles of association which might be suitable for use in respect of a subsidiary company of an OMB. These articles adopt Table A but with the following two stipulations relevant to a subsidiary company:

(a) directors can vote on matters in which they are interested, providing they have disclosed the interest (Article 2);
(b) a parent company may remove a director of the subsidiary by written notice, rather than having to go through the notice requirements of the statutory procedure in s 303 of the Companies Act 1985 (Article 4).

Shareholders' agreements

4.23 In many cases, it will not be possible to provide adequate protection for the interests of owner-managers in the articles of association. This may be because the rights to be protected are not rights as members or that they cannot sensibly be drafted in the form of articles of association. It may then be appropriate to enter into a shareholders' agreement. Such agreements have other advantages over provisions in the articles of association. Firstly, they are not usually subject to registration at Companies House and so can remain confidential. See, however, the Companies Act 1985, s 380(4)(c) which provides that resolutions or agreements which have been agreed to by all the members of a company but which would not have been effective if not so agreed are registrable. For example, a provision of a shareholders' agreement which amounts to an alteration of the articles of association of the company may mean the agreement is registrable. The practice, however, would be not to register the agreement. Secondly, a shareholders' agreement is possibly a more readable document than articles of association, making it more likely that the parties will concentrate on and understand the terms.

4.24 A sample form of shareholders' agreement is included as document 9 in Part II. This is an appropriate starting point for an owner-managed business at the point of start-up or buy-out. Shareholders' agreements vary greatly according to the circumstances and style of the draftsman. They may vary from a very comprehensive document (the starting point from which might in drafting terms be a joint venture agreement) right down to a document which in effect is a formation agreement providing for the steps to be taken towards the incorporation and straightforward matters such as the composition of the board of directors. The particular feature of a shareholders' agreement for an OMB is that it must deal with (either within its terms or by reference to other documents) the relationships between the parties as:

(a) shareholders;
(b) directors; and
(c) employees.

4.25 In relation to share rights, much of this may be contained in the articles of association to be adopted on signature of the shareholders' agreement. The shareholders' agreement will invariably provide that its terms will prevail over any inconsistent provisions to the articles but attempts should still be made to ensure that the articles are tailored to fit. Moreover, provisions such as restrictions on transfer of shares are more appropriately dealt with in the articles. The key feature in relation to shares which is more easily dealt with in shareholder agreements than in articles is provision for put and call options in the event that one of the owner-managers ceases to be directly involved in the business (as to which see below).

4.26 Another key right attaching to shares, which may be varied or extended in the shareholders' agreement, relates to the payment of dividends. In the absence of any contrary provision, dividends will only be payable by a majority decision of the directors (in the case of an interim dividend) or by approval of a resolution of the shareholders (in the case of a final dividend). The shareholders' agreement may provide nothing further but the basic alternatives are that:

(a) no dividends should be declared without the unanimous approval or the approval of a specified majority of the shareholders;
(b) so long as there are available distributable profits, a given percentage or amount of such profits shall be paid out in dividend each year;
(c) by way of a 'fudge' of the issue (which is likely to mean the provision is not legally enforceable in any meaningful way), provision that a specified percentage of available profits will be distributed but only in so far as the company's cash flow and other commitments permit, possibly adding that dividend payments will be 'topped up' to the relevant percentage as soon as cash flow does permit.

4.27 The rights of the owner-managers as directors are usually to remain as such (save where disqualified or removed for good cause), to be involved in the management and control of the company and (potentially) to have a veto on certain matters of importance. So, for example, paragraph 3 of the precedent shareholders' agreement requires unanimity before the company can incur expenditure over a specified amount. The precedent lists only a few restricted matters because:

(a) those restrictions need to be looked at afresh for any given circumstances;
(b) the concept is that these restrictions should only catch really serious decisions as opposed to giving each shareholder a veto on every decision; and
(c) the restriction on expenditure will in any event catch most material transactions.

4.28 The rights and obligations of the owner-managers as employees in the business should preferably be set out in a separate service agreement. However, the parties may wish to tie everything into the same agreement, particularly if they only wish to provide the notice periods and remuneration provisions. Restrictive covenants should preferably be included in the shareholders' agreement as well as in any service agreement because they will be more likely to be enforceable (under the general law relating to restraint of trade) if they relate to the relationship between the parties as shareholders and not just as employees (see *Nordenfelt v Maxim Nordenfelt Guns and Ammunition Co Ltd* [1894] AC 535). It may thus be justifiable to provide a slightly longer period during which those restrictive covenants would continue. Note, however, the possible unfairness of providing that the period for the restrictive covenants only commences once the party ceases to be a shareholder. This would be particularly unfair in circumstances where the owner-manager may leave employment and resign his directorship but remain as a shareholder until put and call options are exercised.

Cross options

4.29 Perhaps the key concept behind the owner-managed business is that each individual's shareholding reflects his contribution as a manager within the business. It follows from this that the parties usually expect the following:

(a) if they leave the business (certainly if they do so involuntarily) they should be in a position to realise the investment, rather than leaving it behind (where the acts of others will affect its value); and
(b) if one of the other shareholders ceases to be involved in the business, they would have the right to purchase the relevant portion of that shareholding so as to avoid the leaver from benefiting from any future uplift in value caused by the efforts of those who remain.

4.30 These principles are very commonly reflected in the form of put and call options over the shares of each owner-manager. The put option relates to the right of a leaving shareholder to oblige the other shareholders to purchase his holding. The call option relates to the right of those remaining with the business to force a leaver to sell his shares to them. The provisions are achieved by means of options as opposed to contingent obligations to purchase and sell for flexibility and tax reasons. The two key features to be dealt with in the drafting of cross options are as follows:

(a) the circumstances in which the options would become exercisable; and
(b) the calculation of the price payable for the shares in each of such circumstances.

4.31 There is not a single correct view on the alternatives for put and call options. There is usually agreement that a lower price should be applied to the shares where the leaving shareholder does not have an adequate reason for going. The following paragraphs run through some typical provisions.

4.32 In the case of voluntary termination of employment (in other words resignation except in circumstances where the leaver was entitled to treat himself as having been constructively dismissed), the other shareholders would have the right to purchase his shares (a call option) but the leaver would have no right to force the sale (a put option). The call option would often be at a restricted value. It might, for example, be at the market value of the shares as a single holding, meaning that a discount would be applied for it being a minority holding. This may in itself be sufficient restriction but, alternatives include restricting the price to the proportion of net asset value which the shares bear to the whole of the share capital (assuming this would be a lesser sum than such market value).

4.33 Similarly in the case of dismissal for gross misconduct or other reason justifying summary dismissal, the leaver would usually have no put option and the remaining shareholders would usually have a call option at some restricted value. It should be noted, however, that this is quite a tough test for the company in that only very serious negligence would justify summary dismissal. This provision would therefore not deal with poor performance. It is submitted that this is fair since that is such a subjective concept. However, the provision may instead stipulate that a restricted price would apply unless the Industrial Tribunal holds the dismissal (or constructive dismissal) to be unfair. This would bring in the test of reasonableness from s 98 of the Employment Rights Act 1996. However, Industrial Tribunal decisions are notoriously unpredictable and in any event take great account of procedural fairness. The dealings between owner-managers are unlikely to have been dealt with within any strict procedure. Also, the remaining shareholders should seek to avoid the matter being taken to an Industrial Tribunal. The best view would be that owner-managers should know each other's qualities before entering into the shareholders' agreement and so only a very major matter should enable them to dismiss one of their number except at a significant cost (see also paragraph 4.41).

4.34 Where one of the owner-managers is dismissed (or is entitled to treat himself as having been constructively dismissed) in circumstances other than in the preceding two paragraphs, the leaving shareholder would normally have a put option at market value translated as a proportion of the value of the whole company (meaning that there is no discount for it being a minority holding). The remaining shareholders would normally retain a call option but at this higher value.

4.35 In the case of death or injury or illness causing permanent incapacity, the usual position would be for put and call options to exist at a full market value (ie the share of whole value). Note, however, that the problem for the remaining shareholders is that they are left in a position requiring funding to make this purchase. This can be alleviated by giving them time to pay by instalments. Subject to having the benefit of exemptions from the prohibition on financed assistance in the Companies Act 1985, s 151, the remaining shareholders will also have the resources and borrowing ability of the company to assist them so that if the shares are valuable this presumably means the company is valuable. In fact, the purchase may be structured as a purchase of own shares by the company. However, obligations arising under options arising on death are commonly covered by insurance. The relevant policies are often referred to as 'shareholder protection' insurance policies. They consist of a policy taken out on the life of each relevant shareholder which is written into trust for the benefit of the other shareholders. The policy premiums are invariably paid by the company although this will amount to a taxable emolument of the relevant insured party and so it may be necessary to increase his remuneration to cover the cost of the premium. The concept is that the insurance policies will pay out for the other shareholders who will have a corresponding obligation to purchase shares from the personal representatives of the deceased shareholder. Thus, the estate of the deceased shareholder benefits in the form of these cash proceeds rather than holding what is perhaps an unsaleable minority stake in a limited company.

4.36 In the event that one of the shareholders is declared bankrupt, it is usual to provide that the other shareholders have a call option at the price originally paid by the bank for the shares or if less, their current market value.

4.37 It can be seen that these option provisions are largely concerned with share valuation. The usual provisions are that the shares are valued by the auditors of the company. The leaving shareholder may feel that the independence of the auditors is compromised because their continuing client is the company. There is, therefore, often provision for the valuation to be conducted by an independent chartered accountant. Valuation of shares at a proportion of the value of the whole company is a fairly straightforward concept although of course share valuation even of whole companies is an art rather than a science. Valuation of a single holding, after applying an appropriate discount to reflect the fact that the holding does not represent total ownership of the company, can seem even more arbitrary. There are no fixed rates of discount to be applied since the level of discount will depend on a number of factors and the particular circumstances of the company. It is worth bearing in mind that a minority stake in an owner-managed business would usually be very difficult to dispose of as the rights attaching to those shares will usually have presupposed that the holder is heavily involved in the business of the company.

4.38 Because of the vagaries of share valuation, the parties may attempt to define value by reference to some sort of formula. This may be based on net asset value or past profit performance or a mixture of both. This seems fair on the face of it and it certainly gives rise to greater certainty (provided the formula is based on historical accounting information). Great caution should, however, be exercised in that the formula could give rise to figures which are grossly unfair because historical accounting information is not an accurate guide to current value or future potential.

4.39 Table 6A, comprises a checklist for taking instructions for shareholders' agreements relevant to OMBs. Where the lawyer is instructed by the company, there is obviously the potential for a conflict of interest to arise when advising the individual owner-managers. This will particularly be the case where one of the owner-managers has a controlling interest or the shareholders are not otherwise equal. In very simple terms, the majority shareholder has less to gain by restrictions on decision making in a shareholders' agreement which is effectively a minority protection measure. Another potential cause for conflict between the individuals is their relative wealth. It is all very well granting put and call options and pre-emption provisions on transfer but it must be remembered that individuals could be required to raise money to operate their rights under such clauses (or indeed to comply with their obligations under any put option). In the case of a smaller OMB, the prospect of each individual obtaining separate legal representation would be unattractive. If this is the case, there are basically two alternatives. The first is for the lawyer to make it clear that he acts for the company and not for any individual shareholders. He is thus able to facilitate a shareholders' agreement by advising on provisions commonly contained in shareholders' agreements and explaining their effects. He is thus acting as an 'honest broker' which is of course a difficult position for a solicitor to adopt both professionally and because of the generally adversarial nature of his training. Note also the potential for conflict in making any judgment about what provisions are 'usually' contained in the shareholders' agreement, particularly where there is a majority shareholder. The second method would be to identify one individual as the client and then advise minority shareholders that in this matter he is not able to advise them and they are recommended to obtain independent legal advice. This method may be more appropriate where there is a majority shareholder. The minority shareholders may take independent legal advice only in the form of a brief overview. One problem with this method is the possibility that the lawyer is seen to have sided too heavily on one side and thus soured the relationship with the minority shareholders and (professionally speaking far more dangerous) the lawyer is swayed by conflicting loyalty to the minority shareholders being persons he has previously regarded as clients.

Majority protection

4.40 The more usual subject of minority protection is dealt with at paragraph 4.41 below. See also the comments on the position of a majority shareholder in paragraph 4.39 above. The issue dealt with in this paragraph is something different. A majority shareholder will not have the same effective powers in the case of an owner-managed business, as he otherwise would because of his reliance on other owner-managers as well as the rights usually held by them to remain involved in the management of the company. It is thus quite often the case that majority shareholders require the minority to further reduce their rights in various ways. This is the opposite of a 'partnership company' where the rights of shareholders are roughly equal. This is the situation where in effect there is one 'owner' but other managers have a shareholding, perhaps as an incentive or as part of a remuneration package. In these cases, the majority shareholder may require additional protection such as the following:

(a) an option to purchase the shareholding back from the individual at any time (but usually limited to an initial period, perhaps a probationary period when the shareholder first acquires his shares) – see the simple option agreement included as document 10 in Part II;
(b) a security power of attorney over the shares, for example where shares are issued to an employee but the majority owner lends the price to the shareholder and wishes to retain voting control on the shares whilst that loan is due but at the same time give the manager the 'badge' of share ownership – see the examples of powers of attorney for use in respect of shares included as document 12 in Part II;
(c) mandatory transfer provisions such as that comprised in document 12 in Part II which is basically a form of call option to deal with cessation of employment which is included in the articles and only applies to one class of shares; and

(d) a 'come along clause' as also included in document 12 which is basically a right (quite difficult to draft and potentially also difficult to enforce) for a majority holder to require the minority to join with him in selling the share capital – note that it is a common misconception amongst owner-managers that the majority can force a sale of shares by the minority. Note also that the compulsory purchase provisions contained in the Companies Act 1985 in respect of minority holdings of less than 10% only apply in the case of a takeover offer and not in the usual case where a purchase is to proceed by a sale and purchase agreement – see Companies Act 1985, Part XIIIA including ss 428 and 429.

The obvious point to make about all of such provisions is that they are generally unsatisfactory from the point of view of both the majority holder and the minority holder. Admission to share ownership should be regarded as a long term commitment not an 'executive perk'. It is true to say however that many owners are 'forced' by commercial factors into offering share ownership to their managers.

TABLE 6A: CHECKLIST FOR SHAREHOLDERS' AGREEMENTS

1 Funding issues

1.1 Share capital v loans
1.2 Interest, repayment terms and security for loans
1.3 Personal guarantees and contribution to joint liabilities

2 Share capital issues

2.1 Pre-emption rights on new issues and share transfers
2.2 Initial period when no transfers permitted
2.3 Possible exceptions for transfers to family etc

3 Cross options

3.1 Put and call options on death and life assurance policies
3.2 Termination of employment (resignation, dismissal for cause and dismissal without cause)
3.3 Bankruptcy
3.4 Valuation of shares (proportion of whole or discount for minority holdings, net asset value, formula value, independent accountant)

4 Decision making and disputes

4.1 Matters reserved for unanimous agreement
4.2 Matters reserved for a qualified majority
4.3 Dividend policy
4.4 Dispute resolution

5 Employment aspects

5.1 Separate service agreements
5.2 Restrictive covenants
5.3 Remuneration
5.4 Termination

Minority protection

4.41 A shareholder is entitled to petition for relief under s 459 of the Companies Act 1985 on the ground that the company's affairs are being or have been conducted in a manner which is unfairly prejudicial to the interests of its members generally or some part of its members (including at least himself). In suitable cases, the minority shareholders may also petition for the company to be wound up on the 'just and equitable' ground under s 122 of the Insolvency Act 1986. Such provisions are of relevance to owner-managed businesses, in particular where one owner-manager is effectively excluded from management or following the death of one of the shareholders, no dividends are paid on the shares whilst the surviving shareholders continue to enjoy very substantial remuneration in the form of salary, benefits and bonuses. It is both difficult and costly to bring a successful petition under s 459 and should be regarded as a last resort once negotiation has failed. The purpose of mentioning it here is twofold. First, one of the purposes of preparing appropriate

TABLE 7: DIRECTORS' DUTIES

Nature of duty	Source	Examples
1. Duty to act in the best interests of the company and not to make a secret profit.	Fiduciary duties under general law	Restricted to taking the benefit of opportunities belonging to the company for the directors' own benefit.
2. Approval required for loss of office payments.	CA 1985, ss 312–316	Any payment by way of compensation for loss of office except for a bona fide payment by way of damages for breach of contract or by way of pension in respect of past service, will require prior shareholder approval.
3. Requirement for approval of service agreements.	CA 1985, s 319	Approval required for an agreement whereby a director's employment cannot be terminated within five years except in specified circumstances.
4. Substantial property transaction involving directors.	CA 1985, s 320	Arrangements between a company and a director of that company or its holding company for the acquisition or disposal of a non-cash asset of the requisite value will require shareholder approval.
5. Directors' loans.	CA 1985, s 330	Detailed provisions restrict the ability of a director and in certain cases persons connected with him from taking loans or similar arrangements from the company.
6. Duties of skill and care.	General law	A director should display such skill as his personal qualifications warrant and a director is treated as having the general knowledge skill and experience that may reasonably be expected of him.

provisions in articles and shareholder agreements is to set out rights so that the parties need not rely on statutory remedies. Secondly, whilst a shareholders' agreement agreed between the relevant parties should prevent a petition running contrary to those provisions from being successful, care should be taken in the enforcement of strict legal rights under the articles where these could run contrary to any understanding between the owner-managers.

4.42 The Law Commission published proposals in October 1997 to amend and simplify the remedy offered by s 459. One proposal would have the effect of giving an owner-manager who is dismissed, other than for serious breach of duty, a right to require the other shareholder to purchase his shares at market value. This sounds fair but could leave the remaining owner-managers in an invidious position if one of their number is underperforming. It might be left to a court to determine whether their decision was justified and left to an expert as to what the market value is. Thus, they might not be able to afford the risk of taking any action against the underperformer. This proposal, if enacted, should at least carry the right for the parties to exclude its operation.

Directors' duties

4.43 Directors of an owner-managed business will of course be subject to the common law and statutory duties which directors owe to the company. In the case of an OMB, particular care should be taken to explain the nature of these obligations given that many of them are designed to give the shareholders (assumed to be a separate body) rights of veto over the actions of directors. Table 7 sets out a checklist of relevant duties.

5 Share capital and finance

Sources of finance

5.1 The methods of financing the owner-managed business will basically comprise the following:

(a) funds provided by the owner-managers, in the form of share capital and/or loans;
(b) investment in share capital by third parties such as venture capitalists or 'business angels'; or
(c) lending by third parties such as banks in the form of term loans, overdraft, invoice discounting facilities and other facilities.

5.2 The choice and/or balance between these sources of finance will be dictated by commercial factors. The first of these to be considered is what is actually available. Looked at from the point of view of owner-managers starting up or developing a business, the questions they must ask themselves are as follows:

(a) have they the personal resources to fund the business themselves?
(b) if they have those resources, to what extent do they wish to use them on the basis that those resources could be committed on a long-term basis and could be at risk?
(c) are the owner-managers prepared to release part of the equity to a third party investor?
(d) are they prepared to accept the financial discipline and loss of outright control which is likely to result from the introduction of a third party investor such as a venture capitalist?
(e) if they wish to borrow, can the business afford to service borrowings?
(f) over what length of time would the business be able to repay borrowings?
(g) what security can be offered to a bank or other lender for borrowings and is this liable to affect the business?
(h) is security likely to involve the giving of personal guarantees by the owner-managers and are they prepared to give them?

5.3 As can be seen from these questions, the owner-managers have to match what is available with their personal objectives/requirements. Many of the considerations centre on the matching of risk and reward. If the owner-managers are not prepared to give up any part of the equity in the business, because they hope to maximise their return on a future sale of the business, they may have difficulty borrowing sufficient amounts to fund the business without personal guarantees to a lender. Introducing outside investment does involve sharing risk with that investor to an extent but it does of course follow that the rate of return for a venture capitalist reflects the risk and the 'cost' of the funding is greater than for secured bank lending.

5.4 Commercial considerations of funding will be different in each case. It may also be that these are addressed principally by accountants taking on the role of lead business advisers. They would usually also deal with advice on taxation considerations. These are complicated and require analysis of the detail in each case. The following paragraphs do, however, set out an overview of major issues.

Taxation considerations

5.5 The following overview assumes that the owner-managed business is conducted through one or more UK resident limited companies.

5.5A It may be that the choice between debt or equity funding has been already made for other tax planning reasons (eg if rollover relief on the transfer of a business has been sought under the Taxation of Chargeable Gains Act 1992, s 162) or for commercial reasons (eg where the promoters wish to rank in priority to other creditors of the company in the event of an insolvency). Assuming a free hand, the choice is prima facie between loan and share capital. However, different types of loan capital and different types of share capital have different tax treatments. Further, UK tax law is sufficiently sophisticated to treat debt which has the characteristics of equity, as equity, and equity which has the characteristics of debt, in some cases, as debt, particularly in the context of groups of companies. Put simply, debt yields income in the form of interest but no capital growth (and indeed, assuming positive rates of inflation, a loss in real terms). The interest is taxable in the hands of the lender and deductible for the borrower. The advance and repayment of principal is usually a non-event for tax purposes. By contrast, an equity investment in a company yields income in the form of dividends and the possibility of unlimited capital growth in line with the success of the business. The taxation of dividends is not straightforward, but basically they are taxed in the hands of the recipient subject to a full or partial credit for tax, but are not tax deductible for the paying company. This can give rise to double taxation. Accordingly, bearing in mind also that the loan interest is tax-deductible, the usual preference tends to be for loan investment.

Taxation of interest

5.6 The new company may be funded by way of loans by the owner-managers. The loans can be interest-free, although where the company is not a UK resident trading company the Inland Revenue might treat a lender which controls the company, particularly a UK resident company, as receiving interest at a market rate. If interest is charged, this is chargeable to income tax under

Schedule D Case III under the Income and Corporation Taxes Act 1988, s 770. Interest paid by a company must be paid after deduction of income tax at the basic rate. The principal exceptions (interest on advances from UK banks and payments of interest on quoted Eurobonds) are not likely to be relevant in this context. A group of companies can elect for payments between members of the group to be made gross (ICTA 1988, s 247). Interest paid by a company on a loan is, subject to the conditions in the Income and Corporation Taxes Act 1988, s 338 being met, allowable as a deduction from profits as a charge on income only and not as a trading expense. Those conditions are primarily that basic rate tax is withheld on payment of the interest; that the liability to pay interest was incurred for a valuable and sufficient consideration; and that the company is either a trading company or an investment company or, if neither, has borrowed money for purposes which would allow relief for the interest to be given if the borrower were an individual.

5.7 In certain circumstances interest payments are re-characterised as distributions and give rise to an obligation to pay advance corporation tax ('ACT'). See the Income and Corporation Taxes Act 1988, s 209(2)(d). Further, the payment is not deductible against profits of the payer company. Interest is treated as a distribution if inter alia:

(a) it represents more than a reasonable commercial return for the use of the principal (only the excess is regarded as a distribution);
(b) it is interest on a redeemable security issued otherwise than wholly for new consideration;
(c) it is interest in respect of securities which are either convertible into shares in the company or carry rights to receive shares or securities of the company;
(d) the amount of interest is in any way dependent on the results of the company's business or any part of it;
(e) it is payable on a security where it is necessary or advantageous to the holder of securities also to hold shares in the company; or
(f) it is interest on equity notes issued by the company (the 'issuing company') and held by a company which is associated with the issuing company.

See ICTA 1988, s 209(2).

Loss incurred on disposal of a debt

5.8 A lender (whether an individual or a company) would usually make the loan on capital account, ie as an investment. No chargeable gain or allowable loss can accrue to the lender as an original creditor, except in the case of a debt on a security (see TCGA 1992, s 251(1)). Original creditors are therefore, subject to the exceptions mentioned below, denied relief for losses on disposals of simple debts. There are anti-avoidance provisions to prevent the creation of losses on disposal of debts between connected persons.

5.9 A 'debt on a security' is not defined in the legislation, although 'security' is defined. It does, however, have a number of identifying characteristics. The debtor must be an institution and not an individual. The debt itself need not be secured nor does it need to be constituted or evidenced in writing. It must, however, be marketable and it must be loan stock or similar. A debt on a security must be in the nature of an investment in the hands of the creditor. See *W T Ramsay Ltd v IRC* [1982] AC 300, [1981] 1 All ER 865, HL (see in particular at p 323 and at p 871, per Lord Wilberforce). Where the debt is a debt on a security, a loss on a disposal is an allowable loss, and a gain is a chargeable gain.

However, if the debt on a security is a qualifying corporate bond then the debt is still not a chargeable asset and no capital gain or allowable loss can arise (see TCGA 1992 s 117). Nearly all sterling debts on a security are qualifying corporate bonds, as in the main they are 'normal commercial loans'. A common device to avoid the qualifying corporate bond legislation was to use a redemption price, which varied between say 99.99% and 100.01% of par, by reference to a currency other than sterling. This will no longer work, however, where the lender is a company, following the Finance Act 1993, Part III, Ch II (ss 125–170). Other methods include making the loan convertible or giving the holder the right to acquire additional securities. Where the borrower is a member of a 75% tax group then the loan is not a qualifying bond.

5.10 The second exception to the general rule arises where the debtor is a trader or where a guarantor of a loan to a trader is called on to pay the loan which has been guaranteed (TCGA 1992, s 253). If the necessary conditions are fulfilled, the creditor or guarantor may obtain relief for losses incurred.

Tax consideration of equity

5.11 For tax purposes, equity is equated to ordinary share capital, which is defined as all of a company's share capital, except preference shares which give the holder a right to participate in profits at a fixed rate but no other right to share in the company's profits (see ICTA 1988, s 832(1)). Accordingly, preference shares which carry other rights to participate in profits are ordinary share capital for tax purposes. Preference shares which are not ordinary share capital for tax purposes are generally treated as shares, ie equity, except for tax grouping purposes.

5.12 An income distribution by a company gives rise to tax consequences for both the company and the shareholder. The most common form of distribution is a dividend, and the way in which a dividend (including, in certain circumstances, interest) is treated for tax purposes is discussed below. A UK resident company paying a dividend is liable to pay to the Inland Revenue advance corporation tax ('ACT'). The rate is fixed in advance and is expressed as a fraction of the amount of the dividend paid. The rate of ACT is currently one-quarter of the amount distributed. Subject to certain restrictions, the amount of ACT paid by the company can be set against the company's mainstream corporation tax liability. Companies are required to issue to a shareholder a statement showing the amount of the dividend and the tax credit due. The foreign income dividend scheme is not considered here. A UK resident individual shareholder is chargeable to tax on the amount of the dividend plus the accompanying tax credit. The tax credit satisfies the shareholder's liability to pay lower or basic rate tax and is equal to the amount of ACT paid on the dividend. An individual investor is therefore only liable to pay tax on the difference between the lower rate and the higher rate on the dividend plus tax credit. A UK corporate shareholder receives income equal to the dividend and the tax credit attached to it. The 1997 Budget has prevented non-chargeable shareholders from reclaiming the amount of tax credit. See paragraph 2.32 above.

5.13 Any disposal of shares is a disposal for capital gains tax purposes and accordingly a chargeable gain arises if the disposal proceeds exceed the shareholder's base cost as increased by indexation allowance. Care needs to be taken if shareholders increase their shareholdings in companies pro rata to their shareholdings, as it is likely that the reorganisation of share capital provisions (TCGA 1992, s 126) will override normal rules as to allowable base cost. The effect of these rules is that the increase in base cost is restricted to the lower of the amount paid for the shares issued and the increase in value of the company as a result of the subscription.

5.14 Where shares are ordinary share capital, and are sold at a loss by the original subscriber who was not associated with the company at the time of subscription then the disposing shareholder can elect to have an income loss instead of a capital loss. (ICTA 1988, ss 573–575). This could be particularly valuable for owner-managers. There are anti-avoidance provisions which generally prevent the creation of a loss on a disposal of shares.

Tax consideration of funding the investment

5.15 A shareholder may have to borrow in order to be able to lend money to the company, and will incur interest costs in so doing. A corporate shareholder should obtain relief for interest paid either as an allowable deduction against trading income or as a charge against total profits. An individual shareholder may obtain relief for interest paid if the company to which he loans money is, broadly, a close company in which he has a material interest and the borrowing company uses the money wholly and exclusively for the purposes of its trade (see the Income and Corporation Taxes Act 1988, ss 360, 360A).

5.16 New shares are usually allotted to a shareholder in return for cash. The shareholder may have to borrow in order to be able to make his investment, and the question then arises whether he will receive any tax relief for interest he pays on these borrowings. A UK resident individual may obtain relief for interest paid on loans taken out to acquire ordinary shares of a close company; or to acquire shares in a co-operative; or to acquire any part of the ordinary share capital of an 'employee-controlled company' where, inter alia, the shareholder is a full-time employee (see the Income and Corporation Taxes Act 1988, s 360). 'Full-time employee' is defined in the ICTA 1988, s 361(8) as 'a person who works for the greater part of his time as an employee or director of the company or of a 51% subsidiary of the company'. Any beneficial interests in shares greater than 10% are treated as not being owned by a full-time employee and relief is denied. All interest is eligible for relief, whether it is paid to a UK resident lender or not. Relief for interest paid on a loan to acquire shares in a close company is used most frequently, and the following discussion concentrates on the detailed requirements to be fulfilled if relief is to be obtained.

5.17 For interest to be eligible for relief under the close company interest relief provisions the following four conditions must all be met:

(a) when interest is paid the payer must have a material interest in a close company. A material interest is, broadly, more than 5% of the ordinary share capital of the company.
(b) The company must, at the time interest is paid, continue to exist wholly or mainly for the purpose of carrying on a trade or certain other activities. However, in *Lord v Tustain* [1993] STC 755, the company was a management buy-out vehicle and the subscription money were used to buy the business. At the time of subscription, therefore, no business was carried on. The court held that this did not matter.
(c) The interest must not be incurred on overdraft, and must not be more than a reasonable commercial return for the principal borrowed. If the return is more than reasonable, relief is only available on the 'reasonable' part and relief is denied on the excess.
(d) The company must be a close company but not a close investment-holding company.

One of two further conditions must be met. The first is that, in the period from the initial investment to the payment of the interest, the shareholder must not have recovered any capital from the company; and, if the company exists wholly or mainly for holding investments or other property, no property is used as a residence by the borrower unless he has worked for the greater part of his time in the actual management or conduct of the company's business. The second of the two conditions is that in the period from the investment to the payment of the interest, the individual has worked full time in the actual management or conduct of the company and the shareholder must not have recovered any capital from the company.

5.18 If a company is neither a close company nor a co-operative nor an employee-controlled company, interest relief is not available to an individual. In this case, it would, in general, be more tax-efficient for the company itself to borrow funds (probably backed up by guarantees from shareholders). The company should obtain a deduction against trading profits for interest paid.

Types of share capital

5.19 The share capital of the company may comprise of more than one class. Each class will carry different rights and entitlements as to such matters as dividend, voting, and distribution of capital on a winding up. Where there is more than one class of share capital, the rights attaching to each must be set out clearly in the articles of association. There are various terms used to describe different types of share capital but these are just a label used for convenience. There is no definition or implied rights of different classes of share capital such as preference shares over and above what is contained in the articles.

5.20 Ordinary shares invariably carry voting rights and entitle the holder to a dividend if declared by the directors. Holders will normally be entitled to any surplus on a winding up after all the liabilities and any preference shareholders have been paid. The articles may provide for different classes of ordinary shares. The different classes normally carry their own entitlement to dividends, voting rights and priority on a winding up. An obvious example is where there are 'A' and 'B' shares, both of which may comprise ordinary share capital, but which have separate rights to protect the interests of different individuals or groups of individuals.

5.21 Preference shares will usually carry a fixed right to dividend (although note that the term merely signifies that the holders have preferred rights to dividend over ordinary shareholders). Sample preference share rights are contained in document 13 in Part II. There are many variants of preference share rights. Venture capitalists, for example, will have their own 'standard' set of rights. Key issues for the drafting of such rights include:

(a) whether the right to a fixed dividend arises automatically (subject of course to the ability of the company to pay a dividend under the Companies Act 1985, s 263) or whether the dividend is to be declared by the directors: how the right is expressed may affect whether the holders can apply to wind up the company on the basis of non-payment or whether their action is merely to require the directors to declare the dividend;
(b) whether the preferential dividend is cumulative, meaning that if dividends are not paid in one year because of the relevant restrictions in the Companies Act 1985, the deficit must be made good in future years before dividends are paid on ordinary shares;
(c) the circumstances in which the preference shares carry votes, quite often limited to the situation where either the preferential dividend is in arrears or where the rights of the preference shareholders are being affected;
(d) whether the preference shares carry participatory dividend rights, or are convertible and/or redeemable.

5.22 Convertible shares are merely shares which either have the right or are subject to conversion into a different class of shares at some future date or on some future contingency. The classic example is convertible preference shares whereby the preference shares have a right to convert into equity shares at a predetermined price or upon a future contingency such as sale or flotation of the company. Convertible preference shares would usually have a lower dividend rate but are obviously more desirable as they carry the potential for participation in higher equity returns. On conversion, no cash is exchanged as conversion merely relates to a change in rights.

5.23 Redeemable shares are shares which are subject to and/or carry the right to redemption in accordance with the Companies Act 1985, Part V, Chapter VII. Financing of that redemption is subject to the same limitations contained in the Companies Act 1985, s 263 as for the payment of dividends. Often shares are to be redeemed in tranches over a period of time. A classic use for redeemable shares is as consideration for the purchase of a company or business, in effect providing for deferred consideration. In the context of an owner-managed business the actual owner-managers are unlikely to invest in redeemable shares. If the owner-managers wished to repay part of the share capital invested by them and this was acceptable to relevant funders, the same effect achieved by redeemable shares could be achieved by a purchase of own shares as with profits or capital.

5.24 No redeemable shares may be issued at a time when there are no issued shares of the company which are not redeemable and a company may not purchase its own shares if as a result of the purchase there would no longer be any member of the company holding shares other than redeemable shares. These provisions contained in s 162 of the Companies Act 1985 ensure that the whole share capital is not redeemable. Redeemable shares may not be redeemed unless they are fully paid and the terms of redemption must provide for payment on redemption (in other words the purchase price cannot be deferred). The Companies Act 1985, s 159A sets out mandatory conditions for the terms and manner of redemption as follows:

(a) the date or dates on which shares are to be redeemed must be specified in the company's articles or, if the articles so provide, fixed by the directors and in the latter case the date or dates must be fixed before the shares are issued;
(b) any other circumstances in which the shares may be redeemed must be specified in the company's articles;
(c) the amount payable on redemption must be specified in or determined in accordance with the company's articles and in the latter case the articles must not provide for the amount to be determined by reference to any person's discretion or opinion; and
(d) any other terms and conditions of redemption (meaning any terms other than statutory requirements) must be specified in the company's articles.

5.25 Deferred shares merely means that the rights attaching to the shares are subject to the rights of other shares. The most common rights attaching to shares of this nature are a right to a certain proportion of surplus profits in each year after payment of a dividend on any shares ranking before them and in the event of the company being wound up, a right to the whole or a certain proportion of surplus assets after repaying the capital paid up on any shares ranking before them.

5.26 Investment by venture capitalists in an owner-managed business would usually comprise some or all of the following:

(a) equity share capital but invariably of a different class from that held by the owner-managers so that the venture capitalist shares would carry rights to appoint a director, special participating dividend rights and the like;
(b) redeemable preference shares (although recent legislation has made it less attractive for venture capitalists to invest in preference shares than in loan capital); and
(c) long-term loan capital.

It is important to match the amount and type of funds to the perceived needs of the business as it develops and grows. Section 6 comprises commentary on venture capital with particular reference to precedents contained in Part II which relate to the largest venture capitalist in the United Kingdom, *3i Group plc*.

Issue of shares

5.27 The leading texts on company law deal extensively with the legal requirements relating to the issue and payment for share capital. The main issues relevant to owner-managed business are, for reference purposes, the following:

(a) shares must not be issued at a discount;
(b) shares allotted by a company and any premium payable on them must be paid in money or money's worth (see ss 99–107 of the Companies Act 1985);
(c) special restrictions apply in respect of the issue of shares in a public limited company (in particular for non-cash consideration);
(d) it is unlawful for a company or any of its subsidiaries to give financial assistance directly or indirectly to any person who is acquiring or proposing to acquire shares for the purpose of that acquisition before or at the same time as the acquisition takes place and it is also unlawful for a company or any of its subsidiaries to give financial assistance directly or indirectly to any person who has acquired any of its shares for the purpose of reducing or discharging any liability incurred by him or any other person for the purposes of that acquisition (see the Companies Act 1985, s 151);
(e) the directors must be authorised to allot shares pursuant to the Companies Act 1985, s 80 (as to which see the appropriate forms of authority contained in document 4 in Part II); and
(f) the issue of shares may be subject to pre-emption provisions in favour of existing shareholders contained in the Companies Act 1985, s 89 (save as excluded by the articles) in the case of issues of shares for cash consideration and/or by the articles themselves in the case of issues for cash or non-cash consideration.

Loans

5.28 Owner-managers will commonly have a loan account which either reflects money introduced to the company by way of loan or amounts which have fallen due for payment to them by the company (for example by way of remuneration) but which had been left in the company to assist with cash flow. In the former case, it may be appropriate to document the loan by way of a simple form of loan agreement. This will be appropriate where it is intended that the loan will not be repayable on demand (which will be the position in the absence of express agreement). The owner-managers may agree between them to commit a level of funds to the company and to permit repayment of those amounts only in certain eventualities and usually only in the same proportions between them as the loans were made. A simple form of loan agreement is included as document 14 in Part II.

5.29 The shareholders may decide to take security from the company for loans made by them. This would invariably rank behind any bank lending money to the company and a deed of postponement may be required. The bank (or indeed any other investor) may require some form of subordination in respect of both the lending by the owner-managers and the security for that lending. The basis for this would be that the lending was 'quasi capital' and that the owner-managers should not be permitted to repay themselves in priority to other investors. Subordination would usually provide that no amounts of the loan capital would be repaid to the owner-managers whilst the company remains indebted to the relevant investor. It may actually be worthwhile providing for the loan agreement in favour of the owner-managers to be repayable by instalments so that (potentially) outside investors would agree that payment of those instalments would not be subject to the provisions for subordination of the lending. The same point could apply in respect of the payment of interest on the loan.

5.30 A simple debenture is included at document 15 in Part II. This is suitable for the situation where the owner-managers simply want to put themselves in a better position than ordinary unsecured creditors. Before granting such a debenture, consideration should be given to the provisions of the Insolvency Act 1986, s 239, concerning preferences. It would obviously be inappropriate to grant such a debenture only when the financial state of the company suggests that it will enter into liquidation or administration. The issue of security should be addressed at the time the loan is originally made, on the basis that the owner-managers are only prepared to give a secured loan. To ensure that the floating charge contained in the debenture is enforceable with immediate effect, the security should be in place before money is transferred into the company, having regard to the Insolvency Act 1985, s 245. However, this can be difficult where funds are being expended by the owner-managers on behalf of the company at the time of its start up.

Other sources of finance

5.31 Mezzanine finance is a debt which is subordinated in that it ranks behind the so-called 'senior debt' both as to repayment and security. It is thus a higher risk form of finance and therefore commands a much higher rate of interest. Mezzanine providers often have the right to acquire shares for a nominal amount in the event of a sale on flotation of the company, to provide them with the high yields required on an investment. This is sometimes known as an 'equity kicker'. This type of finance may be appropriate where there is inadequate security but good cash flow.

5.32 Leasing of equipment is really beyond the scope of this book. Basically, however, an asset is purchased by or for a finance company and leased at an agreed rental over a period reflecting the economic life of the asset. A finance lease exists where the lessee keeps the asset for most of its useful life and experiences all the risks and rewards of ownership including responsibility for maintenance. An operating lease describes (usually) the situation where the lessee keeps the asset for only part of its life and is not responsible for maintenance. Legal title in the asset does not pass to the lessee in either case. The accountancy treatment of such leases differs from financing and operating leases, the detail of which is beyond the scope of this book. The cost of the capital is included in the total cost and spread over the lease payments, frequently resulting in 100% finance of the asset. Medium-term finance (of say three to ten years) is used to finance assets with a similar lifespan such as motor vehicles, plant and machinery. Capital allowances are a key feature in this type of finance and are claimed by the finance company and not by the lessee. A flexible payment package can be designed by the finance house to match the cash flow cycles of the lessee by using low initial rents with a large balloon payment when the asset is sold on at the end of the agreement period. Contract hire is simply a popular form of operating lease used particularly in the case of business motor vehicles.

5.33 Invoice factoring is a method of finance whereby trade debtors are purchased by the factor who assumes responsibility for the sales ledger. A percentage of the invoice value is advanced by the factor (hence improving cash flow) and the remainder is paid on settlement of the debt. The arrangement can be with or without 'recourse'. If it is with recourse, the company is ultimately responsible if the debt turns bad. If without recourse, the factor bears the credit risk.

5.34 Invoice discounting is similar to invoice factoring save that debts are passed to the invoice discounter but the company remains responsible for the sales ledger and for debt collection. The invoice discounter still releases money on the invoicing of debtors against the security offered by those debts.

5.35 Overdraft is a variable finance facility with an agreed limit. It is an on demand facility, meaning that the bank providing the overdraft can require repayment at any time. The bank may confirm a date at which the overdraft limit is to be reviewed although it will strictly reserve the right to require repayment at any time. The applicable rate of interest is usually based on a formula linked to base rates and calculated on a day-to-day basis. It is fairly common for the bank and the company to put in place interest management terms which limit the upper limit (and potentially also the lower limit) of these flexible interest rates.

5.36 Mortgage/term loan is a form of longer-term finance usually used to purchase property or assets.

6 Venture capital

The investment package

6.1 There is set out in forms 7A and 7B in Part II post, standard form documents produced by 3i Group plc ('3i'), a leading venture capital institution. 3i specialises in providing a typical mix of equity capital and loan finance funding to business. Venture capital financing has grown hand-in-hand with the development of corporate finance as a distinct area of professional practice for accountants and solicitors, amongst others. Perhaps the most common example of a venture capital funded acquisition transaction is the 'management buy-out' or 'MBO'. This transaction, as its name suggests, involves the managers acquiring the business from separate owners. It follows from this that a prerequisite to an MBO transaction is a sophisticated target business, with a separately defined class of managers. As these managers are unlikely to have significant personal wealth, venture capital institutions provide a source of funding to enable the acquisition to take place.

6.2 Typically, the management team will require funding both for the acquisition and the subsequent provision of working capital. Usually, a new private limited company (often described in the draft documentation as 'Newco') will be acquired as the vehicle for the acquisition. Venture capitalists will inevitably require a limited company for reasons including:

(a) to secure the benefits of limited liability for their involvement as investor in the business;
(b) the ability of a limited company to offer security in the form of a floating charge;
(c) the institution's investment requirements are most readily met by virtue of the creation of special categories of shares, setting out the special rights to be granted.

The 3i Investment Package comprises of the following:

(a) Investment Agreement (form 7A in Part II, post)
(b) Articles of Association (form 7B in Part II, post)

These documents constitute a contract between 3i, the owners and/or managers of the company, and the company itself.

Development finance

6.3 Venture capital may also be used by businesses to finance business growth. 'Development finance' transactions involve the use of the same investment package documentation, the one distinction being that such transactions involve only the venture capitalist and the business, without the added complication of parallel negotiations with the vendor of the target business. It may be that the commercial terms available to owners of an emerging business in the context of development finance may be more beneficial than would be available to a management buy-out team. This acknowledges the greater risk (and hence commensurately higher reward) that characterises such MBO transactions. It may be considered that the financing of an existing management/business with an established track-record entails less commercial risk, the 'risk/reward ratio' accordingly dictating the commercial reward that may be sought by the venture capital institutions.

Investment Agreement, section 2, Part 1

6.4 Section 2 of the agreement sets out in Part 1 details of the share capital, drawing a distinction between the investment to be made by 3i and that being contributed from other sources. In the sample investment agreement, the directors are to contribute £150,000 for ordinary shares, constituting 60% of the equity share capital, 3i is to contribute £100,000 for 'A' ordinary shares, constituting 40% of the equity share capital. Venture capital institutions will typically seek to have equity participation in the region of 20 to 40% of the equity share capital.

Investment Agreement, section 2, Part 2, clause 1

6.5 Part 2 of section 2 of the Investment Agreement summarises the share rights attaching to 3i's preference shares and 'A' ordinary shares. Typically, the preference shares will exhibit the following characteristics:

(a) They will be redeemable in a number of instalments or tranches, possibly commencing one or two years after the date of investment.

(b) They will be entitled to receive as a first call on profits a fixed dividend, stated as a percentage of the subscription price. Such dividends are commonly paid half-yearly, and again there may be negotiations as to the date upon which the first payment is to be made. Such a dividend entitlement will invariably be 'cumulative' from the date of subscription. The effect of this is that, in the event of the company failing to make a dividend payment (for instance, where it does not have profits available for distribution in accordance with the Companies Act), then the entitlement of 3i to receive its fixed dividend is not extinguished, merely postponed to subsequent years.

6.6 The A ordinary shares to be allocated to 3i are similarly entitled to a fixed dividend, ranking behind the fixed dividend payable on the preference shares, but otherwise having similar characteristics. The A ordinary shares also carry a right to a 'participating dividend' of an amount equal to 7% of group profits, as that expression is defined in the Agreement and (in more detail) in the Articles of Association, after deduction of the fixed dividend. The entitlement to reward is thus closely linked to the fortunes of the business. The appropriate percentage figure is always a matter of negotiation between the venture capital institution and the directors and their advisers. The A ordinary shares also carry a right to a 'compensatory dividend', linked to any payment by the directors of remuneration above pre-ordained agreed levels set out in the Investment Agreement and Articles of Association. The directors are prohibited from paying themselves dividends on the ordinary shares, unless all dividends have been paid up to date to 3i, and all redeemable shares subject to redemption have been redeemed. This Investment Agreement proposes further restrictions on the payment of dividends. Commonly, the directors will be restricted from paying dividends to ordinary shareholders which exceed any dividends which have been paid to the A ordinary shareholders.

Investment Agreement, section 2, Part 2, clause 2

6.7 On a return of capital, the preference shareholders are repaid first their subscription price, then the A ordinary shareholders, with the ordinary shares ranking third. Any surplus is shared by the holders of the ordinary shares and A ordinary shares as if the shares were of a single class.

Investment Agreement, section 2, Part 2, clause 3

6.8 There are restrictions on redemption of preference shares earlier than the due date, unless the holders of such shares agree. This acknowledges that 3i has based its investment decision upon a certain return on its investment; allowing early redemption would directly affect the overall level of this return.

Investment Agreement, section 2, Part 2, clause 4

6.9 There are set out in clause 4 certain class protection provisions. Whilst, whenever a company has shares of different classes, there are contained, within the Companies Act and under common law, restrictions on the variation of class rights, express class protection provisions are invariably included at the behest of the venture capitalist, in part to establish clearly the parameters within which the investors may operate and also to acknowledge the limitations on the restrictions contained by statute or under common law.

Investment Agreement, section 2, Part 2, clause 5

6.10 Clause 5 refers to the pre-emption rights contained in the Articles of Association which restrict the transfer of shares by the directors. Commonly, the venture capital institution will insist upon the right to make inter-group transfers. There may also be a permitted excepted class of 'permitted family transfers', which may be made by the directors to their spouses or other immediate family relations, eg for the purposes of personal tax planning.

6.11 The Agreement and Articles of Association may also include a 'deemed transfer provision' under which a director leaving employment with the company is deemed to serve a transfer notice in respect of his entire holding. In considering provision of this nature, there is necessarily a balancing act to be undertaken between the interests of the venture capitalist (and indeed other director/investors) and the individual concerned. Such clauses are commonly included in management buy-out transactions, acknowledging the underlying owner/manager culture of such companies. There is also commonly included, notwithstanding the existence of pre-emption provisions, an absolute restriction on transfer by the directors of a 'controlling interest' in the company, unless the would-be purchaser also acquires the shares of the venture capital institution. This is commonly known as a 'bring along' clause.

Investment Agreement, section 2, Part 2, clause 6

6.12 As to voting, typically the A ordinary shares are full voting shares, carrying the same rights as the directors' ordinary shares, although the preference shares are non-voting.

Investment Agreement, section 3

6.13 Section 3 sets out certain investor protection terms. Typically, there is included a maximum ceiling on borrowings without prior consent of 3i. Group borrowing is extensively defined to include matters such as hire purchase, leasing etc, and the full ambit of such extended definition will require careful consideration in the context of each individual company.

Investment Agreement, section 4

6.14 Section 4 sets out detailed provisions in relation to the nature and extent of financial and other information required to be provided by the directors on a periodic basis.

Investment Agreement, section 5

6.15 Section 5 sets out a series of warranties to be given by the directors, subject to any agreed disclosures set out in a disclosure letter. The nature of the warranties to be given should be carefully considered with the directors. It should be noted that the nature and the extent of the warranties sought by different venture capital institutions vary. These warranties are designed for use in a typical MBO transaction. A warranty is taken to the effect that the company (ie NewCo) has not traded, with separate warranties being taken with regard to the financial position of the target group (ie the business which is to be acquired by NewCo). It is common for venture capitalists to require extended warranties with regard to information supplied, acknowledging that the investment decision is based largely upon the nature of financial and other information disclosed to it, as opposed to its own searches and enquiries. The directors are not only required to warrant that information supplied was at the time given true and accurate in all material respects, but also:

(a) that such information remains accurate (ie is deemed warranted as accurate as at the date of investment);
(b) the directors are not aware of anything which renders such information misleading; and
(c) the directors are not aware of anything which materially adversely affects the trading prospects of the company or the target group. The effect of this warranty may need to be carefully considered with the directors.

6.16 Part 2 contains the quite typical individual warranties given by each of the directors which regard to their other business interests. There is set out in section 5A the nature and extent of each individual director's several liability. There is also a time-period within which claims may be brought by 3i. It should be noted that the time and financial limits do not relate to claims resulting from a director's fraud, wilful misconduct or wilful concealment.

Investment Agreement, section 6

6.17 Section 6 sets out the fees payable. Typically a negotiation fee is paid on completion, together with reimbursement of all legal fees, and a monitoring fee paid by quarterly instalments during each year of the investment.

Investment Agreement, section 7

6.18 By virtue of s 7, the provision of funding is subject to satisfactory fulfilment of a number of pre-conditions, including commercial matters such as satisfactory bank facilities, financial performance as disclosed by recent audited and/or management accounts and satisfactory references. With regard to the specific legal matters upon which 3i's solicitor is to be satisfied, typically supplemental standard forms of certificate are produced in draft form by the nominated solicitors and are required to be completed by the solicitors advising the directors. Any amendments to these standard forms will need to be individually negotiated with 3i's solicitors.

3i Articles of Association

6.19 The Articles of Association embody many of the special rights granted in favour of the venture capital institution as described in the Investment Agreement. 3i adopts as the basis of its Articles Table A, making the appropriate amendments as necessary. There is set out in Special Article 3 the rights attaching to the respective classes of shares. This, in particular, sets out in full the dividend entitlement relative to the various classes of shares as derived from the summary in the Investment Agreement. In the context of advising upon these Articles, specific attention should be given to the defined terms, in particular 'Net Profit', 'Excess Remuneration', 'Employee Member' and 'Privileged Relation'. The items to be included or disregarded in connection with each definition may well vary from transaction to transaction. It will be noted that the 'A' ordinary shares are stated to be convertible into a like number of ordinary shares. This type of provision is commonly included to facilitate, inter alia, share re-construction considered appropriate in the context of an application for admission to listing on a recognised investment exchange. The statutory pre-emption provisions on the issue of further shares have been modified to facilitate allotments to other companies within the 3i group.

6.20 Depending on the requirements of individual venture capital institutions, the Investment Agreement may well be required to be entered into at an early stage in the negotiations. In such cases, consideration needs to be given as to the liability of the directors to the venture capital institutions in the event that the transaction does not proceed to completion. It is common for the Articles of Association to be adopted by the company on the completion date. This will involve the production of supplemental documents, minutes of board meeting, notice of EGM/written resolutions as appropriate. Commonly, the solicitors to the venture capital institutions will produce draft documentation for approval.

7 Business stationery

Companies

7.1 By statute certain information is required to be specified on a company's business stationery and certain other business documentation. The Companies Act 1985, ss 349 and 351 state as follows:

'349 Company's name to appear in its correspondence, etc

(1) Every company shall have its name mentioned in legible characters:

(a) in all business letters of the company,
(b) in all its notices and other official publications,
(c) in all bills of exchange, promissory notes, endorsements, cheques and orders for money or goods purporting to be signed by or on behalf of the company, and
(d) in all its bills of parcels, invoices, receipts and letters of credit.

(2) If a company fails to comply with sub-s (1) it is liable to a fine.
(3) If an officer of a company or a person on its behalf:

(a) issues or authorises the issue of any business letter of the company, or any notice or other official publication of the company, in which the company's name is not mentioned as required by sub-s (1), or
(b) issues or authorises the issue of any bill of parcels, invoice, receipt or letter of credit of the company in which its name is not so mentioned, he is liable to a fine.

(4) If an officer of a company or a person on its behalf signs or authorises to be signed on behalf of the company any bill of exchange, promissory note, endorsement, cheque or order for money or goods in which the company's name is not mentioned as required by sub-s (1), he is liable to a fine; and he is further personally liable to the holder of the bill of exchange, promissory note, cheque or order for money or goods for the amount of it (unless it is duly paid by the company).

'351 Particulars in correspondence etc

(1) Every company shall have the following particulars mentioned in legible characters in all business letters and order forms of the company, that is to say:

(a) the company's place of registration and the number with which it is registered,
(b) the address of its registered office,
(c) in the case of an investment company (as defined in section 266), the fact that it is such a company, and

(d) in the case of a limited company exempt from the obligation to use the word 'limited' as part of its name, the fact that it is a limited company.

(2) If in the case of a company having a share capital there is on the stationery used for any such letters, or on the company's order forms, a reference to the amount of share capital, the reference must be to paid-up share capital.

(3), (4) (repealed).

(5) As to contraventions of this section, the following applies:

(a) if a company fails to comply with sub-s (1) or (2), it is liable to a fine, and

(b) if an officer of a company or a person on its behalf issues or authorises the issue of any business letter or order form not complying with those sub-sections, he is liable to a fine.'

7.2 There are additional (but corresponding) disclosure requirements where the company adopts a business name other than its full corporate name contained in the Business Names Act 1985.

7.3 These requirements, which relate in part to business stationery alone but in other respects apply more extensively to other documentation, may be summarised as follows:

(a) There must be included on business letters and other documents the full name of the company in legible characters.

(b) There must also be included on business letters and order forms:

(i) the company's place of registration and registered number;

(ii) the address of the company's registered office;

(iii) where a company is an 'investment company' as defined in the Companies Act 1985, s 66 the fact that it is such a company;

(iv) in the case of a company exempt from using the word 'limited' as part of its name, the fact that it is a limited company.

(c) In addition, whilst there is no obligation to refer to the company's share capital where such a reference is made the reference must be made to paid up share capital.

7.4 The registration of a company with a name which gives the impression that the business is connected with HM government or any local authority or which otherwise uses any word or expression specified in the Company and Business Names Regulations 1981, SI 1981/1685, is prohibited without the written approval of the Secretary of State. The relevant words and expressions are set out in Table 8.

TABLE 8: LIST OF WORDS AND EXPRESSIONS REQUIRING APPROVAL FOR USE IN BUSINESS NAME

Abortion	Department of Health (formerly Department of Health and Social Security)
Apothecary	Worshipful Society of Apothecaries of London or Pharmaceutical Society of Great Britain
Association	
Assurance	
Assurer	
Authority	
Benevolent	

TABLE 8: *Cont.*

Board	
British	
Chamber of Commerce	
Chamber of Commerce, Training and Enterprise	
Chamber of Industry	
Chamber of Trade	
Charitable	
Charity	Charity Commission
Charter	
Chartered	
Chemist	
Chemistry	
Contact Lens	General Optical Council
Co-operative	
Council	
Dental	General Dental Council
Dentistry	
District Nurse	United Kingdom Central Council for Nursing, Midwifery and Health Visiting; and the National Boards for Nursing, Midwifery and Health Visiting
Duke	Home Office or Scottish Home and Health Department
England	
English	
European	
Federation	
Friendly Society	
Foundation	
Fund	
Giro	
Great Britain	
Group	
Health Centre	Department of Health (formerly Department of Health and Social Security)
Health Service	
Health Visitor	United Kingdom Central Council for Nursing Midwifery and Health Visiting; and the National Boards for Nursing, Midwifery and Health Visiting
Her Majesty	Home Office or Scottish Home and Health Department
His Majesty	
Holding	
Industrial and Provident Society	
Institute	
Institution	
Insurance	
Insurer	
International	
Ireland	
Irish	

TABLE 8: *Cont.*

King	Home Office or Scottish Home and Health Department
Midwife Midwifery	United Kingdom Central Council for Nursing, Midwifery and Health Visiting; and the National Boards for Nursing, Midwifery and Health Visiting
National	
Nurse Nursing	United Kingdom Central Council for Nursing, Midwifery and Health Visiting; and the National Boards for Nursing, Midwifery and Health Visiting
Patent Patentee	
Police	Home Office or Scottish Home and Health Department
Polytechnic	Department for Education and Employment
Post Office	
Pregnancy Termination	Department of Health (formerly Department of Health and Social Security)
Prince Princess Queen	Home Office or Scottish Home and Health Department
Reassurance Reassurer Register Registered Reinsurance Reinsurer	
Royal Royale Royalty	Home Office or Scottish Home and Health Department
Scotland Scottish Sheffield Society	
Special School	Department for Education and Employment
Stock Exchange Trade Union Trust United Kingdom	
University	The Privy Council
Wales Welsh	
Windsor	Home Office or Scottish Home and Health Department

Directors' names on business letters

7.5 The name of any director of a company may not be stated in any form on any business letter (other than in the text of or as a signatory to such a letter) on which the company's name appears unless there is stated on the letter in legible characters the names of every director of the company (see the Companies Act 1985, s 305(1)). The obligation is satisfied by stating of the christian name (or forename) and surname of the individual (eg Gavin White) although by way or relaxation of this rule an initial (eg G White) or recognised abbreviation (eg Gav White) may be used. Similarly, in the case of peers or other individuals known by a title, the title may be used either in addition to or in substitution for the individual's name.

Companies adopting business names

7.6 The disclosure requirements of the Business Names Act 1985 apply to a company having a place of business in Great Britain and carrying on business in Great Britain under a name other than its corporate name without additions other than additions permitted by the Act.

7.7 A company using a business name must ensure that there is stated in legible letters on all business letters and certain other documents the following:

(a) its corporate name;
(b) an address in Great Britain for service of documents.

7.8 The use by a company of a business name is similarly subject to the Regulations. For an example of business stationery complying with the requirements of the Companies Act 1985 (in the case of a company carrying on business under its corporate name) and in respect of the additional requirements of the Business Names Act 1985 (in the case of a company carrying on business under a business name) see the sample stationery of the publisher of this work and its parent company set out in document 19 in Part II. Table 9 comprises a checklist of matters to be considered in relation to business stationery.

Additional disclosure requirements

7.9 Where a company is registered for value added tax purposes, the VAT registration number is commonly stated upon business letters and other stationery although this is not essential. The VAT registration number must however be stated on invoices issued by a VAT registered company or person.

The name of a company must be painted or affixed in a conspicuous position and in easily legible lettering outside every office or other place in which the company's business is carried on. Where a business name is used by a company then its corporate name and address for service of documents within Great Britain must be displayed in any premises where the business is carried on and to which customers or suppliers of the business have access. Such notice must appear in a prominent position in order that it may easily be read by such customers and suppliers. Details of the company name and an address for service must be given immediately in writing to any person with whom anything is done or discussed in the course of business and who has asked for such name and address.

Penalties

7.10 Any breach of the various publicity requirements gives rise to a liability to penalties on the part of the company and any officer or other person on its behalf who issues business stationery (or other documents) not complying with the statutory requirements. Such penalties basically consist of fines. However, of even more serious consequence is the further sanction for the 'officer or other person' signing on behalf of a company any bill of exchange, promissory note, endorsement, cheque or order for goods or money upon which the company's name is not mentioned as required by the Companies Act 1985, s 349. Such person is not only liable to a fine but is also personally liable to the holder of the bill of exchange etc for the amount of it unless it is duly paid by the company. Liability may attach to officers not only in the situation where the company's name (or part of it) is omitted but also where it is improperly abbreviated. This section is often invoked where the company's insolvent and stationery, and even cheques are improperly printed. There are also civil remedies for breach of the Business Names Act 1985, s 4. The Business Names Act 1985, s 5 states:

> '5 Civil remedies for breach of s 4
>
> (1) Any legal proceedings brought by a person to whom this Act applies to enforce a right arising out of a contract made in the course of a business in respect of which he has, at the time the contract was made, in breach of sub-s (1) or (2) of s 4 shall be dismissed if the defendant (or, in Scotland, the defender) to the proceedings shows:
>
> (a) that he has a claim against the plaintiff (pursuer) arising out of that contract which he has been unable to pursue by reason of the latter's breach of s 4(1) or (2), or
>
> (b) that he has suffered some financial loss in connection with the contract by reason of the plaintiff's (pursuers) breach of s 4(1) or (2), unless the court before which the proceedings are brought is satisfied that it is just and equitable to permit the proceedings to continue.
>
> (2) This section is without prejudice to the right of any person to enforce such rights as he may have against another person in any proceedings brought by that person.'

Publicity requirements – sole traders and partnerships

7.11 The provisions of the Business Names Act 1985 and the Company and Business Names Regulations 1981 are equally applicable to sole traders in so far as the business name chosen contains words or expressions requiring the approval of the Secretary of State or other recognised person.

7.12 The provisions of the Business Names Act apply to a sole trader carrying on business in Great Britain under a name which does not consist of his surname without any addition other than the permitted addition of the individual's forename or his initial.

7.13 The provisions of the Business Names Act again apply in the case of a partnership which carries on business in Great Britain under a name not consisting of all the surnames of the partners who are individuals (and the names of any partners who are bodies corporate) without addition other than permitted additions as follows:

(a) forenames (or their initials) of partners who are individuals; and
(b) where two or more individual partners have the same surname the addition of 's' at the end of that surname.

In the case of both sole traders and partnerships, as with companies, an indication that the business is carried on in succession is permitted.

7.14 The disclosure requirements in s 4 extend to the same business documentation as with companies, and are satisfied in the case of sole traders by a statement in legible letters of the name of the individual and, in the case of a partnership, a statement in legible letters of the names of each partner. The penalties described in paragraph 7.10 would equally apply.

7.15 There is a further exemption in favour of partnerships of more than 20 persons who maintain a list of names of all partners at the principal place of business, provided none of the names of the partners appears in the document (other than in the text or as a signatory) and, further, that the document states in legible letters the address of the partnership's principal place of business and that the list of partners is open to inspection at that place.

TABLE 9: CHECKLIST OF MATTERS TO BE CONSIDERED WHEN ADVISING AS TO THE CONTENTS OF BUSINESS STATIONERY AND OTHER DOCUMENTATION

1. Full name of the company.
2. Place of registration and registered number.
3. Address of company's registered office.
4. Is the company an investment company as defined in the Companies Act 1985, s 266? If so, there are additional disclosure requirements.
5. Is the company exempted from using the word 'limited' within its corporate name? If so, there are additional disclosure requirements.
6. Are the names of any of the directors of the company to be stated? If so, the names of all directors are required to be stated in legible letters.
7. Is the company to use a trading name other than its full corporate name? If so, see the requirements of the Business Names Act 1985.
8. Is the company proposing to use in its company name any words or expressions in respect of which consents are required under the Companies Act 1985 or the Regulations?
9. Is the company registered or to be registered for VAT purposes? If so, consider whether the VAT registration number should be specified.

8 Terms and conditions of trading

Standard terms and conditions of trading

8.1 A small or emerging business will often be confronted with insistence on the part of its suppliers or customers that all contracts between them be formed on the basis of such other party's standard terms and conditions of sale or purchase. Such terms are typically very one-sided in operation, although this practice has been somewhat modified in the light of the Unfair Terms in Consumer Contracts Regulations 1994, SI 1994/309. Accordingly, the primary objective of this chapter is to review the principal terms and conditions commonly incorporated into standard terms of sale and purchase, and to analyse critically the effect of these terms from the perspective of the recipient. If the basic proposition that small or emerging businesses may have difficulties in resisting the pressure to contract on the standard terms of others is accepted, then the recipient needs to consider:

(a) the nature and effect of the clauses in question; and
(b) practical measures that may be taken to minimise potential liabilities, even as to avoiding the effect of incorporation of the other party's standard terms.

A set of draft terms and conditions of sale are included as document 17 (together with a credit application form) in Part II.

'Battle of the forms'

8.2 A seller adopting standard terms and conditions of sale will typically reprint these conditions on a selection of business documentation to include price lists and quotation forms, catalogues, acknowledgement of order forms, invoices and delivery notes. Similarly, a buyer adopting standard conditions of order will print the terms on their standard official order forms. Whether the contract is concluded on the party's conditions will depend upon what the recipient does next. Where the supplier receives a standard order form incorporating buyer's terms and conditions, and simply delivers goods pursuant to the buyer's order then the contract will be concluded on the buyer's conditions. If the buyer receives standard conditions of sale and does nothing more but accept delivery then the contract will be concluded on the seller's conditions. If, however, in either situation, in response to the standard terms the relevant party 'accepts' the offer to supply or purchase by submitting its own confirmatory documentation incorporating its own terms and conditions then this 'acceptance' subject to the incorporation of different conditions is treated as a counter-offer. The result of this is that if the other party then proceeds with the sale or purchase without more he will be deemed to have agreed by conduct to the counter-offer and all its terms which will then become binding. The effect of this 'last shot' rule is that whichever of the seller or buyer is last to get their conditions into the pre-contract negotiations, without objection, should succeed in establishing that his conditions spell out the terms of their agreement.

8.3 This ritual is known as the 'battle of the forms'. From the point of view of the business client the vagaries involved are unsatisfactory in that they provide no commercial certainty to either party. A further particular problem is that of telephone sales often made worse where the sales are conducted by junior members of staff. Far too often it is not appreciated that the contract can be concluded over the telephone without the incorporation of either party's terms and conditions. However, from the point of view of the smaller business unable to formally 'negotiate' any amendment to the standard terms of the more powerful party, the uncertainties in this common law approach can be used to its benefit.

8.4 It may be said that legally the only way in which a party can ensure with certainty that its conditions will apply in relation to a particular contract will be to go to the lengths of obtaining the customer's/supplier's written agreement on each occasion. For commercial reasons this is obviously not practicable. The best available practice may be for the business to circulate its standard conditions together with a form to be returned indicating the customer's/supplier's acceptance to these terms as governing all future contracts between the parties. A party wishing to avoid being tied down to another party's standard terms may be well advised not to return any such form or, alternatively, to 'accept' the conditions set out in such form by means of a covering letter which seeks to reiterate the party's own standard terms.

8.5 A supplier is likely to be in a stronger position as it is submitted that the use of standard conditions of purchase is far less widespread than the use of standard conditions of sale. Accordingly, in this situation, even where the supplier is dealing with ostensibly more powerful customers he may have the opportunity to incorporate standard terms of sale, provided that this is presented in an optically acceptable manner, ie where there is a positive benefit to the recipient in accepting the terms. For instance, where the client is dealing with a new customer, acceptance of the terms may be presented as the basis for allowing the customer to acquire goods on credit terms. Reference could be made to the conditions in a standard credit application form. Upon signing the application, the customer is asked to give an acknowledgment that the supplier's conditions govern orders placed.

Conditions to apply exclusively

8.6 Use can also be made of provisions which are commonly found in both sale and purchase conditions, on the lines of the following:

'Conditions applicable

1 These conditions shall apply to all contracts for the sale of goods by the seller to the buyer to the exclusion of all other terms and conditions including any terms or conditions which the buyer may purport to apply under any purchase order confirmation of order or similar document.

2 All orders for goods shall be deemed to be an offer by the buyer to purchase goods pursuant to these conditions.

3 Acceptance of delivery of the goods shall be deemed conclusive evidence of the buyer's acceptance of these conditions.

4 Any variation to these conditions (including any special terms and conditions agreed between the parties) shall be inapplicable unless agreed in writing by the seller.'

The above clauses may be found in sale conditions. A comparable provision to be contained in purchase conditions is the following:

'Conditions applicable

1 The conditions shall apply to all contracts for the purchase of goods by the buyer from the seller to the exclusion of all other terms and conditions including any terms or conditions which the seller may purport to apply under any sales offer or similar document.

2 Despatch or delivery of the goods by the seller to the buyer shall be deemed conclusive evidence of the seller's acceptance of these conditions.

3 Any variation of these conditions (including any special terms and conditions agreed between the parties) shall be inapplicable unless agreed in writing by the buyer.'

8.7 In either case the intent is the same, namely, an attempt to win the battle of the forms with the first salvo. This is considered a useful approach as it at least enables the party to be in a position to argue that the last shot rule should not apply due to the clear intention of the party to offer to contract on its own terms only, and that such intention survives the assault of any counter-offer from the other party. Of course, the practical problem that ensues is that both buyer and seller may seek to incorporate a similar provision. However, it is submitted that even in this situation the client may benefit from 'muddying the waters', which may be the most that the client is able to achieve bearing in mind the economic strength of the other party. A variation on this theme would be to incorporate a statement in all contractual negotiations to the effect that the client's terms are incorporated in any contract to the exclusion of all other terms.

8.8 The final sub-clause of both sale and purchase conditions printed above represents a further attempt to win the battle of the forms by reference to variations. Again such provision is, it is submitted, inconclusive. Firstly, the provision pre-supposes incorporation of the standard terms and secondly, where it can be established that a party has waived its strict contractual rights (eg by conduct in agreeing verbally to variations) then it may be very difficult for the party to rely upon a provision of this nature.

8.9 The client should be encouraged to establish checklists which will form the basis of dealings with customers/suppliers conducted by more junior members of staff. It is submitted that the party with economic strength is less likely to become the victor in the battle of the forms than the party who can demonstrate the tighter procedures. However, unless the client does have the administrative resources and commercial willingness to seek to win the battle of the forms, the costs and inconvenience of the exercise are likely to be prohibitive. In other cases, merely taking part in the ritual may at least serve to muddy the waters and leave open doubts as to incorporation which can be utilised as a bargaining lever should problems be encountered.

Price and payment

8.10 The seller will seek to establish the price to be paid and payment terms, eg:

> '1 The price shall be [the seller's quoted price *or* the price set out overleaf]. The price is exclusive of VAT which shall be due at the rate ruling on the date of the seller's invoice.
>
> 2 Payment of the price and VAT shall be due within [30] days of the date of the date of the invoice. [Time for payment shall be of the essence.]
>
> 3 Interest on overdue invoices shall accrue from the date when payment becomes due from day to day until the date of payment at a rate of [2]% above *(name)* bank plc's base rate from time to time in force and shall accrue at such a rate after as well as before any judgment.'

Under the Sale of Goods Act 1979 the time for payment is not generally of the essence. Accordingly, a provision, commonly included by sellers, is that time is to be of the essence, ie any failure to pay on the due date will represent a breach of a contract condition entitling the seller to rescind the contract for breach of condition and/or to claim damages.

8.11 The seller's conditions may also seek to reserve the right to make unilateral variations in the price to be charged, usually by reference to external events giving rise to an increase in the seller's costs of supply, eg:

> 'The price of the goods shall be the seller's quoted price which shall be binding on the seller provided that the buyer shall accept the seller's quotation within [30] days. The seller may by giving notice to the buyer at any time up to [7] days before delivery increase the price of the goods to reflect any increase in the cost to the seller which is due to factors occurring after the making of the contract of sale which are beyond the reasonable control of the seller (including, without limitation, foreign exchange fluctuations, taxes and duties and the cost of labour, materials and other manufacturing costs). Provided that the buyer may cancel this contract within [7] days of any such notice from the seller. The price is exclusive of VAT which shall be due at the rate ruling on the date of VAT invoice.'

The effect of the above clause needs to be explained to the client. The client should also watch for any provision which provides for price to be determined by any prevailing prices at the date of dispatch of goods rather than the date the buyer placed the order, eg:

> 'The price of the goods shall be the price stipulated in the seller's published price list current at the date of delivery of the goods. The price is exclusive of VAT which shall be due at the rate ruling on the date of VAT invoice.'

Again the buyer here is vulnerable to unilateral increases in the seller's standard prices. Of course, commercially, the ability of the seller to get away with imposing unilateral variations (notwithstanding the reservation of appropriate rights within its terms and conditions) will depend upon a number of factors including the availability of alternative supply sources.

8.12 The buyer may seek to incorporate a term allowing it to set-off against moneys due to the seller any amounts owed by the seller to the buyer, eg:

> 'The buyer may set off against the price (including any applicable VAT payable) amounts due from the seller whether under the applicable contract of sale or otherwise.'

The buyer's extended wording would, it is submitted, include claims not only under the present contract but also claims in relation to other contracts and tortious claims.

Seller's exclusion of liability – limiting the down side

8.13 By virtue of the Sale of Goods Act 1979 (as amended by the Supply of Goods and Services Act 1994) there is implied into every contract for the sale of goods a number of implied conditions and warranties including the following:

(a) A condition that the seller has title to sell the goods.
(b) A condition that the goods will be of satisfactory quality.
(c) A condition that the goods be reasonably fit for purpose.
(d) A condition that goods will correspond with any description attached to them or sample previously supplied.

These implied conditions apply in all contracts for sale, including contracts between businesses. There is also a potential liability on sellers (and indeed manufacturers and other parties involved in the chain of distribution) under the common law tort of negligence and, in favour of consumers, liability under the Consumer Protection Act 1987. Most sellers will seek to exclude or limit their liability by reference to a standard term of contract. Such terms are known as exclusion clauses. From a commercial point of view the seller will not usually be relying on the exclusion clause to supply to the buyer goods which by any standard are unsatisfactory. No business is likely to survive which supplies its customers late, with defective goods. Typically, the exclusion clause will come into play where the seller is attempting to recover the price of the goods sold and the buyer resists payment by invoking unmeritorious claims that the goods are in some way not suitable.

8.14 Three key areas need to be addressed by the adviser to the seller, in order to maximise the prospects of the seller being entitled to rely upon the benefit of an exclusion clause:

(a) *Incorporation*

If the clause is not included within the contract because the seller's terms as a whole are not incorporated, then it will provide no protection.

(b) *Interpretation*

It is important to have a comprehensively drafted exclusion clause to eliminate arguments that the cause of action alleged is not covered by the clause. The so-called 'contra proferentem' rule operates against the party seeking to rely upon standard terms. Particularly in the case of exclusion clauses any provision will be interpreted in favour of the recipient.

(c) *Statutory intervention*

Clauses seeking to exclude or restrict liability are subject to regulation by the Unfair Contract Terms Act 1977 and more recently by the broader requirements of the Unfair Terms in Consumer Contracts Regulations 1994.

Under the terms of the Unfair Contract Terms Act 1977 a person cannot exclude or restrict liability for death or personal injury resulting from negligence.

Requirement of reasonableness

8.15 In his 'written standard terms of business' a seller of goods may only seek to exclude or restrict liability for breach of any of the implied conditions in the Sale of Goods Act 1979, ss 13–15, or for any breach of an express term of contract, as against a business customer if the term excluding or restricting liability satisfies the requirement of reasonableness. There is a similar restriction upon the seller seeking to claim to supply substantially different goods or indeed supplying no goods at all. The ability of the seller to exclude or restrict liability in favour of consumers is very limited.

8.16 The key question arising from this is 'what is reasonable?' The Unfair Contract Terms Act 1977, s 11 requires that the clause 'shall have been a fair and reasonable one to be included having regard to the circumstances which were, or ought reasonably to have been, known to or in the contemplation of the parties when the contract was made'. Schedule 2 to the Act lays down a number of guidelines to determine whether the test of reasonableness is satisfied, it being upon the seller to prove that the contract term excluding or restricting liability is reasonable. There are five matters to be taken into account and which will therefore need to be carefully considered by the seller. They are as follows:

(a) *Relative bargaining strength*

This refers to such matters as whether the buyer could have bought the goods elsewhere.

(b) *Whether the buyer received an inducement to agree to the clause or whether he had the opportunity of entering into a similar contract with other suppliers without a limitation/exclusion clause*

This would typically cover the situation where the buyer realised he was getting a bargain or discount on the price for whatever reason, or where a 'two tier' service was offered, one option at a higher price containing no exclusion of liability and the second, cheaper, option containing the exclusion clause.

(c) *The buyer's knowledge of the term excluding liability*

It will, for example, be more difficult for the buyer to claim that the term is unreasonable where the seller has been dealing on his terms and conditions for a long period of time.

(d) *Exemption if conditions not complied with*

This refers to the situation, for example, where the seller stipulates an unreasonably short period of time in which to return defective goods, thereby allowing the buyer limited time to examine them.

(e) *Whether the goods were manufactured, processed or adapted to the special order of the buyer*

8.17 A further major factor in determining the reasonableness of a clause seeking to limit liability will be the ability of the seller to obtain product liability insurance cover in respect of possible claims. Accordingly, it would be prudent, subject to the costs involved, for such cover to be maintained. Product liability insurance may be available as part of a comprehensive business insurance policy or may need to be acquired as a bolt-on element to the client's existing public liability insurances. A short form exclusion clause to be included in sale conditions might typically comprise the following:

> 'All terms, conditions and warranties (whether implied or made expressly) whether by the seller or its servants or agents or otherwise (other than those express warranties set out in the current edition of the seller's specification) relating to the quality and/or fitness for purpose of the goods or any of the goods are excluded.'

Omnibus limitation clauses

8.18 Alternatively, an 'omnibus' type clause will deal separately with the various implied conditions.

Description

'1 The goods shall be [manufactured and] supplied in accordance with the description contained in the seller's specification and manufactured in accordance [with all applicable British standards which relate specifically to the goods *or* with British standard *(number)*].

2 The seller may from time to time make changes in the specification of the goods which are required to comply with any applicable safety or statutory requirements or which do not materially affect the quality or fitness for purpose of the goods.'

Sales by sample

'1 The bulk of the goods will correspond with the sample in quality provided that the seller shall have no liability to the buyer unless more than [5]% of the goods do not so correspond.

2 The buyer shall be deemed to have had a reasonable opportunity of comparing the bulk of any consignment of goods with the sample after [2] days from delivery have expired.

3 Upon the buyer having been deemed to have had a reasonable opportunity of comparing the bulk of any consignment with the sample the buyer will also be deemed to have notice of any defect rendering the goods not in accordance with the contract and to have accepted all the goods so delivered.'

Allowable discrepancies in quantity

'1 The buyer shall take delivery of the goods tendered notwithstanding that the quantity so delivered shall be either greater or less than the quantity purchased provided that:

1.1 such discrepancy in quantity shall not exceed [5]%
1.2 the price shall be adjusted pro rata to the discrepancy.'

Limitation imposing time limits upon bringing claims for defects, damage, loss or non-delivery

'1 The buyer shall inspect the goods on delivery and shall within [3] days of delivery notify the seller of any alleged defect, shortage in quantity, damage or failure to comply with description or sample. The buyer shall afford the seller an opportunity to inspect the goods within a reasonable time following delivery and before any use is made of them. If the buyer shall fail to comply with these provisions the goods shall be conclusively presumed to be in accordance with the contract and free from any defect or damage which would be apparent on a reasonable examination of the goods and the buyer shall be deemed to have accepted the goods.

2 The buyer shall notify the seller of any non-delivery of a whole consignment of complete cartons within [14] days of the date of dispatch (as stated on the invoice). Notwithstanding the receipt by the seller of any such notice a clear signature on a carrier's delivery advice sheet shall be deemed to signify receipt of the quantity of cartons indicated on the advice sheet.

3 If the goods are not in accordance with the contract for any reason the buyer's sole remedy shall be limited to the seller making good any shortage by replacing such goods or, if the seller shall elect, by refunding a proportionate part of the price.'

General exclusion of seller's liability for indirect (consequential) loss

'The seller shall be under no liability whatever to the buyer for any indirect loss and/or expense (including loss of profit) suffered by the buyer arising out of a breach by the seller of this contract.'

General limitation of seller's liability

'In the event of any breach of this contract by the seller the remedies of the buyer shall be limited to damages. Under no circumstances shall the liability of the seller exceed the price of the goods.'

The clause above dealing with exclusion of indirect or consequential losses is commonly included by sellers but will not always be enforceable. The clause prescribing a financial ceiling on claims operates as a limitation of liability, the reasonableness of which may be determined by reference to the insurance question.

Residual exclusion of causes of actions

'All warranties and conditions whether implied by statute or otherwise are excluded from this contract provided that nothing in this contract shall restrict or exclude liability for death or personal injury caused by the negligence of the seller or affect the statutory rights of a buyer dealing as consumer.'

It is usual to include a provision of the above nature, particularly where express guarantees are being given. Note the acknowledgment of the position of a consumer.

The buyer's perspective – increasing liability

8.19 Whilst the purpose of incorporating an exclusion clause in sales conditions is to eliminate or reduce the impact of liabilities which would otherwise arise, in purchase conditions the buyer will typically seek to impose upon the seller even greater liabilities than would otherwise arise under law. The scope of liabilities contained in the Sale of Goods Act 1979 have already been mentioned. This liability may be extended in a number of ways:

(a) By requiring goods, as a matter of contract, to conform to all national and international standards and be of the highest standard of quality.

> 'The seller shall ensure that all the goods shall be manufactured, stored, tested and packed in accordance with [all British standards applicable to them *or* British standard (*number*)] and that all the goods are of satisfactory or the very best quality and [fit for purpose *or* fit for the purposes for which the buyer intends to use such goods].'

(b) To conform with all applicable packaging and labelling requirements.

> 'The goods shall be marked in accordance with [the buyer's instructions *or* the specifications] and all lawful requirements and properly packed and secured for delivery to the buyer in an undamaged condition.'

(c) To incorporate as a matter of contract all pre-contract representations given in negotiations.

> 'All representations, statements or warranties made or given by the seller, its servants and agents (whether orally in writing or in any of the seller's brochures catalogues and advertisements) regarding the quality and fitness for purpose of the goods or any of the goods shall be deemed to be express conditions of the contract of sale.'

(d) To compel the seller to submit the goods to testing either by the buyer or independently.

> '1 The seller shall comply with the specification and all applicable British Standards and legal requirements concerning the design, manufacture, processing, storage and testing of the goods.
> 2 The seller shall permit the buyer to inspect and test the goods during their manufacture and processing.
> 3 If the buyer is not reasonably satisfied that the goods or their manufacture or processing comply in all material respects with the contract the seller without extra cost to the buyer shall take all steps necessary to ensure due compliance.'

and prior to delivery:

> 'The goods shall within [14] days prior to despatch be tried by the seller in the presence of a representative of the buyer by working the goods in the usual manner. If the goods shall fail to work in accordance with their specification the seller shall remedy the defects within [7] days after the trial and the goods shall then be tried again in the manner set out above. Provided that the trial shall fail to disclose any defects then the goods shall be deemed to conform to the contract and the buyer shall be bound to accept the goods.'

and in relation to loss or damage in transit:

> 'The seller upon receiving notice to that effect from the buyer shall repair or replace free of charge goods damaged or lost in transit and due delivery of the goods shall not be deemed to have taken place until replacement or repaired goods have been delivered by the seller to the buyer. The buyer reserves the right to hold such damaged goods at the seller's risk or to return them at the risk and expense of the seller.'

(e) Right to reject goods not conforming with the contract.

> '1 The seller agrees to permit the buyer to return any of the goods which are not in accordance with the contract at any time up to [6] months after delivery notwithstanding that the goods may have already been accepted by the buyer.
>
> 2 The buyer may set off against any payment due to the seller (whether under this contract or otherwise) the price of such goods. Unless within a reasonable time of receipt of notice of rejection the seller collects such goods the buyer may dispose of them as the buyer shall think fit (provided that if the buyer sells such goods the buyer shall account to the seller for the net proceeds of such sale).'

(f) An indemnity in respect of claims made by sub-buyers or end-users of the products.

> 'The seller shall indemnify the buyer against all claims by the customers of the buyer and their sub-buyers arising out of any breach whatever by the seller of this contract of sale [due to want of satisfactory quality or lack of fitness for purpose of the goods or any of the goods].'

This clause includes an obligation to repair or replace defective goods even after they have been the subject of sub-sales or installation. Where the seller is asked voluntarily to accept liability beyond that which would otherwise arise by operation of law the insurance position must be carefully examined. It may be that insurance is not available under the terms of the seller's policy against such voluntarily assumed risk and enquiry should be made of the insurers to ascertain the position.

Warranties as exclusion clauses

8.20 The seller may seek to exclude or limit liability under the guise of offering a limited form of indemnity subject to the exclusion of other statutory remedies. If the effect of the clause is to limit any liability otherwise arising by the operation of the Sale of Goods Act 1979 then the 'warranty' will be treated in the same way as any exclusion clause. For instance, a seller may seek to limit liability for infringement of third party intellectual property rights by reference to an 'indemnity' subject to the seller retaining the right to conduct the action.

> 'If the buyer shall be subject to any claim from a third party that the goods infringe such third party's intellectual property rights then the seller shall indemnify the buyer against such claim(s) subject to the buyer allowing the seller to conduct any proceedings or negotiation (in the name of the buyer if the seller so requests) provided that this indemnity shall not extend to any loss to the extent covered by any policy of insurance maintained by the buyer.'

It is submitted that this is an attempt to exclude liability under the implied condition as to title under the Act. The seller may also seek to impose upon the buyer an obligation to indemnify the seller against third-party claims, including claims arising out of the seller's breach of contract or negligence.

Property and risk – retention of title

8.21 The provisions concerning risk of damage or destruction to the goods sold can be shortly stated. Unless otherwise agreed, the goods remain at the seller's risk until they become the buyer's property. When ownership is transferred, the goods are at the buyer's risk whether delivery has been made or not. It is obviously desirable from the seller's viewpoint to ensure that risk in the goods passes at the earliest possible time, which will often be stipulated to be on delivery. In the absence of agreement, statutory rules contained in the Sale of Goods Act 1979 will spell out the position. A failure to reach agreement can therefore lead to unforeseen and undesired consequences.

Retention of title – an important right

8.22 The question of retention of title has been the subject of substantial legal debate. The limits on the efficacy of such provisions may need to be carefully explained to the seller, proceeding from basic principles. Firstly, what is retention of title and what is its significance? It is the right of the seller to retain ownership of the goods sold and until payment notwithstanding that he has parted with possession of the goods to the buyer. It is vital to bear in mind that, as a general rule, where a contract for the sale of goods has been entered into between the parties for goods in a deliverable state then under the Act ownership of the goods will pass to the buyer at the time the contract is made, irrespective of whether the goods have been paid for or delivered. It will therefore be obvious that retaining ownership in goods delivered to the buyer but not paid for will be an extremely important right in the event of the buyer becoming bankrupt or going into liquidation. The consequences of an insolvency practitioner disposing of the goods or interfering with them would mean the seller could bring legal proceedings against the practitioner for wrongful interference with the goods and claim damages for their market value.

A typical clause might comprise the following:

> '1 In spite of delivery having been made property in the goods shall not pass from the seller until:
> 1.1 the buyer shall have paid the price plus VAT in full; and
> 1.2 no other sums whatever shall be due from the buyer to the seller.
>
> 2 Until property in the goods passes to the buyer in accordance with clause [1] the buyer shall hold the goods and each of them on a fiduciary basis as bailee for the seller. The buyer shall store the goods (at no cost to the seller) separately from all other goods in its possession and marked in such a way that they are clearly identified as the seller's property.
>
> 3 Notwithstanding that the goods (or any of them) remain the property of the seller the buyer may sell or use the goods in the ordinary course of the buyer's business at full market value for the account of the seller. Any such sale or

dealing shall be a sale or use of the seller's property by the buyer on the buyer's own behalf and the buyer shall deal as principal when making such sales or dealings. Until property in the goods passes from the seller the entire proceeds of sale or otherwise of the goods shall be held in trust for the seller and shall not be mixed with other money or paid into any overdrawn bank account and shall be at all material times identified as the seller's money.

4 The seller shall be entitled to recover the price (plus VAT) notwithstanding that property in any of the goods has not passed from the seller.

5 Until such time as property in the goods passes from the seller the buyer shall upon request deliver up such of the goods as have not ceased to be in existence or resold to the seller. If the buyer fails to do so the seller may enter upon any premises owned occupied or controlled by the buyer where the goods are situated and repossess the goods. On the making of such request the rights of the buyer under clause [3] shall cease.

6 The buyer shall not pledge or in any way charge by way of security for any indebtedness any of the goods which are the property of the seller. Without prejudice to the other rights of the seller, if the buyer does so all sums whatever owing by the buyer to the seller shall forthwith become due and payable.

7 The buyer shall insure and keep insured the goods to the full price against "all risks" to the reasonable satisfaction of the seller until the date that property in the goods passes from the seller, and shall whenever requested by the seller produce a copy of the policy of insurance. Without prejudice to the other rights of the seller, if the buyer fails to do so all sums whatever owing by the buyer to the seller shall forthwith become due and payable.'

8.23 So far as the effectiveness of the retention of title clause is concerned, apart from the obvious remedy of recovering possession of goods on the buyer's premises which can be clearly identified as belonging to the seller (a 'simple' retention of title), a typical clause will provide further extension on the rights of the seller as follows:

(a) The clause may seek to secure not just the price of the particular goods which have been sold but all other goods supplied which will include goods supplied and paid for by the buyer but which can still be identified (an 'all monies' or 'current account' clause). Such provisions have been upheld.

(b) A provision may entitle the seller to trace the proceeds of sale of goods sold by the buyer which are the subject of the retention of title clause. Such a provision has been upheld, but as its exercise is dependent on the seller establishing a 'fiduciary relationship' with the buyer (arguably not a common feature of a buyer/seller relationship) such clauses are usually resisted by insolvency practitioners. Further, the courts will not readily infer the necessary fiduciary relationship. Where a fiduciary relationship can be established, it means that the seller of the goods does have a proprietary claim or vested right to money, typically in a bank account, which represents the sale proceeds of the goods. In practice, this right is not going to be of much value. The reason for this is that if the buyer is insolvent it is unlikely that he will have a credit balance in his bank account. It will also not help if the buyer has factored his debts or charged debts to his bank.

(c) Clauses commonly seek to extend a claim to retain ownership of goods which have become mixed, processed or applied to other goods supplied by other suppliers. This raises extremely complicated issues of personal property law. If the goods sold have only suffered minor adaptation, then there is some prospect of asserting a valid claim. If the process goes further than this so that the goods lose their original identity, then the courts are likely to hold that the true nature of the arrangement between the parties with regard to such down-stream products was not one of sale and purchase, but that the buyer was creating a charge over goods supplied to secure sums owing to the seller. This charge would only be effective in law as against a limited company buyer if registered as such at Companies House under the Companies Act 1985, s 395. The following provision may be appropriate to be included in sale conditions:

> 'The buyer shall promptly deliver the prescribed particulars of this contract to the registrar in accordance with the Companies Act 1985, Part XII as amended. Without prejudice to the other rights of the seller, if the buyer fails to do so all sums whatever owing by the buyer to the seller shall forthwith become due and payable.'

It is, however, extremely unlikely that either the buyer or the seller would have taken the trouble to register.

Traps for the unwary

8.24 Having gone to the time and trouble of adopting new sale conditions, it often comes as a shock when the seller experiences practical problems in enforcing his rights to ownership of goods or in securing their return, or payment of their value, by the relevant insolvency practitioner. There may be a number of reasons for this:

(a) The seller fails to establish that his conditions of sale have in fact been incorporated into the agreement for sale. This situation is likely to occur where the seller has failed to obtain the written confirmation of the buyer that he agrees to the seller's condition of sale and only a handful of transactions have taken place between the parties so that the seller is unable to rely on a 'course of dealings' to establish that his conditions of sale represent the terms of the agreement for sale.

(b) The seller fails to identify that the goods present on the buyer's premises on insolvency have in fact been supplied by him. The moral here is to ensure that all goods supplied have some form of coding or marking, preferably placed upon the goods themselves, and not merely upon packaging, which can then be cross-checked with the seller's own records. It will also be useful to have a credit controller in the seller's organisation who will be able to go quickly to the business premises of the insolvent buyer to identify and schedule the goods before the relevant insolvency practitioner has had a chance to dispose of them.

(c) The retention of title clause itself may be subject to attack on conceptual grounds. As mentioned above, it is common, for example, to build in all sorts of stipulations such as a requirement on the buyer to store the goods separately and pay the proceeds of sale of the goods into a separate designated bank account in the name of the seller. However, where these events do not occur in practice and in fact were never intended to be carried into effect, the clause may be ineffective. Sub-clauses 3 and 7 of the clause cited above are regarded as being vulnerable to attack on these grounds. It is therefore advisable to err on the side of brevity and reflect the factual situation rather than to indulge in 'overkill'.

Retention of title – the buyer's perspective

8.25 How should the buyer respond to a seller's request to incorporate a retention of title provision? It may be argued that such a requirement in a contract on a credit sale can scarcely be objected to, on the basis that if the buyer wants title at the outset he should pay for the goods in full. However, failure on the part of the seller to establish incorporation of his standard terms (as much as any attack on conceptual grounds) may result in his being unable to rely upon the retention of title clause. It may be that the buyer would benefit, indirectly, from this. If the retention of title provision is ineffective, the goods or proceeds of sale will be treated as part of the company's assets available to meet the claims of all creditors. The effect of this may, whilst incurring the liability of the seller to the supplier as unsecured creditor, reduce in overall terms the liability to creditors generally and indeed may mean that additional sums are available to meet the claims of creditors who hold personal guarantees from the individual business proprietors.

Delivery of goods

8.26 In the absence of agreement to the contrary between buyer and seller there are implied under the Sale of Goods Act 1979 a number of rules regarding delivery. It is important that the client is aware of the rules that will apply unless the matter is specifically addressed. These include:

(a) Delivery of goods and payment of price to be concurrent.
(b) Right of buyer to reject goods where incorrect quantity delivered.
(c) Buyer to collect goods from seller's premises.
(d) Delivery to be made within a reasonable time.
(e) Buyer not bound to accept delivery by instalments.
(f) Expense of delivery to be borne by seller.
(g) Where goods will be subject to transit from seller to buyer, buyer must bear the risk of incidental deterioration.
(h) In the case of delivery involving sea transit where it is usual to insure against loss, seller must give notice to the buyer such as will enable him to insure the goods.
(i) If buyer fails within a reasonable time to accept delivery where seller ready willing and able to deliver, then buyer is liable for any loss occasioned by seller.

Accordingly, the arrangements for delivery should be clearly spelt out in the contract. In particular, are goods to be collected from the seller's premises or is delivery to be made by the seller to the buyer's carrier or by the seller or the seller's carrier to the buyer direct?

Two of the possible alternatives are set out below:

> 'Delivery of the goods shall be made to the buyer's address on the delivery date. The buyer shall make all arrangements necessary to take delivery of the goods whenever they are tendered for delivery.'

> '1 The goods shall be delivered to the buyer at the seller's address. The risk in the goods shall pass to the buyer upon such delivery taking place.

2 The seller shall arrange for carriage of the goods to the buyer's address. The costs of carriage and any insurance which the buyer reasonably directs the seller to incur shall be reimbursed by the buyer [without any set-off or other withholding whatever] and shall be due on the date for payment of the price. The carrier shall be deemed to be the buyer's agent.'

There are often included ancillary obligations on the buyer to ensure that qualified personnel are in attendance to accept delivery, and an express right to reclaim costs of storage and/or redelivery where the buyer fails to collect or accept delivery of goods. Risk of accidental loss or damage, and as a consequence responsibility for obtaining insurance, passes as a general rule only when property passes. By virtue of the incorporation of a retention of title provision, this may be some time later than actual delivery. Accordingly the seller may wish risk to pass upon physical delivery.

'The goods shall be at the buyer's risk as from delivery.'

This provision is commonly included as an opening sub-clause in a comprehensively drafted retention of title provision.

If the seller wishes to reserve the right to deliver by instalments an express term is necessary, eg:

'1 The seller [shall *or* may] deliver the goods by separate instalments [in accordance with the agreed delivery schedule]. Each separate instalment shall be invoiced and paid for in accordance with the provisions in this contract of sale.

2 The failure of the seller to deliver or the failure of the buyer to pay for any one or more of the said instalments of the goods on the due dates shall not entitle either party to treat this contract as repudiated.'

The seller may seek to exclude or limit liability for failure to meet delivery dates, eg:

'1 The seller shall not be liable for any loss or damage whatever due to failure by the seller to deliver the goods (or any of them) promptly or at all.

2 Notwithstanding that the seller may have delayed or failed to deliver the goods (or any of them) promptly the buyer shall be bound to accept delivery and to pay for the goods in full provided that delivery shall be tendered at any time within [3] months of the delivery date.'

In any event the seller will want protection against delays occasioned by reason of circumstances of 'force majeure', eg:

'Neither party shall be liable for any default due to any act of God, war, strike, lock-out, industrial action, fire, flood, drought, storm or other event beyond the reasonable control of either party.'

To counter the general presumption that time of delivery is not of the essence, the buyer may seek to make this an express term of the contract, eg:

'1 The delivery date is of the essence of this contract.

2 If the seller fails to deliver all of the goods in accordance with the contract on the delivery date then without prejudice to the buyer's rights for the breach of contract:

2.1 The buyer may terminate the contract. In this event without prejudice to the buyer's other remedies the seller shall promptly collect any goods which have been delivered.
2.2 Where delivery of a quantity of the goods which correspond to the contract which is less than the agreed quantity has been tendered and the buyer has not exercised its rights of termination under clause [2.1] the buyer may accept the goods which correspond to the contract and recover for the seller's breach in respect of the failure to deliver the remainder of the goods.
2.3 The buyer may require the seller promptly to deliver sufficient goods which correspond to the contract to comply with the quantity required.

The buyer may exercise these rights by [written] notice to the seller.'

Exports

8.27 In relation to export sales, reference is commonly made to a series of standard conventions laid down in INCOTERMS. Many expressions contained in INCOTERMS such as 'ex works' and 'FOB (free on board)' are common expressions of international trade. The use of each expression necessarily involves an allocation between the seller and buyer of various responsibilities for matters such as risk of loss (and thus responsibility for insurance), costs of delivery, obtaining of necessary import/export licences. By way of comparison of the various conventions under an FOB contract the principal duties of the seller are:

(a) to provide goods in conformity with the contract;
(b) to obtain at his risk any export licence/authorisation;
(c) to deliver the goods on board the vessel named by the buyer at the named port of shipment on the date stipulated;
(d) to bear the costs incurred until the goods pass the ship's rail and any official charges payable upon exportation;
(e) to give sufficient notice to the buyer that the goods have been delivered on board.

The buyer must:

(a) pay the price as provided in the contract;
(b) obtain at his own risk any import licence/authorisation;
(c) contract at his expense for the carriage of goods and arrange a contract of insurance;
(d) bear all risks of loss of or damage to the goods from the time they have passed the ship's rail.

This INCOTERM may be regarded as benefiting the seller who fulfils all delivery obligations as soon as the goods pass the ship's rail. By contrast, use of other conventions place more extensive obligations on the seller. For example, under the DDP (Delivery Duty Paid) INCOTERM, in addition to the obligations on the part of the seller listed above the seller must:

(a) contract at his own expense for a contract of carriage;
(b) place the goods at the disposal of the buyer on the date or within the period stipulated;

(c) pass all the costs of delivery including importation duties;
(d) bear all the risks of loss of or damage to the goods until such time as they have been placed at the disposal of the buyer.

Another INCOTERM commonly encountered is CIF (Cost Insurance and Freight). The obligations upon the seller are less onerous than DDP but more extensive than FOB. In particular, the seller must arrange contracts of carriage and insurance. Risk still passes at the ship's rail.

Specimen clauses:

'Delivery – FOB contract

1 The goods shall be delivered to the buyer by delivery on board the [named vessel] lying at [named port] on the delivery date. The seller shall promptly notify the buyer that the goods have been delivered aboard. Title to and risk in the goods shall pass to the buyer upon such delivery being effected. The seller shall promptly provide the buyer with a clean shipped bill of lading in respect of the goods.

2 The buyer shall reserve the necessary space on board the [named vessel] and give the seller due notice of the loading berth and any revised delivery dates to the [named vessel]. The buyer shall bear any additional costs caused due to the failure of the [named vessel] to be available to load the goods on the delivery date.

3 No claim for damaged goods for shortages or for non-delivery will be accepted by the seller unless written notice of such damage or shortage is received by the seller within [28] days of receipt of the goods by the buyer, or within [28] days of the defect being discovered where the defect could not reasonably have been discovered earlier, or (in the case of non-delivery) [28] days from the date on which the goods could in the normal course of events have been expected to be received by the buyer.'

'Delivery – CIF Contract

1 The goods shall be delivered to the buyer at [named port] on or before the delivery date. The seller shall procure a contract of carriage and insure the goods from dispatch until delivery on terms current in the trade for the benefit of the buyer. The goods shall be at the risk of the buyer as they are loaded on board. The seller shall promptly tender to the buyer a clean shipped bill of lading, the insurance policy and an invoice in respect of the goods.

2 The buyer shall accept the documents tendered by the seller if they correspond to this contract and take delivery of the goods at [named port] and bear all other costs and charges arising out of shipment of the goods to [named port].'

Whether or not expressions defined in INCOTERMS are relied upon, the responsibility of the respective parties for matters such as insurance and the obtaining of any necessary export/import licences should be clearly spelt out.

Boilerplate provisions

8.28 There are usually contained within standard conditions seemingly innocuous administrative provisions, but these clauses often have serious impact upon the rights of the respective parties.

Governing law

8.29 Clients involved in dealings with foreign businesses will be concerned as to which law will govern the contract. There will obviously be no problem from a jurisdictional viewpoint where all relevant parties are resident in the UK and all aspects of the contract were formed in the UK. The matter does, however, become relevant where goods are being sold and delivered outside the UK. In the absence of an agreement between the seller and the buyer the proper law of the contract will be the system of law with which the agreement has the closest and most substantial connection. It goes without saying that the English seller of goods, unless some other legal system has particular advantages for him, will ordinarily wish to ensure that the contract is governed by English law and not by the law of the country of residence of the buyer being a law with which he may be entirely unfamiliar and which may be more beneficial or advantageous for the buyer. In the absence of specific agreement, all sorts of problems are likely to arise and the moral is an obvious one: agree at the outset with the foreign buyer what the law of the contract is going to be. Again, in considering the issue of forum, the English seller will ordinarily wish to be in a position to bring proceedings before an English court, although he may wish to reserve rights to bring proceedings in foreign jurisdictions.

Specimen clause:

> '0.1 This contract is subject to the law of England and Wales.
>
> [0.2 All disputes arising out of this contract shall be subject to the [exclusive] jurisdiction of the courts of England and Wales.
>
> *or*
>
> The parties submit to the [exclusive] jurisdiction of the courts of England and Wales and irrevocably agree that proceedings issued out of the said courts may without prejudice to the rules of service of such courts be served on them by delivering such proceedings in an envelope addressed to the party to be served at the address for such party set out in this contract.]'

And where one party, here the buyer, wishes to reserve the right to bring proceedings in a foreign court, the following provision may be considered:

> 'Nothing in this clause . . . shall prevent the buyer from commencing proceedings against the seller in any other court of competent jurisdiction nor shall the commencement of proceedings in one or more jurisdictions preclude the commencement of proceedings in any other jurisdiction whether concurrently or not.'

Where the client is not in a position to influence the choice of law or jurisdiction the obtaining of local legal advice would be advisable. As an absolute minimum, the client needs to be clear that its insurances will afford cover against claims which may be brought by foreign nationals under the laws of other jurisdictions.

Assignment

8.30 Is the contract to be capable of being assigned by either of the parties? As a general rule with commercial as opposed to 'personal' contracts, unless the contract provides that assignment is prohibited then the benefit of the contract may be assigned. Further, is either party to be free to sub-contract any part of its obligations? Again, the answer depends upon whether personal performance by the party was required, expressly or impliedly, under the contract. Alternative provisions are set out below:

> 'The seller may license or sub-contract all or any part of its rights and obligations under this contract without the buyer's consent.'
>
> *or*
>
> 'The seller shall not assign sub-contract license or otherwise dispose of any part of its rights or obligations under this contract without the prior written consent of the buyer.'

Further, whilst a sale of the business will necessarily involve the assignment of contracts this will not be the case on the sale of issued share capital by the owner of a limited company. Consideration thus needs to be given as to whether to accept, or impose, a provision entitling termination in the event of change of control of a company.

Insolvency

8.31 Either party may wish to be excused further performance of the contract in the event of the insolvency of the other. A comprehensive provision, in this case drafted for the benefit of the seller, would look as follows:

> 'If the buyer fails to make payment for the goods in accordance with this contract of sale or commits any other breach of this contract of sale or if any distress or execution shall be levied upon any of the buyer's goods or if the buyer offers to make any arrangement with its creditors or if any petition in bankruptcy is presented against the buyer or the buyer is unable to pay its debts as they fall due or if being a limited company any resolution or petition to wind up the buyer (other than for the purpose of amalgamation or reconstruction without insolvency) shall be passed or presented or if a receiver administrative receiver or manager shall be appointed over the whole or any part of the buyer's business or assets or if any petition for the appointment of an administrator is presented against the buyer or if the buyer shall suffer any analogous proceedings under foreign law all sums outstanding in respect of the goods shall become payable immediately. The seller may in its absolute discretion and without prejudice to any other rights which it may have:
>
> 1 suspend all future deliveries of goods to the buyer and/or terminate the contract without liability upon its part; and/or
> 2 exercise any of its rights pursuant to clause *(number of clause relating to the seller's retention of title)*.'

Cancellation

8.32 The client will be concerned as to the presence in any standard contract of any provision entitling the other party to cancel the contract without liability.

> 'The seller may cancel this contract at any time before the goods are delivered by giving written notice. On giving such notice the seller shall promptly repay to the

buyer any sums paid in respect of the price. The seller shall not be liable for any loss or damage whatever arising from such cancellation.'

'The buyer may cancel this contract at any time before all of the goods are delivered by giving written notice. On giving such written notice:

1 the seller shall cease to be bound to deliver and the buyer shall cease to be bound to receive delivery of any further goods;
2 the buyer shall cease to be bound to pay that part of the price which relates to goods which have not been delivered;
3 the buyer shall not be liable for any loss or damage whatever arising from such cancellation.'

Intellectual property

8.33 Where intellectual property rights (particularly trade marks, patents or copyright) subsist in the goods then the seller may seek to impose restrictions on the use to which the buyer may put the goods other than straightforward retail sale in the seller's packaging. For example:

'1 All goods sold in retail packaging may be resold by the buyer only in the packaging supplied by the seller and in no case may any trade mark other than those applied by the seller be marked on or applied in relation to the goods.
2 No right or licence is granted under this contract of sale to the buyer under any patent, trade mark, copyright, registered design or other intellectual property right except the right to use or resell the goods.'

Similarly where specifications, drawings etc are used in the production of goods which have been supplied by the buyer then the buyer's purchase conditions will commonly include an acknowledgment:

'Where any specification[s] and design[s] of the goods or any of the goods have been provided by the buyer the copyright, design right or other intellectual property in them shall remain the property of the buyer.'

Conversely, in such a situation, where the buyer has supplied drawings, the seller in its sale conditions may look for an indemnity:

'The specification[s] and design[s] of the goods (including the copyright, design right or other intellectual property in them) shall as between the parties be the property of the seller. Where any designs or specifications have been supplied by the buyer for manufacture by or to the order of the seller then the buyer warrants that the use of those designs or specifications for the manufacture, processing, assembly or supply of the goods shall not infringe the rights of any third party.'

Similarly a buyer may look for an indemnity against third-party claims for infringement of intellectual property rights:

'The seller will indemnify the buyer against any claim that the sale or use of the goods by the buyer contravenes any third-party's intellectual property rights.'

Personal guarantee

It will often be desired to obtain some form of personal commitment or security for debts owed to the company. Document 18 in Part II comprises a simple form of personal guarantee which may be appropriate in these sort of situations. It envisages that the individual may not take personal legal advice. The rules on duress and undue influence should be considered in appropriate cases.

TABLE 10: CHECKLIST OF MATTERS TO BE CONSIDERED WHEN ADVISING A CLIENT AS BUYER UPON TYPICAL STANDARD TERMS AND CONDITIONS OF SALE

1 Basis of sale

1.1 Do the terms apply to the entire exclusion of any other terms and conditions?

1.2 Have any express terms been agreed which are not embodied in the standard sale conditions?

1.3 Do the terms contain an entire agreement clause purporting to exclude liability for pre-contract statements? Check whether the client is contracting in reliance upon anything said during the course of negotiations. If so, this should be reduced to writing and incorporated in the contract.

1.4 Are there are any provisions relating to the manner in which terms may be modified (eg approval of a director or other authorised representative of the seller required)?

1.5 Is the buyer relying upon any advice or recommendation of the seller with regard to the suitability of goods or otherwise?

1.6 Has the buyer made known in writing to the seller:

1.6.1 the particular purpose for which the goods are to be used/resold?

1.6.2 any special losses that would be suffered by the buyer as a result of any non-compliance by the seller with the terms of the contract?

1.7 Under what circumstances (if any) is the order cancellable by

1.7.1 the seller?

1.7.2 the buyer?

What are the consequences of either party exercising rights of cancellation?

2 Specification of goods and/or services

2.1 Is the specification for goods/services to be prepared by the seller or the buyer? Where it is the buyer, is there any time limit within which this is to be made available? Consider with the client the practicalities of the buyer complying with this requirement. What are the consequences of the buyer defaulting?

2.2 Is the buyer required to give any indemnity to the seller in respect of infringement of intellectual property rights arising out of the seller's use of the buyer's specification? If so, check with the buyer whether it is aware of any problems. Is the giving of the indemnity covered by the buyer's business insurances?

2.3 Does the seller reserve the right to depart from the agreed specification and, if so, in what circumstances (eg non-availability of supply of particular raw materials)? Check with the client what effect if any, this would have upon the buyer having regard to such matters as the purpose for which the goods are being acquired (eg components to be incorporated in a finished product. In this case the buyer will need to be able to comply with particular specification of the buyer's own customer).

TABLE 10: *Cont.*

2.4 Where the seller reserves the right to depart from the agreed specification is the buyer to be given any prior notice? If so, will the buyer be granted a right of cancellation? Will this right only be exercisable within a limited time period? What sum, if any, will be payable to the seller in this situation?

3 Price

3.1 Is the buyer buying by reference to:
- 3.1.1 A quoted price? If so, has the quotation been confirmed in writing? Is the quoted price still open for acceptance?
- 3.1.2 A price list? If so, is the listed price still current?

3.2 Is the price quoted inclusive or exclusive of:
- 3.2.1 value added tax?
- 3.2.2 carriage and delivery?
- 3.2.3 other costs and expenses (including packaging and insurance)?

3.3 Does the seller reserve the right:
- 3.3.1 to charge by reference to a price list/standard charge rate prevailing at the date of delivery?
- 3.3.2 to make unilateral price variations?

3.4 Is there any requirement to return pallets or other returnable or re-usable containers/packaging (or to make payment therefor in default of return)?

4 Payment terms

4.1 Is the buyer required to pay any sum upon placing the order otherwise than before delivery?

4.2 If answer to 4.1. is yes, is such sum a deposit or pre-payment of the price?

4.3 If a deposit, in what circumstances is the deposit returnable and what are the arrangements of the seller for holding customer deposits?

4.4 When is the purchase price (or balance) payable? Is payment conditional upon delivery, installation or commissioning of goods (where appropriate)?

4.5 Is there any provision in the terms providing for prompt payment discount? Has any discount been agreed by the client direct?

4.6 Is time of payment of the essence?

4.7 Will the seller issue a receipt for payment/appropriate VAT invoice?

4.8 What are the seller's remedies in default of payment on the due date? Is there any restriction upon the buyer's rights of set-off?

4.9 Where credit terms are available to the buyer is the particular order when taken in conjunction with other current orders, within agreed credit limits?

5 Delivery

5.1 Under the terms are the goods:
- 5.1.1 to be delivered by the seller or the seller's carrier?
- 5.1.2 to be delivered by the seller to the buyer's carrier?
- 5.1.3 to be collected from the seller's premises by the buyer or the buyer's carrier?

5.2 Does the answer to 5.1 above accord with the buyer's understanding?

5.3 At whose risk are the goods to be transported?

5.4 Where the answer to 5.3 is the buyer, does the buyer hold insurance cover?

5.5 Where the answer to 5.3 is the seller, does the seller hold insurance cover? Has evidence of the existence of cover been produced to the buyer?

5.6 Is delivery by a due date of fundamental importance to the buyer (eg to enable it to comply with delivery requirements under the contract with its own customer)? If so, consider making time of delivery of the essence.

TABLE 10: *Cont.*

5.7 Does the supplier reserve the right to delay delivery?

5.8 Does the seller reserve the right to deliver more or less than the contract quantity ordered? If so, is there to be a proportionate alteration to the price? Will this provision present any problems to the buyer (eg pre-packaged goods in stated quantities which are purchased for re-sale)?

5.9 Does the seller reserve the right to deliver by instalments?

5.10 Where the seller is resident overseas:

- 5.10.1 What are the arrangements for obtaining import/export licences/ consents, and at whose cost?
- 5.10.2 Do any quotas operate? What duties are payable?
- 5.10.3 Is use being made of any internationally recognised convention (eg FOB, CIF) derived from INCOTERMS? Do the conditions of the convention accord with the client's own understanding of the allocation of risks/responsibilities between the parties?
- 5.10.4 Are there any special payment terms (eg irrevocable letter of credit)? If so check that the client has advised its bankers of the requirement.

6 Retention of title

6.1 Are the goods to be supplied on retention of title terms?

6.2 Are there included any obligations upon the buyer with regard to storage and insurance?

6.3 Does the retention of title provision extend to all goods supplied including goods previously supplied and identifiable as the seller's goods but which have been paid for in full by the buyer?

6.4 Does the seller purport to place any restrictions on the right of re-sale by the buyer?

6.5 Is the buyer as a condition of the contract required to register the terms of the supply agreement as a charge under the provisions of the Companies Act 1985, s 395?

7 Seller's liability

7.1 Does the seller make any attempt to exclude or limit the extent of its liability under statute or at common law?

7.2 Does the seller offer a guarantee:

- 7.2.1 in addition to other rights or remedies of the buyer, or
- 7.2.2 in substitution for other rights and remedies?

7.3 Is the liability of the seller under the contract or otherwise arising by law covered by the seller's insurances? Has evidence been supplied as to the nature and extent of insurance cover held?

7.4 Does the seller seek to limit liability by reference to offering the buyer the benefit of any warranties given by its own supplier? If so, have such warranties been given and are they capable of assignment?

7.5 Does the seller seek to impose time limits within which the buyer may bring claims alleging the supply of defective goods, non-delivery or short delivery?

7.6 Is the liability limited to:

- 7.6.1 a stated sum, or
- 7.6.2 the purchase price?

If a stated sum check that this is a sum not less than the applicable maximum liability under the seller's insurance.

7.7 Advise the client of the consequences if the seller is seeking to exclude liability for indirect or consequential losses.

TABLE 10: *Cont.*

7.8 Is the seller resident outside the European Union?
7.9 Has the seller maintained comprehensive records of supplies and obtained from its own supplier of components and raw materials a contractual obligation to maintain such comprehensive records?
7.10 Can the buyer insist upon the testing of goods prior to delivery or upon delivery as a pre-requisite for acceptance?
7.11 Has the seller purported to exclude liability for mis-description/misrepresentation in respect of data, photographs, illustrations, catalogues or otherwise comprised in the seller's advertising previously supplied to the buyer?

8 Miscellaneous

8.1 Has the seller reserved the right to cancel in the event of the buyer's insolvency? Does this include insolvency procedures used for the purposes of amalgamation or reconstruction of a solvent company?
8.2 Are any particular formalities to be complied with in relation to the giving of notices under the contract?
8.3 Does the contract provide for a governing law? Where this is not English law has the buyer received the benefit of local legal advice?
8.4 Does the contract provide which legal system will have jurisdiction to resolve disputes? Is this jurisdiction to be exclusive or non-exclusive?
8.5 Does the contract include an agreement to refer disputes to arbitration?

TABLE 11: CHECKLIST OF MATTERS TO BE CONSIDERED WHEN ADVISING A CLIENT AS SUPPLIER UPON TYPICAL STANDARD TERMS AND CONDITIONS OF PURCHASE

1 Basis of sale

1.1 Do the terms apply to the entire exclusion of any other terms and conditions?
1.2 Have any express terms been agreed which are not embodied in the standard purchase order conditions?
1.3 Do the terms contain an entire agreement clause or otherwise provide that the supplier's liability under the warranties contained in the agreement (or otherwise implied by law) will not be affected by any statements made to the buyer unless the same has been reduced to writing and agreed with the buyer? Check the position with the client.
1.4 Any provision relating to the manner in which terms may be modified (eg approval of a director or other authorised representative of the buyer)?
1.5 Has the supplier given any advice or recommendation to the buyer with regard to the suitability of goods or otherwise?
1.6 Has the supplier been made aware of any particular purpose for which the goods are to be used and/or any special losses that would be suffered by the buyer as a result of non-compliance by the seller with the terms of the contract? If so, explain to the client potential liabilities.
1.7 Under what circumstances, if any, is the order cancellable by
1.7.1 the buyer?
1.7.2 the supplier?
What are the consequences of either party exercising its right of cancellation?

TABLE 11: *Cont.*

2 Specification

2.1 Is the specification for goods/services to be prepared by the buyer or supplier? Where the buyer is relying upon any specification derived from the supplier's advertising or other promotional literature is the supplier content that this is up-to-date?

2.2 Does the buyer restrict the ability of the supplier to depart from the agreed specification in any respect? Consider including an express reservation of right to do this in the event of difficulties in obtaining particular components, raw materials etc.

2.3 Does the contract provide for any tolerance (with regard to dimensions, quantities, weights etc) from strict contractual specification? If not, consider including an appropriate acceptable tolerance.

2.4 If the supplier is required to indemnify the buyer in respect of intellectual property infringement actions arising out of the supply of goods pursuant to the supplier's specification, check the availability of insurance cover.

2.5 If the supplier is to produce goods to a specification of the buyer, consider seeking an indemnity against intellectual property infringement actions.

2.6 Does the order require that the goods be manufactured/assembled at a particular designated location of the supplier?

3 Price

3.1 Does the order form correctly state the agreed price?

3.2 Does the stated price include:

3.2.1 value added tax?

3.2.2 carriage and delivery (where appropriate)?

3.2.3 other costs and expenses (eg packaging and insurance)?

3.3 Does the purchase preclude any price variation by the supplier?

3.4 Does the buyer reserve the right to claim any discounts which the supplier customarily has on any particular occasion granted to other buyers (eg prompt payment or volume discounts) whether or not such discounts are shown on the supplier's terms and conditions?

3.5 Is there any restriction upon the supplier charging for additional work necessarily undertaken, save with the formal authorisation of the buyer in the manner provided by the order?

3.6 Is the buyer required to produce, at no additional cost, any other supporting documentation (eg materials certificates, letters of conformity or other documentation)?

3.7 Is payment to be conditional upon the supplier strictly complying with formalities such as the furnishing of delivery/invoice documentation in any prescribed form (eg cross-referenced to purchase order number)?

3.8 Is there any express prohibition upon the supplier's invoices relating to more than one order?

3.9 What are the arrangements for return of pallets or other returnable or re-usable containers/packaging (or for payment therefor in default of return)?

4 Payment

4.1 Does the order provide for the supply on credit terms? Are the terms (eg 60 days from delivery) acceptable? Do the standard terms (eg 60 days from delivery) accord with the agreement between the clients?

4.2 Does the supplier require a deposit or pre-payment before delivery? If so, consider including an express provision to this effect.

TABLE 11: *Cont.*

4.3 Are there any restrictions on the remedies available to the supplier in the event of late payment by the buyer? For instance, may interest be charged on outstanding amounts? Consider incorporating reference to an appropriate default rate.

4.4 Has the buyer expressly reserved the right to deduct or set off against sums payable under the order?

4.5 Is the supplier required to issue any receipt for payment?

4.6 Consider making time of payment of the essence (express term needed).

4.7 Where the goods are to be supplied on credit terms is the particular contract within any agreed credit limit, and have appropriate searches and enquiries been made by the supplier as to the financial standing of the buyer (eg credit reference search, search of company's registration office, search of the Companies Court)?

5 Delivery

5.1 Is time of delivery of the essence?

5.2 If the answer to 5.1 is yes, is there any exception in respect of circumstances of force majeure?

5.3 Is delivery to be made to a location designated by the buyer? Is the supplier required to deliver to a specified person and obtain his formal acceptance? Is a formal inspection to take place on delivery?

5.4 Are goods to be delivered:

5.4.1 by the supplier or the supplier's carrier?

5.4.2 by the supplier to the buyer's carrier?

5.4.3 to be collected from the supplier's premises by the buyer or the buyer's carrier?

Is this understanding reflected in the standard terms of order? Are there any restrictions upon the supplier utilising the services of a carrier? (see question 8 below).

5.5 At whose risk are goods to be transported?

5.6 Where the answer to 5.5 is supplier, does the supplier hold insurance cover?

5.7 Where the answer to 5.5 is buyer, does the buyer hold insurance cover? Has evidence of the existence of cover been produced to the supplier?

5.8 Is the supplier restricted from making delivery by instalments?

5.9 Where the buyer is resident overseas:

5.9.1 What are the arrangements for obtaining export/import licences/consents and at whose cost?

5.9.2 Do any quotas operate? Are any duties payable?

5.9.3 Is use being made by the buyer of any internationally recognised conventions (eg DDP) derived from INCOTERMS? Do the requirements of the stated convention accord with the supplier's understanding of the allocation of risks/responsibilities between the parties?

5.10 Is the supplier to be subject to any sanction if delivery is made to the buyer in advance of the due date?

5.11 Are there any stipulations as to the qualification of employees/agents of the supplier who are to be involved in delivery/installation/ commissioning of goods?

5.12 Is the supplier aware of any legal requirements regarding packaging and/or labelling of the goods? Is compliance with such requirement made a term of the contract?

TABLE 11: *Cont.*

6	**Property in goods**
6.1	Is title in goods to pass to the buyer on delivery or at any other point in time prior to payment in full by the buyer?
6.2	Are there any other contracts between the buyer and supplier in respect of which payment is outstanding?
6.3	If the answer to either 6.1 or 6.2 is yes, consider incorporation of a retention of title provision.
6.4	Where a retention of title provision is to be incorporated ensure that the goods supplied are correctly marked in a permanent form and appropriately cross-referenced to seller's and buyer's order documentation in order to clearly identify goods as property of the supplier.
7	**Supplier's warranty**
7.1	Does the buyer seek to impose upon the supplier warranties or indemnities the effect of which is to extend the liability of the supplier beyond that otherwise arising by operation of law?
7.2	If the answer to 7.1 is yes. is this extended liability covered by the supplier's product liability insurances?
7.3	Is the supplier obliged to submit goods for testing or inspection prior to delivery? Is approval to be obtained from the buyer or an independent third party? In either event, at whose cost will the testing be undertaken?
7.4	Where the supplier is obliged to manufacture in accordance with any quality compliance procedures of the buyer has the supplier had the opportunity to satisfy itself with such procedures?
7.5	Is the benefit of any express warranty/indemnity or guarantee to be capable of being assigned by the buyer? If so, will the supplier's insurances extend to such additional potential exposure?
7.6	Is the supplier required to obtain any performance bond in respect of the performance of its obligations under the order?
7.7	Is the buyer resident in the European Union?
7.8	In connection with prospective liabilities under the Consumer Protection Act 1987 has the buyer placed any contractual obligations on the supplier to maintain records in respect of goods supplied? Consider a reciprocal requirement on the buyer to maintain similar records regarding its own supplies.
8	**Miscellaneous**
8.1	Has the buyer sought to impose confidentiality obligations on the supplier and in particular restricted any subsequent use of designs, drawings, specifications, etc comprised within the order?
8.2	Has the buyer imposed any restriction upon the ability of the supplier to supply goods manufactured to the same specification (or similar goods) to any competitor of the buyer?
8.3	Is the supplier restricted from publicising its business connection with the buyer?
8.4	Are there any restrictions upon the supplier assigning the rights and obligations under the order? Is there any restriction on sub-contracting the performance of the order in whole or in part?
8.5	Has the buyer reserved any remedies for breach of contract which would not otherwise necessarily be implied by law (eg a liquidated damages provision)?

TABLE 11: *Cont.*

8.6	Is there any requirement on the supplier to maintain stocks/manufacturing capacity for production of the goods as against prospective repeat orders?
8.7	Where the buyer has supplied parts or equipment (including free issue materials) to be utilised in the manufacturing process at whose risk are these items to be held? If the answer is the supplier's, does the supplier's existing insurances cover the holding of third-party property in transit and at the supplier's premises?
8.8	Is the supplier obliged to nominate a suitably qualified person to act as dedicated support to the buyer in connection with the performance of the order?
8.9	Has the buyer reserved the right to cancel in the event of the supplier's insolvency?
8.10	Are there any particular formalities to be complied with in relation to the giving of notices under the contract?
8.11	Does the contract provide for a governing law? Where this is not English law, has the supplier received the benefit of local legal advice?
8.12	Does the contract provide which legal system will have jurisdiction to resolve disputes? Is this jurisdiction to be exclusive or non-exclusive?
8.13	Does the contract include an agreement to refer disputes to arbitration?

Part II

Precedents

1 Incorporation agreement

THIS AGREEMENT is made the day of 199

PARTIES:

(1) *(names and addresses of partners)* ('the Vendors') and
(2) *(purchaser of business)* whose registered office is at *(address)* (registered in England no......) ('the Purchaser')

BACKGROUND

(A) The Vendors have carried on business in partnership as *(description of business)* under the name of *(firm name)* ('the Business')
(B) The Purchaser has an authorised share capital of £... divided into *(number)* ordinary shares of [£...] each *(number)* of which have been issued fully paid and are held and beneficially owned as shown in the first schedule
(C) The Purchaser has as one of its objects the acquisition and management of the Business and the Vendors have agreed to transfer the same to the Purchaser as a going concern with effect from the Transfer Date

OPERATIVE PROVISIONS

1 Definitions

1.1 'Consideration Shares' means the ordinary shares of £... each in the Purchaser credited as fully paid up and to be allotted to the Vendors in consideration for the sale of the Business
1.2 'Transfer Date' means the close of business on *(date)*
1.3 'Vendors' Pension Scheme' means *(name of vendors' pension scheme)*

2 Sale and purchase

The Vendors agree to sell with [full] title guarantee and the Purchaser agrees to purchase with effect from the Transfer Date the Business as a going concern comprising the following assets used in the conduct of the Business [for the following sums]:
2.1 the Goodwill of the Business [for the sum of £...]
2.2 the freehold property known as *(description)* registered at HM Land Registry under Title no... [for the sum of £...]
2.3 the leasehold property known as *(description)* comprised in a lease dated *(date)* made between *(parties)* [for the sum of £...]
2.4 the plant machinery vehicles and equipment of the Vendor relating to the Business [for the sum of £...]
2.5 the stock and work in progress of the Vendor relating to the Business at the Transfer Date [for the sum of £...]

2.6 the benefit (subject to the burden) of the contracts and engagements of the Vendor in relation to the Business [for the sum of £...]

2.7 without in any way limiting the generality of the foregoing all other assets and rights of whatever nature employed in the Business at the Transfer Date [other than cash] [for the sum of £1]

3 Title

The Purchaser accepts such title as the Vendors have to the freehold [and leasehold] properties to be transferred without investigation and shall not be entitled to make any objections or requisitions in relation to the same

4 Liabilities

The Purchaser agrees to purchase the Business subject to all debts owing by the Vendors in respect of the same and all other liabilities of the Business subsisting as at the Transfer Date but excluding any liability of the Vendors in respect of income tax or capital gains tax. The Purchaser agrees to indemnify the Vendors and each of them against all claims demands actions or other proceedings in respect of such debts or liabilities

5 Consideration

The consideration for the sale of the Business (in addition to the Purchaser's assumption of the debts and liabilities referred to in clause 4) shall be the sum of £... which shall be satisfied by the allotment to the Vendors of the number of Consideration Shares set opposite their respective names in the second schedule

6 Completion

The sale of the Business shall be completed in *(date)* at the offices of *(name and address of Vendors' solicitors)* when the Purchaser shall deliver to the Vendors the certificates for the Consideration Shares and the Vendors shall execute and do all such deeds and things as may be necessary to vest effectively the Business and its assets in the Purchaser

7 Employees

The parties acknowledge and agree that pursuant to the Transfer of Undertakings (Protection of Employment) Regulations 1981 as amended the contract of employment between the Vendors and each of the employees of the Business will (save in so far as such contract relates to any occupational pension scheme) have effect from completion as if originally made between the Purchaser and each such employee

8 Pensions

The Purchaser shall establish a suitable pension scheme approved by the Inland Revenue and capable of providing the equivalent benefits in respect of the continuing employment of the employees of the Business as are provided under the Vendors' Pension Scheme

9 Costs

The costs of the Vendors and the Purchaser of and incidental to this agreement and the formation and registration of the Purchaser shall be borne by the Purchaser

10 Filing

The Purchaser shall file this agreement duly stamped and Companies Form 88(2) with the Registrar of Companies within one month of the date of allotment of the Consideration Shares

FIRST SCHEDULE

Existing Shareholdings in the Purchaser

(set out particulars)

SECOND SCHEDULE

Consideration Shares to be allotted to Vendors

(set out particulars)

SIGNED by the said)
in the presence of:)

SIGNED by the said)
in the presence of:)

SIGNED by)
on behalf of the Purchaser)
in the presence of:)

2 Company law papers for incorporation of business

2a Minutes of board meeting to approve transfer

MINUTES OF A MEETING OF THE BOARD OF DIRECTORS
OF *(name)* LTD

Held at *(address)* on (date)

PRESENT:
(insert details)

IN ATTENDANCE:
(insert details)

1 Quorum

The Chairman declared that a quorum was present.

2 Minutes

The minutes of the last meeting of the Directors held on (date) were produced, approved and signed by the Chairman.

3 Proposed contract with *(names of proprietors of unincorporated business)* ('the Vendors')

There was reported the proposal to acquire from the Vendors the business and assets of (name). The Vendors declared their interest in the transaction as required by the Companies Act 1985, s 317.

It was further reported that as the transaction qualified as a substantial property transaction for the purposes of the Companies Act 1985, s 320 the approval of the members by ordinary resolution was required.

There was produced a form of Notice of Extraordinary Meeting to consider and if thought fit pass the following resolutions:

ORDINARY RESOLUTIONS

1 THAT in accordance with the Companies Act 1985, s 320 the sale of the business and assets of *(name)* owned by *(name)* [a] [the] director[s] of the company [upon the terms of the sale and purchase agreement

produced to the meeting and signed by the Chairman for the purposes of identification] be approved.

[2 THAT in accordance with the provisions of Regulation 96 of Table A (which Regulation is comprised within the Company's Articles of Association) the provisions of Regulations 94 and 95 of Table A (which Regulations are comprised in the Company's Articles of Association) shall be suspended in respect of the consideration by the Board of Directors of the arrangements described in Resolution 1 above.]

3 THAT the capital of the Company be increased to £...... divided into ... [Ordinary Shares of ... each] by the creating of ... [Ordinary Shares of ... each] to rank pari passu in all respects with the existing Ordinary Shares in the Company.

4 THAT the directors are [generally *or* specifically] authorised pursuant to the Companies Act 1985, s 80 [for a period of 5 years from the date of the adoption of this article or up to the next annual general meeting of the company or until otherwise resolved by the company in general meeting] to exercise the power of the company to allot relevant securities (within the meaning of the Companies Act 1985, s 80(2)) in respect of all shares for the time being unissued, but the maximum aggregate nominal amount of ordinary shares which may be allotted pursuant to this authority shall be £... and this authority may be varied or revoked by an ordinary resolution of the company. [This authority is given [subject to the following conditions *(specify)* or for the following purposes *(specify)*].]

SPECIAL RESOLUTION

5 THAT [subject to the consent of the Registrar of Companies] the name of the company be changed to *(name)*.

4 EGM

IT WAS RESOLVED that an Extraordinary General Meeting of the Company be convened to consider the Resolutions set out in the Notice produced to the Meeting.

The Secretary was instructed to despatch the Notices to the members together with the form of agreement signed by the Chairman by way of identification and, all members being in attendance and subject to their consenting thereto, the EGM be held forthwith.

5 Adjournment

The meeting be adjourned to enable the EGM to take place.

6 Resumption

When the meeting resumed it was reported that the Resolutions had been duly passed.

7 Contract

The form of agreement [and property transfer] to effect the sale and purchase above referred to was produced to the meeting and approved. The transaction was then completed.

8 Allotment

In accordance with the terms of the agreement IT WAS RESOLVED to allot shares as follows:

(name) ...... Ordinary Shares
(name) ...... Ordinary Shares

9 Disclosure

(name) and (name) disclosed their interest in the shares allotted to them in accordance with the Companies Act 1985, s 324.

10 Returns

The Secretary was instructed to make all necessary returns to Companies House.

There being no further business the meeting was closed.

....

Chairman

2b Notice of Extraordinary General Meeting

(name) LIMITED

NOTICE IS HEREBY GIVEN that an Extraordinary General Meeting of *(name)* Ltd will be held at *(address)* on *(date)* at *(time)* for the purpose of considering and (if thought fit) passing the Resolutions set out below which will be proposed, as to resolutions 1, 2, 3 and 4 as Ordinary Resolutions, and as to resolution 5 a Special Resolution.

ORDINARY RESOLUTIONS

1 THAT in accordance with the Companies Act 1985, s 320 the purchase by the company of the business and assets of *(name)* owned by *(name)* [a] [the] director[s] of the company [upon the terms of the sale and purchase agreement produced to the meeting and signed by the Chairman for the purposes of identification] be approved.

[2 THAT in accordance with the provisions of Regulation 96 of Table A (which Regulation is comprised within the Company's Articles of Association) the provisions of Regulations 94 and 95 of Table A (which Regulations are comprised in the Company's Articles of Association) shall be suspended in respect of the consideration by the Board of Directors of the arrangements described in Resolution 1 above.]

3 THAT the capital of the Company be increased to £...... divided into ... [Ordinary Shares of ... each] by the creating of ... [Ordinary Shares of ... each] to rank pari passu in all respects with the existing Ordinary Shares in the Company.

4 THAT the directors are [generally *or* specifically] authorised pursuant to the Companies Act 1985, s 80 [for a period of 5 years from the date of the adoption of this article *or* up to the next annual general meeting of the company or until otherwise resolved by the company in general meeting] to exercise the power of the company to allot relevant securities (within the meaning of the Companies Act 1985, s 80(2)) in respect of all shares for the time being unissued, but the maximum aggregate nominal amount of ordinary shares which may be allotted pursuant to this authority shall be £... and this authority may be varied or revoked by an ordinary resolution of the company. [This authority is given [subject to the following conditions *(specify)* or for the following purposes *(specify)*].]

SPECIAL RESOLUTION

5 THAT [subject to the consent of the Registrar of Companies] the name of the company be changed to *(name)*.

A member entitled to attend and vote at the Meeting is entitled to appoint a Proxy to attend and vote in his or her place. A Proxy need not be a member of the Company.

DATED: [ ]

BY ORDER OF THE BOARD

....

Secretary

3 First board meeting minutes

LIMITED

MINUTES of a Meeting of the Directors held at

on 19

Present :

In Attendance :

1 Incorporation of the Company

The incorporation of the Company on 19 was reported and the Certificate of Incorporation produced to the Meeting.

2 Directors

It was reported that the first Director of the Company, having resigned and had been appointed Directors of the Company with effect from

3 Secretary

It was reported that the first Secretary of the Company, London Law Secretarial Limited, having resigned had been appointed Secretary of the Company with effect from

4 Chairman

IT WAS RESOLVED that Mr be and is hereby appointed Chairman of the Board of Directors of the Company.

5 Auditors

IT WAS RESOLVED that Messrs be and they are hereby appointed Auditors of the Company at a remuneration to be hereafter agreed between them and the Board.

6 Bankers

IT WAS RESOLVED that be and they are hereby appointed bankers of the Company. Resolutions in the form of the attached print were passed.

7 Common Seal

IT WAS RESOLVED that the Common Seal, an impression whereof appears in the margin, be and it is hereby adopted as the Common Seal of the Company.

8 Dispensation with Distinguishing Numbers

IT WAS RESOLVED that so long as all the issued shares in the capital of the Company are fully paid up and rank pari passu for all purposes with all shares of the same class for the time being issued and fully paid up none of those shares need hereafter bear a distinguishing number.

9 Accounting Reference Date

IT WAS RESOLVED that the accounting reference date of the Company be in each year.

10 Registered Office

It was reported that the registered office of the Company is at

OR

IT WAS RESOLVED that the registered office of the Company be changed to

11 Registration of Subscribers

IT WAS RESOLVED that the names of and being the subscribers of the Memorandum of Association of the Company, be entered in the Register of Members as the holders of one Share each.

12 Transfer of Shares

IT WAS RESOLVED that the following transfers of Shares, duly stamped, be approved and registered in the books of the Company:

Transferor	*Transferee*	*Number of Shares*
		1
		1

and that Share Certificates be sealed and issued accordingly.

13 Issue of Shares

IT WAS RESOLVED that the Company issue Shares for cash at par and that, in response to applications accompanied by the subscription moneys in full received from the following persons for the numbers of Shares set out opposite their respective names, the Company do allot such Shares accordingly:

Allottee	*Number of Shares*

14 Directors' Interests in Contracts

The following Directors gave notice pursuant to s 317(3) of the Companies Act 1985 that, either by reason of being a member or the holder of an office, they had an interest in any contract made with any of the companies shown below opposite their respective names:

Name of Director	*Names of Companies*

Mr gave notice that he was a partner in the firm of and accordingly had an interest in any contract made with that firm.

15 Directors' Interests in the Company and Associated Companies

Pursuant to s 324 of the Companies Act 1985 the undermentioned Directors respectively furnished in writing particulars for inclusion in the Register of Directors' Interests as follows:

Name of Director	*Nature of Interest*	*Name of Company*	*Amount/number of Shares/Debentures*

16 Filing at Companies Registry

The Secretary was instructed to file the following forms with the Registrar of Companies:

(i) form 288 (Notice of change of Directors and Secretary)
(ii) form 224 (Notice of Accounting Reference Date)
(iii) form 88(2) (Return of Allotments)
(iv) form 287 (Notice of change in situation of registered office).

....

Chairman

4 Shareholders' resolution package and sample company resolutions

4a Notice of EGM

LIMITED

NOTICE IS HEREBY GIVEN that an EXTRAORDINARY GENERAL MEETING of the above-named Company will be held at on the 19 at am/pm for the purpose of considering and, if thought fit, passing the following Resolution/Resolutions which will be proposed as an Ordinary/a Special Resolution/Resolutions [which will be proposed as to the Resolutions numbered and as Ordinary Resolutions and as to the Resolutions numbered and as Special Resolutions]

RESOLUTION(S)

BY ORDER OF THE BOARD

....

Secretary

Registered Office:

19

NOTE :

Any member entitled to attend and vote at the above Meeting is entitled to appoint a proxy to attend and vote in his stead. A proxy need not be a member of the Company

CONSENT TO SHORT NOTICE

We, the undersigned, being a majority in number of the members having a right to attend and vote at the Extraordinary General Meeting convened by the attached Notice, and together holding not less than ninety-five per cent in nominal value of the shares giving a right to attend and vote thereat, HEREBY AGREE that the said meeting shall be called and the Resolution[s] set out therein may be proposed and passed notwithstanding that shorter notice than that specified in the Companies Act 1985 or in the Company's Articles of Association, as the case may be, has been given therefor

Dated 19

....

....

4b Copy Resolution(s)

Company Registered No.

THE COMPANIES ACTS 1985 AND 1989

COMPANY LIMITED BY SHARES

ORDINARY/SPECIAL RESOLUTION(S)

of

LIMITED

Passed 19

At an EXTRAORDINARY GENERAL MEETING of the above-named Company duly convened, and held on 19 , the following Resolution/Resolutions was/were passed as a SPECIAL/an ORDINARY RESOLUTION/RESOLUTIONS [as to the Resolutions numbered and as ORDINARY RESOLUTIONS and as to the Resolutions numbered and as SPECIAL RESOLUTIONS]

RESOLUTION[S]

....

Chairman

4c Minutes of EGM

LIMITED

MINUTES of an Extraordinary General Meeting of the Company held at
on 19 at am/pm

Present:

In Attendance:

1. It was agreed that the Notice convening the Meeting be taken as read.
2. It was reported that a majority in number of the members having a right to attend and vote at the Meeting, being a majority together holding not less than 95 per cent in nominal value of the shares giving a right to attend and vote thereat, had given their consent to the Meeting being convened on short notice.
3. The following Resolution was duly proposed as a Special/an Ordinary Resolution and carried unanimously:

There being no further business the Meeting was closed.

....

Chairman

4d Written Resolution(s)

Company registered no.

THE COMPANIES ACTS 1985 AND 1989

COMPANY LIMITED BY SHARES

WRITTEN RESOLUTION OF THE
MEMBERS OF LIMITED
PURSUANT TO s 381A
of the COMPANIES ACT 1985

Passed 199

By a Written Resolution of the Members pursuant to s 381A of the Companies Act 1985 and dated 19 IT WAS RESOLVED as follows:

RESOLUTION

....

Chairman

4e Sample Resolution(s)

(a) Resolution to Change Name

That the name of the Company be changed to ' Limited'.

(b) Resolution to adopt new Articles of Association

That the regulations contained in the document produced to the Meeting and signed for identification by the Chairman be adopted as the Articles of Association of the Company in substitution for and to the entire exclusion of the existing Articles of Association.

(c) Resolution to increase capital by creation of Ordinary Shares

That the authorised share capital of the Company in increased from £ to £ by the creation of additional Ordinary Shares of £ each.

(d) Resolution to increase capital by creation of Preference Shares

That the capital of the Company be increased to £ by the creation of Preference Shares of £ each to which shall be attached the special rights privileges and restrictions following, that is to say:

(i) The right to a fixed cumulative preferential dividend at the rate of per cent per annum on the capital for the time being paid up thereon;
(ii) The right in a winding up to have the capital paid up thereon, and all arrears of dividend up to the date of the commencement of the winding up [*or* calculated to the date of payment] paid off in priority to any payment of capital on the Ordinary Shares, but with no further or other right to participate in the profits or assets of the Company;
(iii) The said shares shall not confer upon the holders thereof the right to receive notices of General Meetings of the Company or to attend or vote thereat unless the dividend on such Shares is [twelve months] in arrear (and so that for this purpose the same shall be deemed to be due twice yearly on the 1st day of January and the 1st day of July whether declared or not) or a Resolution has been passed for the winding up of the Company.

(e) Ordinary Resolution pursuant to s 80 of the Companies Act 1985

That with effect from the date of this Resolution the directors are, pursuant to s 80 of the Companies Act 1985, generally and unconditionally authorised to allot unissued shares in the authorised share capital of the Company at the date of this Resolution in accordance with the provisions of Article in the Articles of Association of the Company at any time or times during the period of five years from the date hereof.

[NOTE: This form of Resolution is appropriate in cases where the Articles of Association of the Company contain a pre-emption article or an article which is otherwise inconsistent with ss 89 and 90 of the Companies Act 1985 and therefore there is no need to pass a Special Resolution to dis-apply the statutory pre-emption rights].

(f) Alternative Ordinary Resolution pursuant to s 80 of the Companies Act 1985

That the Directors of the Company be and they are hereby generally and unconditionally authorised to exercise all the powers of the Company to allot relevant securities (within the meaning of s 80 of the Companies Act 1985) up to an aggregate nominal amount of [£] provided that this authority shall determine at the expiry of the period of five years from the date of passing of this Resolution

AND

Special Resolution pursuant to s 95(1) of the Companies Act 1985

That subject to the passing of the previous Resolution the Directors be and they are hereby empowered pursuant to s 95(1) of the Companies Act 1985 to allot equity securities (within the meaning of s 94 of that Act) pursuant to the authority conferred by the previous Resolution as if s 89(1) of that Act did not apply to any such allotment.

Alternative Special Resolution pursuant to s 95(1) of the Companies Act 1985

(For use in cases where there is an existing 's 80 authority' and therefore no 'previous Resolution')

That pursuant to s 95(1) of the Companies Act 1985 the Directors be and they are hereby empowered to allot equity securities (within the meaning of s 94 of that Act) pursuant to their authority under s 80 of that Act as if s 89(1) of that Act did not apply to the allotment.

[NOTE: These forms of Resolution are appropriate in cases where the statutory rights of pre-emption in ss 89 and 90 of the Companies Act 1985 apply because there is no article in the Company's Articles of Association which excludes the statutory rights or is otherwise inconsistent with them, and it is desired that the shares should be at the disposal of the Directors to allot as they may decide].

5 Sample memorandum

THE COMPANIES ACT 1985

A PRIVATE COMPANY LIMITED BY SHARES

MEMORANDUM OF ASSOCIATION

of

C LIMITED

1 The Company's name is 'C Limited'

2 The Company's Registered Office is to be situated in England and Wales

3 The Company's objects are:

(A) (i) To carry on the trade or business of general merchants and traders, to manufacture, buy, sell, import, export, supply and deal in goods and services of all kinds, to act as distributors or agents, and to purchase and sell or deal in plant and equipment of any description

(ii) To carry on any other trade or business which may in the opinion of the directors of the Company be conveniently carried on by it

(B) To purchase, take on lease or in exchange, hire or otherwise acquire and hold for any estate or interest any real or personal property of any kind necessary or convenient for the Company's business and any rights, privileges or easements over or in respect of any such property

(C) To erect, construct, enlarge, alter, maintain, remove or replace any plant and machinery, buildings, shops, offices, factories, roads and other works of any kind necessary or convenient for the Company's business, to clear sites for the same, and to contribute to or subsidise any such activities

(D) To purchase or otherwise acquire and undertake all or any part of the business, property, assets, liabilities and transactions of any person, firm or company possessed of property suitable for the purposes of this Company or carrying on or proposing to carry on any business which this Company is authorised to carry on, or which can be carried on in conjunction with any such business or which is capable of being conducted so as directly or indirectly to benefit the Company

(E) To apply for, register, purchase or by other means acquire and protect, prolong and renew any patents, patent rights, licences, trade marks, designs, protections and concessions and to use, turn to account, manufacture under or grant licences or privileges in respect of the same

(F) To borrow or raise money in such manner as the Company shall think fit for the purposes of or in connection with the Company's business

(G) For the purposes of or in connection with the Company's business or to secure the repayment of any moneys borrowed, raised or owing by it, to mortgage and charge the undertaking and all or any of the Company's property and assets, present and future, and all or any of its uncalled capital for the time being, and to issue at par or at a premium or discount and for such consideration and with and subject to such rights, powers, privileges and conditions as may be thought fit, debentures or debenture stock, either permanent or redeemable or repayable, and collaterally or further to secure any securities of the Company by a trust deed or other assurances

(H) To lend money and give credit to any company, firm or person and to give all kinds of guarantees and indemnities and in particular to guarantee either by personal covenant or by mortgaging or charging all or any part of the undertaking, property and assets present and future and uncalled capital of the Company or by both such methods, the performance of the obligations and the payment of the capital or principal (together with any premium) of and dividends or interest on any debenture, stocks, shares or other securities of any company, firm or person, including (but without limiting the generality of the foregoing) any company which is for the time being the Company's holding or subsidiary company. To do all such things whether or not the Company receives directly or indirectly any consideration or advantage from the same

(I) To establish and maintain or procure the establishment and maintenance of any non-contributory or contributory or superannuation funds for the benefit of, and give or procure the giving of donations, gratuities, pensions, allowances, or emoluments to any persons who are or were at any time in the employment or service of the Company, or of any company which is for the time being the Company's holding or subsidiary company or otherwise associated with the Company in business or who are or were at any time directors or officers of the Company or of any such other company, and the wives, widows, families and dependants of any such persons, and also to establish and subsidise or subscribe to any institutions, associations, clubs or funds calculated to be for the benefit of or to advance the interests and well-being of the Company or of any such other company, or of any such persons, and to make payments for or towards the insurance of any such persons, and to subscribe or guarantee money for charitable or benevolent objects or for any exhibition or for any public, general or useful object; and to establish, set up, support and maintain share purchase schemes or profit sharing schemes for the benefit of any employees of the Company, or of any company which is for the time being the Company's holding or subsidiary company and to do any of the matters aforesaid either alone or in conjunction with any such other company

(J) To draw, make, accept, endorse, negotiate, discount and execute promissory notes, bills of exchange and other negotiable or transferable instruments

(K) To invest and deal with the moneys of the Company not immediately required for the purposes of its business in or upon such investments or securities and in such manner as may from time to time be determined

(L) To pay for any property or rights acquired by the Company, either in cash or fully or partly paid-up shares, with or without preferred or deferred or special rights or restrictions of any kind, or by any securities which the Company has power to issue, or partly in one mode and partly in another, and generally on such terms as the Company may determine

(M) To accept payment for any property or right sold or otherwise disposed of or dealt with by the Company, either in cash, by instalments or otherwise, or in fully or partly paid-up shares of any company or corporation, with or without deferred or preferred or special rights or restrictions of any kind, or in debentures or debenture stock, mortgages or other securities of any company or corporation, or partly in one mode and partly in another, and generally on such terms as the Company may determine, and to hold, dispose of or otherwise deal with any shares, stock or securities so acquired

(N) To amalgamate or enter into any partnership, joint venture or profit-sharing arrangement with any company, firm or person carrying on or proposing to carry on any business within the objects of this Company, and to acquire and hold, sell, deal with or dispose of shares, stock or securities of any such company, and to guarantee the contracts or liabilities of, or the payment of the dividends, interest or capital of any shares, stock or securities of and to subsidise or otherwise assist any such company

(O) To establish or promote or concur in establishing or promoting any other company whose objects shall include the acquisition and taking over of all or any of the assets and liabilities of this Company or the promotion of which shall be in any manner calculated to advance directly or indirectly the objects or interests of this Company, and to acquire and hold or dispose of shares, stock or securities and guarantee the payment of dividends, interest or capital of any shares, stock or securities issued by or any other obligations of any such company

(P) To sell, improve, manage, develop, turn to account, exchange, let on rent, grant royalty, share of profits or otherwise, grant licences, easements and other rights in or over, and in any other manner deal with or dispose of the undertaking and all or any of the property and assets for the time being of the Company for such consideration as the Company may think fit

(Q) To subscribe for, purchase or otherwise acquire, and hold shares, stock, debentures or other securities of any other company

(R) To distribute among the members in specie any property of the Company, or any proceeds of sale or disposal of any property of the Company, but so that no distribution amounting to a reduction of capital be made except with the sanction (if any) for the time being required by law

(S) To give such financial assistance directly or indirectly for the purpose of the acquisition of shares in the Company or the Company's holding company or for the purpose of reducing or discharging any liability incurred by any person for the purpose of the acquisition of shares in the Company or the Company's holding company as may be lawful

(T) To purchase and maintain a policy or policies of insurance to cover any potential liability of the officers of the Company or any of them attaching to such person or persons by reason of any of their acts or omissions performed in relation to the Company

(U) To do all or any of the above things in any part of the world, and either as principals, agents, trustees, contractors or otherwise, and either alone or in conjunction with others, and either by or through agents, trustees, sub-contractors or otherwise

(V) To do all such things as are incidental or conducive to the above objects or any of them

And it is hereby declared that each of the paragraphs of this Clause shall be regarded as specifying separate and independent objects and accordingly shall not be in any way limited by reference to or inference from any other paragraph. None of the objects mentioned in any paragraph of this Clause shall be deemed to be merely subsidiary to the objects mentioned in any other paragraph

4 The liability of the Members is limited

5 The Company's share capital is £1,000 divided into 1,000 shares of £1 each

We, the Subscribers to this Memorandum of Association, wish to be formed into a Company pursuant to this Memorandum; and we agree to take the number of Shares shown opposite our respective names

NAMES AND ADDRESSES OF SUBSCRIBERS	Number of Shares taken by each Subscriber
	One
	One
Total Shares taken	Two

Dated the day of 199

Witness to the above Signatures:

6 Standard articles suitable for owner-managed business

Articles of association

THE COMPANIES ACTS 1985 TO 1989

COMPANY LIMITED BY SHARES

ARTICLES OF ASSOCIATION

of

LIMITED

(Adopted by Special Resolution passed on 199)

PRELIMINARY

1 The Company is a private company within the meaning of the Companies Act 1985, s 1 ('the Act') and, accordingly, it may not offer to the public any shares in or debentures of the Company or allot or agree to allot the same with a view to all or any of those shares or debentures being offered for sale to the public.

2.1 The regulations contained or incorporated in Table A in the Schedule to the Companies (Tables A-F) Regulations 1985 ('Table A') shall apply to the Company (save in so far as they are excluded or varied hereby) and such regulations (save as so excluded and varied) and the Articles contained below shall be the regulations of the Company.

2.2 The following regulations of Table A shall not apply to the Company, namely regulations 8, 50, 64 to 69 (inclusive), 73 to 80 (inclusive), 94, 95, 116 and 118.

SHARES

3 At the date of adoption of these articles the share capital of the company is £... divided into ...... Ordinary Shares of £1 each which shall rank pari passu in all respects.

4.1 Subject to s 80 of the Act and save as provided by contract or any other provision in these Articles to the contrary all unissued Shares of the Company (whether forming part of the original or any increased capital) shall, before issue, be offered either at par or at a premium to such of the existing members as at the date of the offer shall be entitled to receive notice from the Company of general meetings upon the terms that the Shares shall be allotted to the members accepting the offer in the proportions (as nearly as may be and without increasing the number allotted to any member beyond the number applied for by him) that their existing holdings of shares in the Company bear to each other. The offer shall be made by notice specifying the number of Shares offered and whether at par or at a premium and, if at a premium, the amount of such premium, and limiting a time (being not less than 28 days from the date of dispatch of the offer) within which the offer, if not accepted, will be deemed to have been declined, and after the expiration of that time, or on the receipt of an intimation from any member to whom the offer shall have been made that the offer of all or part of the Shares so offered is declined, the Directors may thereafter in accordance with the provisions of paragraphs 4.2 to 4.7 of this Article dispose of those Shares which shall not have been accepted provided that no such Shares may be disposed of at a lower price than that at which they were offered to members.

4.2 Unless otherwise agreed in writing by all the members for the time being or determined by Ordinary Resolution of the Company in General Meeting the Directors are unconditionally authorised for a period of 5 years from the date of the adoption of this Article generally to allot or grant rights to subscribe for or convert any securities into or otherwise dispose of the unissued shares or relevant securities for the time being of the Company up to an aggregate maximum amount of the authorised but unissued share capital of the Company immediately preceding the passing of the resolution adopting this Article to such persons on such terms and in such manner as they think fit but subject to the provisions of paragraph 4.1 of this Article and of any agreement binding on the Company.

4.3 The authority granted by paragraph 4.2 above may be renewed for a further period (whether or not it has been previously renewed under this paragraph) not exceeding 5 years as may be authorised by Ordinary Resolution of the Company in General Meeting which must state the amount of Shares of relevant securities which are subject to the renewal of the said authority and specify the date on which the renewed authority will expire.

4.4 Any shares which the Directors are not authorised to deal with by virtue of paragraphs 4.2 or 4.3 above may, with the consent of the Company in General Meeting, be dealt with by the Directors who may allot or otherwise dispose of the same to such persons and in such manner as they think fit subject to paragraph 4.1 for a period not exceeding 5 years from the date of such consent.

4.5 The Company may before the expiry of the authority created by paragraph 4.2 above or any renewal of the same made pursuant to paragraph 4.3 above make any offer or agreement which will or might require Shares or relevant securities to be allotted after the expiry of such authority or renewed authority and the Directors may, notwithstanding the expiry of such authority or renewed authority, allot Shares or relevant securities pursuant to any such offer or agreement.

4.6 For the purposes of this Article, the expression 'Shares' shall include options to subscribe for Shares or obligations of the Company convertible into share capital or any other rights which may be capable of being granted to any person to subscribe for or acquire Shares in the capital of the Company and the expression 'relevant securities' shall be construed in accordance with sub-s 80(2) of the Act.

4.7 Sub-sections 89(1) and 90(1) to (6) of the Act shall be excluded from applying to the Company.

LIEN

5 The Company shall have a first and paramount lien upon every share (whether a fully paid-up share or not) registered in the name of any member, either alone or jointly with any other person, for his or his estate's debts, liabilities and engagements, whether solely or jointly with any other person, to or with the Company, whether the period for the payment, fulfilment or discharge thereof shall have actually arrived or not. Such lien shall extend to all dividends from time to time declared or other moneys payable in respect of every such share, but the Board may at any time declare any share to be exempt, wholly or partially, from the provisions of this Article.

TRANSFER OF SHARES

6 The Directors may, in their absolute discretion and without assigning any reason therefor, decline to register the transfer of any Share, not being a fully paid share, or any Share (whether fully paid or not) where the Company has a lien on such Share.

7.1 Subject to the provisions of Article 6 above a member (or person entitled to a share in consequence of the death or bankruptcy of a member) may at any time transfer any of the shares registered in the name of such member to any person with the consent in writing of all other members of the Company.

7.2 The Directors may require from any person lodging a transfer pursuant to this Article such evidence as they may think fit of the consent to such transfer of the other members of the Company.

8 Except in the case of a transfer of shares expressly authorised by Article 7 above the right to transfer Shares of the Company shall be subject to the following restrictions, namely:

8.1 Before transferring any Shares a member proposing to transfer the same (hereinafter called 'the proposing transferor') shall give notice in writing (hereinafter called a 'transfer notice') to the Company that he desires to transfer the same and by the giving of the transfer notice the Company shall be constituted his agent for the sale of the shares therein mentioned (together with all rights then attached thereto) at the prescribed price to any member or members selected in the manner hereinafter appearing. The transfer notice may provide that unless all the shares comprised in it are sold to a member or members of the Company, none shall be so sold (hereinafter called 'a total transfer provision'). A transfer notice once given or deemed to be given shall not be revocable except with the consent of the Directors.

8.2 All such shares included in a transfer notice shall be offered by the Company to all members of the Company other than the member by whom or in respect of whose shares that transfer notice shall have been given or deemed to be given and such offer shall be made for the members concerned to purchase such shares at the prescribed price on the terms that in the case of competition the shares so offered shall be sold to the members accepting the offer in the proportions (as nearly as may be and without increasing the number sold to a member beyond the number applied for by him) that their existing holdings of shares in the Company bear to each other. All offers of shares under this paragraph shall be made by notice in writing and every such offer shall limit a time (not being less than 21 days from the date of dispatch of the offer) ('the prescribed period') within which the offer must be accepted or in default will lapse.

8.3.1 If the Company shall within the prescribed period find members as aforesaid (hereinafter called 'purchasers') willing to purchase the shares concerned or (unless the transfer notice contained a total transfer provision which the proposing transferor shall not have waived) any of them (as the case may be) and shall give notice in writing thereof to the proposing transferor he shall be bound, upon payment of the prescribed price, to transfer such shares to the prospective purchasers thereof. Every such notice shall state the name and address of the purchaser or purchasers and the number of shares agreed to be purchased by him or them and the purchase shall be completed at a place and time to be appointed by the Directors not being less than 7 days nor more than 28 days after the date of such notice or (where necessary) so soon thereafter as the prescribed price shall have been determined.

8.3.2 If in any case a proposing transferor after having become bound to transfer any shares to a purchaser, shall make default in transferring such shares the Directors may authorise some person to execute on behalf of and as attorney for the proposing transferor any necessary transfers and may receive the purchase money therefor and shall thereupon cause the name of the purchaser to be entered in the register as the holder of such shares and hold the purchase money in trust for the proposing transferor. The receipt of the Company for the purchase money shall be a good discharge to the purchaser (who shall not be bound to see to the application thereof) and after the name of the purchaser has been entered in the register in purported exercise of the aforesaid powers the validity of the proceedings shall not be questioned by any persons.

8.4 If:

8.4.1 the Company shall not have given notice in writing to the proposing transferor within the prescribed period that it has found purchasers willing to purchase all the shares as aforesaid or any of them or

8.4.2 the Company shall within the prescribed period give to the proposing transferor notice in writing that the company has no prospect of finding purchasers of such shares, or any of them,

the proposing transferor at any time thereafter up to the expiration of two months after the end of the prescribed period shall be at liberty (subject only to the provisions of Article 6 above and paragraph 8.5 below) to transfer to any person on a bona fide sale (a 'third party transfer') at any price not being less than the prescribed price (after deducting, where appropriate, any net dividend or other distribution declared or made after the date or the transfer notice and to be retained by the proposing transferor), those shares which the proposing transferor shall not be obliged hereunder as at the expiry of the prescribed period or, if notice is given under paragraph 8.4.2 above, on the date of service of such notice to transfer to purchasers.

8.5 No third party transfer may be effected unless:

8.5.1 not less than one month's written notice (expiring on or before the day preceding the expiration of the 2 month period specified in paragraph 8.4 above) of the proposal to make the same, including details of the number of shares to be transferred, the proposed transferee and the relevant price and reasonable evidence of the bona fide intention of the proposed transferee to purchase the said shares at a price being not less than the prescribed price shall first have been given to the Directors and

8.5.2 the Directors shall not have notified the proposing transferor during such period that the shares are required for purchase by any other person or persons (whether or not existing members of the Company). If the Directors shall so notify the proposing transferor, the person or persons indicated by the Directors as requiring to purchase the shares which are subject to the proposed third party transfer shall constitute 'purchasers' for the purposes of paragraph 8.3.1 of this Article which shall (save for references therein to the prescribed period) apply accordingly (mutatis mutandis).

Nothing herein shall oblige the Directors to inform members of details of any proposed third party transfer but the Directors may take such steps (if any) as they may in their absolute discretion decide in order to ascertain whether following receipt by the Directors of notice of a proposed third party transfer any members require to purchase the Shares which are the subject thereof.

8.6 The expression 'the prescribed period' shall mean a period of 2 months from the date on which the transfer notice is given or deemed to be given.

8.7 Subject to Article 9 below the expression 'the prescribed price' shall mean such sum per share as may be specified in the transfer notice by the proposing transferor.

8.8 For the purposes of these Articles a renunciation of the allotment of any share by the allottee in favour of some other person shall be deemed to be a transfer of such share.

9.1.1 Subject to the provisions of Article 7 above, a person entitled to a share in consequence of the bankruptcy of a member shall be bound, at any time if and when required in writing by a majority in value of the other members so to do, to give a transfer notice to the company in respect of all the shares then registered in the name of the bankrupt member.

9.1.2 Subject to the provisions of Article 7 above, a person entitled to a share in consequence of the death of a member shall be bound at any time after the expiration of one year from the date of such death, if and when required in writing by a majority in value of the other members so to do, to give a transfer notice to the Company in respect of all the shares then registered in the name of the deceased member.

9.1.3 Subject to paragraph 9.2 of this Article, the provisions of Article 8 above shall apply in relation to any such transfer notice as if the person serving notice under paragraphs 9.1.1 and 9.1.2 above were defined as the proposing transferor.

9.2 The prescribed price in respect of any transfer notice given pursuant to paragraph 9.1 of this Article shall be the amount which the Auditors for the time being of the Company (acting as experts and not as arbitrators, at the cost of the proposing transferor and whose decision shall be final and binding) shall certify in writing to be in their opinion the fair selling value therof as between a willing seller and a willing buyer Provided that in any case where a transfer notice has been duly required to be given hereunder in respect of any shares and such transfer notice is not given within a period of one month, such transfer notice shall (except and to the extent that a transfer of any of such shares in favour of a person to whom they may be transferred pursuant to the next but one preceding Article shall have been lodged prior to the expiration of the said period) be deemed to have been given at the expiration of the said period and all the provisions of Article 8 above shall thereupon apply as if a transfer notice had been duly served by a proposing transferor and the amount of capital paid up on such shares shall (if less than the prescribed price calculated as above in this paragraph 9.2) be deemed to be the prescribed price and the provisions of these presents shall take effect accordingly.

10 Upon receipt of a written application from any member holding Shares in the Company, and upon payment by him of the costs thereby incurred, the Directors shall request the Auditors of the Company for the time being to state the sum which in their opinion is the fair value of the Share or Shares being the subject of such application and such statement shall be certified in writing by the Auditors (acting as experts and not as arbitrators). Any member holding Shares in the capital of the Company shall be entitled at any time to make an application to the Directors in pursuance of this Article and such application shall not be deemed to constitute a notice of his intention to transfer Shares within the meaning of these Articles.

11 It shall be obligatory (subject to Article 5) for the Directors to register any share transfer permitted by Articles 7, 8 or 9 and it shall also be obligatory for the Directors to refuse to register any share transfer not so permitted.

GENERAL MEETINGS AND RESOLUTIONS

12 Every notice convening a General Meeting shall comply with the provisions of sub-s 372(1) of the Act as to giving information to members in regard to their right to appoint proxies.

13 If at an adjourned meeting of the Company a quorum is not present

within half an hour from the time appointed for the meeting, the meeting shall be dissolved, and Regulation 41 of Table A shall be modified accordingly.

14 One member present in person or by proxy may demand a poll and Regulation 46 of Table A shall be modified accordingly.

DIRECTORS

15.1 Unless and until the Company in General Meeting shall otherwise determine, the number of Directors shall not be less than ...... nor more than ....

15.2 In the case of an equality of votes, the chairman shall not be entitled to a second or casting vote and Regulation 88 of Table A shall be modified accordingly.

PROCEEDINGS OF DIRECTORS

16 A Director need not hold any Shares in the Company as a qualification for his office but nevertheless shall be entitled to attend and speak at all General Meetings of the Company.

17.1 A Director may at any time nominate any other person (whether a Director or Member of the Company or not) approved for that purpose by a resolution of the Board to act as Alternate Director at any Meeting of the Board at which the Director is not present, and may at any time revoke any such appointment. An Alternate Director so appointed shall not be entitled as such to receive remuneration from the Company, but shall otherwise be subject to the provisions of Table A and of these presents with regard to Directors.

17.2 An Alternate Director shall be entitled to receive notices of all Meetings of the Board and to attend and vote as a Director at any such Meeting at which the Director appointing him is not personally present, and shall perform all the functions, rights, powers and duties of the Director by whom he was appointed. Where a Director who has been appointed to be an Alternate Director is present at a Meeting of the Board in the absence of his appointor such Alternate Director shall have one vote in addition to his vote as Director but shall not be considered as two Directors for the purpose of making a quorum of Directors. An appointment of an Alternate Director shall not prejudice the right of the appointor to receive notices of and to attend and vote at meetings of the Board.

17.3 An Alternate Director shall ipso facto cease to be an Alternate Director if his appointor ceases for any reason to be a Director.

17.4 Every appointment and revocation of appointment of an Alternate Director shall be made by instrument in writing under the hand of the Director making or revoking such appointment and subject to paragraph 17.1 above such instrument shall only take effect on the service thereof at the office.

17.5 The remuneration of any such Alternate Director shall be payable out of the remuneration payable to the Director appointing him and shall consist of such portion of the last-mentioned remuneration as shall be agreed between the Alternate Director and the Director appointing him.

17.6 Every person acting as an Alternate Director shall while so acting be deemed to be an officer of the Company and shall alone be responsible to the Company for his own acts and defaults and he shall not be deemed to be the agent of or for his appointor.

18.1 A Director may, subject to s 317 of the Act, vote as a Director in regard to any contract or arrangement in which he is interested or upon any matter arising thereout, and if he shall so vote his vote shall be counted and he shall be reckoned in estimating a quorum when any such contract or arrangement is under consideration.

18.2 Any Director may continue to be or become a director of, or hold any other office or place of profit under any other company in which the Company may be interested and no such Director shall be accountable for any remuneration, salary, profit or other benefits received by him as a director of, or holder of any other office or place of profit under, or member of any such other company. The Directors may exercise the voting power conferred by the shares in any company held or owned by the Company in such manner in all respects as they think fit (including the exercise thereof in favour of any Resolution appointing themselves or any of them directors of such company,or voting or providing for the payment of remuneration to the directors of such company) and any Director of the Company may vote in favour of the exercise of such voting rights, in manner aforesaid, notwithstanding that he may be, or be about to be, appointed a director of such other company, and as such is or may become interested in the exercise of such voting rights in manner aforesaid.

MANAGING DIRECTOR

19 The Directors may from time to time appoint one or more of their number to an executive office (including that of Managing Director, Manager, or any other salaried office) for such period and upon such terms as they think fit, and subject to the provisions of any agrement entered into in any particular case, may revoke such appointment. A Director so appointed as a Managing Director shall (without prejudice to any claim he may have for damages for breach of contract of service between him and the Company) ipso facto cease to be Managing Director if he cease from any cause to be a Director.

20 The Managing Director, Manager or other such executive officer shall receive such remuneration whether by way of salary, commission or participation in profits or otherwise (either in addition to or in lieu of his remuneration as a Director), as the Directors may determine.

21 The Directors may entrust to and confer upon a Managing Director, Manager or other such executive officer any of the powers exercisable by them upon such terms and conditions with such restrictions as they think fit, and either collaterally with or to the exclusion of their own powers, and may from time to time (subject to the terms of any

agreement entered into in any particular case) withdraw, alter or vary all or any of such powers.

BORROWING POWERS

22 The Directors may exercise all the powers of the Company to borrow money, and to mortgage or charge its undertaking, property and uncalled capital, or any part thereof, and, subject to Article 3 above, to issue Debentures, Debenture Stock, and other securities, whether outright or as security for any debt, liability or obligation of the Company or of any third party.

INDEMNITY

23 Every Director or other officer of the Company shall be entitled to be indemnified out of the assets of the Company against all losses or liabilities which he may sustain or incur in or about the execution of the duties of his office or otherwise in relation thereto, including any liability incurred in which judgment is given in his favour or in which he is acquitted or in connection with any application under s 727 of the Act, in which relief is granted to him by the Court, and no Director or other officer shall be liable for any loss, damage or misfortune which may happen to or be incurred by the Company in the execution of the duties of his office or in relation thereto. But this Article shall only have effect insofar as its provisions are not avoided by s 310 of the Act.

7 Articles of association with 'A' and 'B' shares and simple class rights

The Companies Act 1985

COMPANY LIMITED BY SHARES

ARTICLES OF ASSOCIATION

of

LIMITED

(Adopted by Special Resolution passed on 199)

PRELIMINARY

1.1 The regulations contained in Table A as prescribed by the Companies (Tables A to F) Regulations 1985 as amended by the Companies (Table A to F) (Amendment) Regulations 1985 (hereinafter called 'Table A') shall apply to this Company save in so far as they are varied or excluded by or are inconsistent with these Articles.

1.2 Regulations 2, 32, 33, 50, 54, 64, 73 to 80 (inclusive), 81(e), 88 to 90 (inclusive), 94 to 98 (inclusive) and 118 of Table A shall not apply to the Company.

1.3 In these Articles 'the Act' means the Companies Act 1985 including any statutory modification or re-enactment thereof for the time being in force.

SHARE CAPITAL

2 The capital of the Company at the date of adoption of these Articles is £ divided into 'A' Shares of £1 each and 'B' Shares of £1 each, which shall, save as hereinafter expressly provided rank pari passu in all respects.

3 If at any time the share capital is divided into different classes of shares, the rights attached to any class (unless otherwise provided by the terms of issue of the shares of that class) may be varied with the consent in writing of the holder or holders of three-fourths of the issued shares of that class, or with the sanction of an Extraordinary Resolution passed at a separate general meeting of the holders of the shares of the class. To every such separate general meeting the provisions of these Articles relating to general meetings shall mutatis mutandis apply, but so that the necessary quorum shall be two persons at least, holding or representing by proxy one-third of the issued shares of the class.

4 The Company may from time to time by Special Resolution whether or not all the shares for the time being authorised shall have been issued, or all the shares for the time being issued shall have been fully paid, increase its capital by the creation of new shares of such amount

as may be deemed expedient and unless otherwise determined by Special Resolution the new shares created upon any such increase of capital shall consist of equal numbers of 'A' Shares and 'B' Shares all of £1 each.

5 All 'A' Shares and 'B' Shares shall before issue be offered to such persons as at the date of the offer are respectively the holders of the 'A' Shares and of the 'B' Shares then in issue for subscription of them, in proportion to their respective holdings of 'A' and 'B' Shares, but the provisions of this Article may be waived in any particular case with the written consent of all the shareholders for the time being.

TRANSFER OF SHARES

6.1 Table A shall be read subject to the following provisions of this Article.

6.2 For the purpose of this Article, where any person is unconditionally entitled to be registered as the holder of a share he and not the registered holder of such share shall be deemed to be so registered and a member of the Company in respect of that share.

6.3 [Subject to paragraph 12 hereof] no shares in the Company shall be transferred unless and until the rights of pre-emption hereinafter conferred shall have been exhausted.

6.4 Every member who desires to transfer any share or shares (hereinafter called 'the Vendor') shall give to the Company notice in writing of such desire (hereinafter called a 'transfer notice'). No transfer notice shall relate to more than one class of shares. Subject as hereinafter mentioned, a transfer notice shall constitute the Company the Vendor's agent for the sale of the share or shares specified therein (hereinafter called 'the said shares') in one or more lots at the discretion of the directors to the members other than the Vendor at a price to be agreed upon by the Vendor and the directors, or, in the case of difference, at the price which an accountant nominated by agreement between the Vendor and the Company, or in default of such agreement, by the President for the time being of the Institute of Chartered Accountants in England and Wales shall, by writing under his hand, certify to be in his opinion the fair value thereof as between a willing seller and a willing buyer. The transfer notice may contain a provision that unless all the shares comprised therein are sold by the Company pursuant to this Article, none shall be so sold and any such provision shall be binding on the Company.

6.5 If an accountant is asked to certify the fair value as aforesaid, his certificate shall be delivered to the Company and as soon as the Company receives the certificate it shall furnish a certified copy thereof to the Vendor [and the Vendor shall be entitled, by notice in writing given to the Company within ten days of the service upon him of the said certified copy, to cancel the Company's authority to sell the said shares].

6.6 Upon the price being fixed as aforesaid [and provided the Vendor shall not give notice of cancellation as aforesaid] the Company shall forthwith by notice in writing inform each member other than the Vendor of the number and price of the said shares and invite each such member to apply in writing to the Company within fourteen days of the date of despatch of the notice (which date shall be specified therein) for such maximum number of the said shares (being all or any thereof) as he shall specify in such application.

6.7 If the said members shall within the said period of fourteen days apply for all or (except where the transfer notice provides otherwise) any of the said shares, the directors shall allocate the said shares (or so many of them as shall be applied for as aforesaid), first to and amongst the applicants who are registered in respect of shares of the same class (and in case of competition pro rate (as nearly as possible) according to the number of shares of such class of which they are registered or unconditionally entitled to be registered as holders), and secondly (if any of the said shares shall remain after such applicants have been satisfied in full) to and amongst the applicants who are registered in respect of shares of any other class (and in the case of competition pro rata according to the number of shares of such other class or classes in respect of shares of any other class or classes in respect of which they are registered as holders), provided that no applicant shall be obliged to take more than the maximum number of shares specified by him as aforesaid; and the Company shall forthwith give notice of such allocations (hereinafter called 'an allocation notice') to the Vendor and the persons to whom the shares have been allocated and shall specify in such notice the place and time (being not earlier than fourteen and not later than twenty-eight days after the date of the notice) at which the sale of the shares so allocated shall be completed.

6.8 The Vendor shall be bound to transfer the shares comprised in an allocation notice to the purchasers named therein at the time and place therein specified; if he shall fail to do so, the Chairman of the Company or some other person appointed by the directors shall be deemed to have been appointed attorney of the Vendor with full power to execute, complete and deliver, in the name and on behalf of the Vendor, transfers of the shares to the purchasers thereof against payment of the price to the Company. On payment of the price to the Company the purchaser shall be deemed to have obtained a good quittance for such payment and on execution and delivery of the transfer the purchaser shall be entitled (subject to the transfer being duly stamped) to insist upon his name being entered in the Register of Members as the holder by transfer of the shares. The Company shall forthwith pay the price into a separate bank account in the Company's name and shall hold such price in trust for the Vendor.

6.9 During the three months following expiry of the said period of fourteen days referred to in paragraph (6) of this Article, the Vendor shall be at liberty to transfer to any persons and at any price (not being less than the price fixed under paragraph (4) of this Article) any share not allocated by the directors in an allocation notice. Provided that, if the Vendor stipulated in his transfer notice that unless all the shares comprised therein were sold pursuant to this Article, none should be so sold, the Vendor shall not be entitled to sell hereunder only some of the shares comprised in his transfer notice].

6.10 If a member shall die or become bankrupt he shall be deemed to have given to the Company a transfer notice on the day immediately preceding the date of death or adjudication of bankruptcy in respect of all the shares held by him in the Company and the foregoing provisions of this Article shall thereupon apply].

6.11 An employee of the Company holding shares who leaves the Company's employment for whatsoever reason shall be deemed on the date of cessation of his employment to have given to the Company a transfer notice in respect of all the shares held by him and the foregoing provisions of this Article shall thereupon apply. [In this Article 'employee of the Company' means and includes a director, manager or other person in the employment of the Company or any subsidiary company of the Company (as defined in s 736 of the Act) holding in the aggregate less than two and one-half per cent of the issued share capital of the Company)].

6.12 The pre-emption provisions contained in this Article shall not apply

(i) to a transfer by a member of other person entitled to transfer the same of any share or shares to another member holding shares of the same class in the capital of the Company; or

(ii) to a transfer by a member to any child or other issue, son-in-law, daughter-in-law, father, mother, brother, sister, husband, wife, nephew or niece of such a member or to the trustee or trustees of any settlement made or intended to be made by a member principally for the benefit of himself or any of the foregoing persons; to a transfer for the purpose of effectuating any change of trustees of any such settlement as aforesaid or to any person or persons related to the settlor as aforesaid who shall be a beneficiary or beneficiaries under such settlement; or to a transfer by a corporate member to a controlling shareholder thereof; and any share of a deceased member may be transferred to any such relative as aforesaid of the deceased member or to the executors or administrators of any such deceased member. Any share standing in the name of the trustees of the Will of any deceased member may be transferred upon any change of trustees to the trustees for the time being of such Will or to a person to whom such member or deceased member would have been entitled to transfer the same; or

(iii) to a transfer to which all the members of the Company have consented in writing.]

6.13 Notwithstanding the foregoing provisions of this Article, the directors may decline to register any transfer of any share on which the Company has a lien and any transfer of a share (not being a fully paid share) to a person of whom they do not approve. Subject thereto, the directors shall be bound to register any transfer made pursuant to and in accordance with the provisions of this Article but may, in their absolute discretion and without assigning any reason therefor, decline to register any transfer not so made].

PROCEEDINGS AT GENERAL MEETINGS

7 One member holding an 'A' Share and one member holding a 'B' Share present in person or by proxy or (in the case of a corporation) by a duly authorised representative shall form a quorum and reg 40 of Table A shall be modified accordingly.

8 Any member present in person or by proxy may demand a poll and reg 46 of table A shall be deemed to be varied accordingly.

9 In the case of an equality of votes, whether on a show of hands or on a poll, the chairman shall not be entitled to a casting vote.

10 Subject to any rights or restrictions for the time being attached to any class or classes of shares, on a show of hands every member present in person shall have one vote and on a poll every member shall have one vote for every £1 in nominal amount of the 'A' Shares of which he is the holder and one vote for every £1 in nominal amount of the 'B' Shares of which he is the holder provided that:

(i) no 'A' Shares shall confer any right to vote upon a resolution for the removal from office of a 'B' Director;
(ii) no 'B' Shares shall confer any right to vote upon a resolution for the removal from office of an 'A' Director;
(iii) if at any meeting any holder of any 'A' Shares is not present in person or by proxy the votes exercisable on a poll in respect of the 'A' Shares held by members present in person or by proxy shall be pro tanto increased so that such 'A' Shares shall together entitle such members to the same aggregate number of votes as could be cast in respect of all the 'A' Shares if all the holders thereof were present; and
(iv) if at any meeting any holder of any 'B' Shares is not present in person or by proxy the votes exercisable on a poll in respect of the 'B' Shares held by members present in person or by proxy shall be pro tanto increased so that the 'B' Shares shall together entitle such members to the same aggregate number of votes as could be cast in respect of the 'B' Shares if all the holders thereof were present.

DIRECTORS

11 The number of directors (other than alternate directors) shall not, unless otherwise determined by a Special Resolution of the Company, be less than two or more than six and shall always be an even number. At the date of adoption of these Articles of Association the directors of the Company are (who shall be designated as 'A' directors and shall be deemed to have been appointed under the next following Article by the holders of the 'A' Shares) and (who shall be designated as 'B' directors and shall be deemed to have been appointed under the next following Article by the holders of the 'B' Shares).

12.1 (a) The holders for the time being of the 'A' Shares may from time to time nominate and appoint not more than three persons to be directors of the Company (herein referred to as the 'A' directors) and so that not more than three persons shall at any time hold office by virtue of appointment under this paragraph.

(b) The holders for the time being of the 'B' Shares may from time to time nominate and appoint not more than three persons to be directors of the Company (herein referred to as the 'B' directors) and so that not more than three persons shall at any one time hold office by virtue of appointment under this paragraph.

12.2 Any director appointed in accordance with paragraph (1) of this Article or in accordance with Article 15 may from time to time be removed by the holders for the time being of the shares by or upon whose nomination he was or was deemed to be appointed and any vacancy for any reason occurring in the office of director so appointed or deemed to be appointed may from time to time be filled up by the holders for the time being of the shares by or upon whose nomination the director so vacating office was appointed or deemed to be appointed.

12.3 Any appointment or removal under paragraph (1) or (2) of this Article shall be made in writing under the hands of the holder or holders for the time being of the shares in whom the power is vested, a corporation holding any such shares acting by resolution of its directors certified by the signature or signatures of its chairman or two of its directors. Any such appointment or removal shall take effect on and from the date on which notice in writing thereof is lodged at the Registered Office of the Company or delivered to the Secretary.

POWERS AND DUTIES OF DIRECTORS

13 A director who is in any way, whether directly or indirectly, interested in a contract (which in this Article shall be construed as including any transaction or arrangement, whether or not constituting a contract) or proposed contract with the Company shall declare the nature of his interest at a meeting of the directors in accordance with s 317 of the Act. Subject to such disclosure as aforesaid, a director may vote in respect of any contract or arrangement in which he is interested (and if he do so vote his vote shall be counted) and he shall be counted in ascertaining whether a quorum is present at any meeting at which any such contract or proposed contract shall come before the directors for consideration.

PROCEEDINGS OF DIRECTORS

14.1 The directors may meet together for the despatch of business, adjourn, subject as hereinafter provided, and otherwise regulate their meetings as they think fit. A director may, and the Secretary on the requisition of a director shall, at any time summon a meeting of the directors. Not less than seven days' notice of every meeting of the directors shall be given to all directors unless notice of the meeting shall have been waived by all the directors. Until otherwise determined by Special Resolution of the Company, one 'A' director and one 'B' director shall be a quorum. A committee of the directors must include at least one 'A' director and one 'B' director and the quorum for a meeting of any such committee shall be one 'A' director and one 'B' director. A person who holds office as an alternate director shall, if his appointor is not present, be counted in the quorum. A director who is also an alternate director shall be entitled in the absence of his appointor to a separate vote on behalf of his appointor in addition to his own vote.

14.2 All business arising at a meeting of the directors or of any committee of the directors shall be determined only by resolution and no resolution shall be effective unless carried by a majority including at least one 'A' director and at least one 'B' director. The Chairman shall not be entitled to a second or casting vote.

14.3 If within half an hour from the time appointed for the holding of a meeting of directors or of any committee of the directors a quorum be not present, the meeting shall be dissolved.

15 The continuing directors at any time may act notwithstanding any vacancy in their body provided always that in case the directors shall at any time be reduced in number to less than the minimum number fixed by these Articles and the holders of the shares who appointed the director who has vacated office and thereby caused the number of directors so to be reduced shall not fill such vacancy within twenty-one days after notice in writing shall have been given by the remaining director to such holders requiring such appointment to be made, it shall be lawful for the remaining director to act as director for the purpose of filling up the vacancy, but not for any other purpose, and the person so appointed shall for all the purposes of these Articles be deemed to be appointed by the holders to whom such notice is given.

INDEMNITY

16 Every director or other officer of the Company shall be indemnified out of the assets of the Company against all losses or liabilities which he may sustain or incur in or about the execution of the duties of his office or otherwise in relation thereto, including any liability incurred by him in defending any proceedings, whether civil or criminal, in which judgment is given in his favour or in which he is acquitted or in connection with any application under s 727 of the Act in which relief is granted to him by the Court, and no director or other officer shall be liable for any loss, damage or misfortune which may happen to or be incurred by the Company in the execution of the duties of his office or in relation thereto. But this Article shall only have effect in so far as its provisions are not avoided by s 310 of the Act.

8 Articles of association for a subsidiary company

The Companies Act 1985

COMPANY LIMITED BY SHARES

ARTICLES OF ASSOCIATION

of

LIMITED

(Adopted by Special Resolution passed)

PRELIMINARY

1.1 The regulations contained in Table A as prescribed by the Companies (Tables A to F) Regulations 1985 as amended by the Companies (Table A to F) (Amendment) Regulations 1985 (hereinafter called 'Table A') shall apply to this Company save in so far as they are varied or excluded by or are inconsistent with these Articles.

1.2 Regulations 73 to 80 (inclusive), 81(e), 94 to 98 (inclusive) and 118 of Table A shall not apply to the Company.

1.3 In these Articles 'the Act' means the Companies Act 1985 including any statutory modification or re-enactment thereof for the time being in force.

DIRECTORS

2 A director who is in any way, whether directly or indirectly, interested in a contract (which in this Article shall be construed as including any transaction or arrangement, whether or not constituting a contract) or proposed contract with the Company shall declare the nature of his interest at a meeting of the directors in accordance with s 317 of the Act. Subject to such disclosure as aforesaid, a director may vote in respect of any contract or arrangement in which he is interested (and if he do so vote his vote shall be counted) and he shall be counted in ascertaining whether a quorum is present at any meeting at which any such contract or proposed contract shall come before the directors for consideration.

3 No person shall be disqualified from becoming a director by reason of his attaining or having attained the age of seventy or any other age.

4 A member or members holding a majority in nominal value of the issued ordinary shares for the time being in the Company shall have power from time to time and at any time to appoint any person or persons as director or directors either as an additional director or to fill any vacancy and to remove from office any director howsoever appointed. Any such appointment or removal shall be effected by an instrument in writing signed by the member or members making the same, or in the case of a member being a company signed by one of its

directors on its behalf, and shall take effect upon lodgement at the registered office of the Company.

INDEMNITY

5 Every director or other officer of the Company shall be indemnified out of the assets of the Company against all losses or liabilities which he may sustain or incur in or about the execution of the duties of his office or otherwise in relation thereto, including any liability incurred by him in defending any proceedings, whether civil or criminal, in which judgment is given in his favour or in which he is acquitted or in connection with any application under s 727 of the Act in which relief is granted to him by the Court, and no director or other officer shall be liable for any loss, damage or misfortune which may happen to or be incurred by the Company in the execution of the duties of his office or in relation thereto. But this Article shall only have effect in so far as its provisions are not avoided by s 310 of the Act.

9 Shareholders' agreement for start-up or buy-out company

DATED 199

(1)
(2)
(3)
(4)
(5) LIMITED

SHAREHOLDERS' AGREEMENT

relating to Limited

THIS AGREEMENT is made the day of 199

PARTIES

(1) of ('A')

(2) of ('B')

(3) of ('C')

(4) of ('D')

(5) LIMITED registered in England number whose registered office is at ('the Company')

BACKGROUND

(A) The Company has at the date of this Agreement an authorised share capital of £ divided into ordinary shares of £1 each of which such shares are issued fully paid and are beneficially owned by A

(B) A, B, C and D ('the Founders') being all the current directors of the Company wish to invest in the Company upon and subject to the terms of this agreement in order to [enable the Company to complete the purchase of the entire issued share capital of Limited ('Target')] [enable the Company to carry on business in relation to [ ] ('the Business')]

[(C) To assist with [the purchase of Target] [the financing of the Company] it is also proposed that the Company should create and issue to [the current shareholders of Target] [proposed investors] a certain number of redeemable preference shares in the capital of the Company]

(D) The Company has entered into this Agreement for the purpose of receiving the benefit of the covenants in its favour set out in clause 7 below

DEFINITIONS

In this Agreement:

(1) 'the Shareholders' shall mean the Founders and the other parties to this agreement (other than the Company) from time to time

(2) 'Completion' shall mean the occurrence of the events referred to in clause 1.1 below

(3) 'In the agreed terms' shall mean in the form agreed by or on behalf of the Founders, and

(4) 'Subsidiary' shall have the meaning given to that term by s 736 of the Companies Act 1985, and 'subsidiaries' shall be construed accordingly

OPERATIVE PROVISIONS

1 Investment

1.1 On the date of this Agreement (or on such other day as the Founders shall otherwise agree in writing) ('the Completion Date'):

1.1.1 A [and B] shall procure that resolutions are passed by [him/them] as the current shareholder[s] of the Company to (inter alia):

1.1.1.1 increase the Company's authorised share capital to £ divided into ordinary shares of £1 each [and redeemable preference shares of £1 each]

1.1.1.2 confer upon the directors of the Company the general and unconditional authority pursuant to s 80 of the Companies Act 1985 to allot ordinary shares [and redeemable preference shares] in the Company up to a maximum nominal value of £ , and

1.1.1.3 adopt as the new articles of association of the Company the articles in the agreed form ('the Articles');

1.1.2 the Founders shall subscribe at par for a total of ordinary shares of £1 each in the capital of the Company (in the proportions set opposite their respective names in the Schedule) and shall each complete, sign and deliver to the Company an application form for their shares accompanied by payment of the subscription monies due from them;

1.1.3 A [and B] shall [each] pay to the Company the sum of £1 being the amount due on [each] of the ordinary shares currently in issue which are nil-paid;

1.1.4 the Founders shall procure a board meeting of the Company's directors to be held at which, inter alia, there shall be issued to each of them credited as fully paid the number of ordinary shares in the capital of the Company respectively applied for by them pursuant to sub-clause 1.1.2 of this clause; and

1.2 The Founders shall procure that within the time limits prescribed by statute those documents and forms required to be filed with the Registrar of Companies in consequence of any of the events referred to in clause 1.1 shall be so filed

1.3 A [and B] shall [each] waive all rights of pre-emption that they may have over any of the shares to be allotted pursuant to clause 1.1.2 and 1.1.4, whether conferred by the Articles or otherwise

2 Directors

2.1 Subject to clause 2.3, each of the Founders shall be entitled to remain a director of the Company and of each subsidiary of the Company for so long as he shall remain the beneficial owner and registered holder of the shares to be issued to him pursuant to clause 1

2.2 With effect from the Completion Date, each of the Founders shall be employed by the Company and/or any subsidiary of the Company at salaries of £ per annum each (subject to periodic review by the board of directors) and with benefits commensurate with the duties of his employment, such employment to be terminable either way on six months' notice or summarily on the occurrence of conduct justifying the same, but otherwise to be subject to the standard terms and conditions of employment from time to time in force in relation to the Company or the relevant subsidiary

2.3 The Founders shall each exercise the functions and have the responsibilities of office from time to time vested in them by the board of directors, and in performing their duties shall comply with the reasonable directions of the board and the provisions of this Agreement

2.4 None of the Founders may be removed as a director of the Company or of any of its subsidiaries unless and until he shall have ceased to comply with the shareholding qualification referred to above or shall be in breach of this Agreement or in the case of any Founder who is an employee of the Company or any subsidiary of the Company, he shall be guilty of conduct justifying his summary dismissal at common law

2.5 No additional directors of the Company or of any of its subsidiaries shall be appointed without the unanimous written consent of all the Founders

3 Management

3.1 The Shareholders shall each exercise their powers in relation to the Company so as to procure that neither the Company nor any company which is from time to time a subsidiary of the Company shall, without the unanimous written consent of all the Founders:

- 3.1.1 dispose of the whole or any material part of its business or assets or change the nature or scope of its business;
- 3.1.2 issue, allot, redeem, purchase or grant options over any share or other securities or reorganise its share capital in any way;
- 3.1.3 save in the ordinary course of its business mortgage or charge or part with possession or control of any of its assets, give any guarantee or indemnity or stand surety for the obligations of any third party;

3.1.4 other than as contemplated by this Agreement alter the provisions of its memorandum or articles of association or pass any resolution for winding up;

3.1.5 enter into any transactions or series of connected transactions involving capital expenditure in respect thereof in aggregate in excess of £ ; or

3.1.6 acquire any new premises or make any investment in another company or business or incorporate any new subsidiary

3.2 [Other specific limitations or provisions]

4 Confidentiality

Each of the Shareholders covenants and undertakes with the other Shareholders that he shall in all respects keep the secrets of the Company and its subsidiaries and shall not during the period of this Agreement or at any time thereafter (except with the consent of the proper officers of the Company or under the authority of the board or the court) divulge or make known to anyone or use for the benefit of himself or any other person firm or corporation any of the secrets of the Company or its subsidiaries or any information of a confidential nature relating to any of their respective customers or to the businesses (including prospective businesses) from time to time carried on by them other than information or knowledge which comes into the public domain otherwise than by reason of his default

5 Transfer of shares

5.1 None of the Shareholders shall dispose of any interest in or create any encumbrance over any of his shares in the Company except:

5.1.1 by a transfer of the entire legal and beneficial interest therein; and

5.1.2 to a transferee as permitted by this Agreement and the Company's articles of association for the time being in force

5.2 The Shareholders shall procure that before any person (other than a person who is already a Shareholder) is registered as a holder of any share in the Company such person shall enter into a deed of adherence (in a form satisfactory to the Shareholders) covenanting with the parties to this Agreement from time to time to observe, perform and be bound by all the terms of this Agreement which are capable of applying to such person and which have not then been performed. Upon being so registered that person shall be deemed to be a party to this Agreement

5.3 The Shareholders shall exercise their powers in relation to the Company so as to procure that the Company shall not register any transfer made in breach of clauses 5.1 or 5.2. The shares comprised in any transfer so made shall carry no rights whatsoever unless and until, in each case, the breach is rectified

6 Put and call options

6.1 In certain circumstances, one of the Shareholders ('the Seller') may be required to sell all (but not some only) of the shares in the capital of the Company held by him ('the Option Shares') to the other Shareholders ('the Buyers') on the terms of this clause 6 ('Call Options'). In certain of those circumstances, the Seller may require the Buyers to purchase all (but not some only) of the Option Shares on the terms of this clause 6 ('Put Options')

6.2 Call Options may be exercised by the Buyers (or any of them) by notice to the Seller given at any time within six months following any of the following events:

6.2.1 the death of the Seller;

6.2.2 the Seller ceasing to be employed within the Company and any of its subsidiaries; or

6.2.3 the bankruptcy of the Seller

6.3 The Put Options may be exercised by the Seller (or his personal representatives) by notice to the Buyers given at any time within six months after any of the following events:

6.3.1 the death of the Seller;

6.3.2 the retirement of the Seller from employment with the Company and any of its subsidiaries on or after his 60th birthday or earlier due to ill health causing permanent incapacity; or

6.3.3 the dismissal of the Seller (or resignation in circumstances where the Seller is entitled to treat himself as having been constructively dismissed) from employment with the Company and any of its subsidiaries where the dismissal (or constructive dismissal) is held by an industrial tribunal or court of competent jurisdiction (or otherwise agreed) to be unfair or wrongful (as the case may be)

6.4 The price to be paid for the Option Shares on exercise of any of the Put Options or Call Options shall be as follows:

6.4.1 the price on exercise of a Put Option or a Call Option following the occurrence of any of the events specified in clauses 6.3.1 through to 6.3.3 (inclusive) shall be the fair value of the Option Shares as at the date of Option exercise as between a willing seller and a willing buyer but ignoring any reduction in value which may be ascribed to the Option Shares by virtue of the fact that they represent a minority interest;

6.4.2 the price on exercise of a Call Option following the bankruptcy of the Seller shall be the lower of the original subscription price paid for the Option Shares and their fair value as a single holding as at the date of Option exercise as between a willing seller and a willing buyer; and

6.4.3 the price on exercise of a Call Option in any of the other permitted circumstances shall simply be the fair value of the Option Shares as a single holding as at the date of Option exercise as between a willing seller and a willing buyer

In each case the price payable for the Option Shares shall be agreed between the Seller and the Buyer on the basis of these provisions, but in default of such agreement, shall be calculated in accordance with these provisions, by the Independent Accountants

6.5 The 'Independent Accountants' as referred to in clause 6.4 shall be a firm of chartered accountants (other than the auditors for the time being of the Company) nominated by agreement between the Seller and the Buyers, or in default of such agreement, by the President for the time being of the Institute of Chartered Accountants in England and Wales. In calculating the price payable for the Option Shares as aforesaid the Independent Accountants:

6.5.1 shall be entitled to obtain professional valuations in respect of any of the Company's assets; and

6.5.2 shall be considered to be acting as experts and not as arbitrators or arbiters and accordingly any provisions of law or statute relating to arbitration shall not apply

6.6 The fees and other costs of and incurred by the Independent Accountants in calculating the price payable for the Option Shares as aforesaid shall be apportioned between the Seller and the Buyers or borne by any one or more of them as the Independent Accountants shall in their absolute discretion decide

6.7 Where the Seller exercises a Put Option, the Buyers shall be obliged to purchase the Option Shares in the proportions in which they hold shares in the capital of the Company at such time save as may otherwise be agreed. On the exercise of a Call Option by one of the Buyers, the Buyers shall be entitled to purchase the Option Shares in the proportions which they hold shares at such time but if any one or more of the Buyers does not wish to purchase any of the Option Shares and gives notice within 14 days of being notified of the exercise of the Call Option, the Buyer exercising the Call Option (and any other Buyers willing to purchase the Option Shares) shall be obliged to purchase all of the Option Shares (in proportion to their holdings of shares at such time, if there is competition between them)

6.8 On any exercise of the Put Options or the Call Options, the party exercising the same shall give notice to each of the other Shareholders and to the Company. Completion of the sale and purchase of the Option Shares shall take place within one month of the price payable for the Option Shares being determined pursuant to clause 6.4, when the Seller shall deliver executed share transfers in respect of all of the Option Shares in favour of the Buyers (or such of them as are obliged to purchase the Option Shares) together with the share certificates for the Option Shares (or an indemnity in respect of any lost share certificates in such form as the Buyers may reasonably require) against payment of the price for the Option Shares provided always that if the price of the Option Shares exceeds £[100,000], the price shall be paid by four equal and successive half-yearly instalments over two years the first instalment being paid within six months of the price of the Option Shares being determined in accordance with clause 6.4

6.9 The Seller hereby irrevocably appoints the eldest of the Buyers to act as his attorney and agent in relation to the sale and transfer of the Option Shares on the terms of this clause 6 so that such Buyer shall be entitled to execute deliver complete and do any act deed document or thing to complete the sale of the Option Shares and to perfect title thereto of the Buyers provided that this power of attorney shall not be exercisable unless the Seller fails to execute deliver complete or do any such act deed document or thing within 30 days after notice requiring the Seller to do so

6.10 The Seller shall sell the Option Shares pursuant to the Call Options and Put Options free from any charge lien or other encumbrance together with all rights attached thereto at the date of exercise of the Option

7 Restrictive covenants

7.1 Each of the Shareholders (each of whom is in this sub-clause called 'the Covenantor') covenants with each of the others and separately with the Company that the Covenantor (whether alone or jointly with any other person, and whether directly or indirectly, and whether as shareholder, participator, partner, promoter, director, officer, agent, manager, employee or consultant of, in or to any other person) shall not at any time ('the date in question') whilst the Covenantor is the holder of any shares in the Company and for a period of [one year] after the date on which the Covenantor ceased to be a shareholder in the Company ('the Termination Date'):

7.1.1 solicit or endeavour to entice away from or discourage from dealing with the Company any person who was at any time during the period of one year preceding the Relevant Date a manufacturer for or supplier, customer or client of the Company;

7.1.2 supply or provide any goods or services to any person who was at any time during the period of one year preceding the Relevant Date a customer or client of the Company to whom the Company had during that period supplied or provided goods or services in the ordinary course of its business;

7.1.3 solicit or endeavour to entice away from or discourage from being employed by the Company any person who was at the Relevant Date an officer or employee of the Company whether or not such person would commit a breach of contract by reason of leaving service; or

7.1.4 employ or engage or attempt to employ or engage or negotiate or arrange the employment or engagement by any other person, firm or company of any person who was at the Relevant Date, or was at any time during the period of one year prior thereto, an officer or employee of the Company

7.2 Each of paragraphs 7.1.1 to 7.1.4 of sub-clause 7.1 shall be deemed to constitute a separate agreement and shall be construed independently of the others

7.3 The expression 'the Company' where used in sub-clause 7.1 includes each of the Company's subsidiaries for the time being to the intent and effect that each of the paragraphs thereof shall apply (as a separate covenant in each case) in relation to each such company as they apply in relation to the subsidiary

7.4 The parties consider the restrictions in sub-clauses 7.1 and 7.3 to be reasonable, but if a court of competent jurisdiction finds any of them to be unenforceable the parties agree to accept any modification as to the area, extent or duration of the restriction concerned which the court sees fit to impose or, if it does not see fit, which is reasonably necessary to render the restriction enforceable

7.5 For the purposes of this clause 'the Relevant Date' means the date in question or the Termination Date (whichever shall be the earlier)

8 The company's articles of association

8.1 If, during the continuance of this Agreement, there shall be any conflict between the provisions of this Agreement and the provisions of the Articles or any subsequent articles of association of the Company then, during such period, the provisions of this Agreement shall prevail

8.2 Each of the parties hereto undertakes with each of the others to fully and promptly observe and comply with the provisions of the Articles and any subsequent articles of association of the Company to the intent and effect that each and every provision thereof shall be enforceable by the parties hereto inter se and in whatever capacity

8.3 Nothing contained in this Agreement shall be deemed to constitute an amendment of the Articles or of any previous articles of association of the Company

9 General

9.1 This Agreement represents the entire agreement between the Shareholders in connection with the Company and each of the Shareholders hereby acknowledges that save as herein provided he has not entered into this Agreement in reliance upon any representation express or implied written or oral

9.2 Where any matter or thing herein contained is expressed to be an obligation on the part of the Company (whether to do or refrain from doing any such matter or thing) the parties hereto shall exercise their respective powers in relation to the Company so as to procure that the Company shall observe the same

9.3 Where this Agreement provides that any particular transaction or matter requires the consent, approval or agreement of any Shareholder, such consent, approval or agreement may be given subject to such terms and conditions as that Shareholder may impose and any breach of such terms and conditions by any person subject thereto shall ipso facto be deemed to be a breach of the terms of this Agreement

9.4 Where any Shareholder is required under this Agreement to exercise his powers in relation to the Company so as to procure a particular matter or thing, such obligation shall be deemed to include an obligation to exercise his powers both as a shareholder and as a director (where applicable) of the Company and to procure that any director appointed by him (whether alone or jointly with any other person) shall procure such matter or thing

9.5 This Agreement shall be binding on and shall enure for the benefit of the successors and assigns and personal representatives (as the case may be) of each of the parties hereto

9.6 None of the parties hereto may assign his rights or obligations in whole or in part hereunder without the prior written consent of the other parties hereto; Provided that nothing in this clause 9.6 shall prevent a transfer of shares pursuant to clause 5

9.7 All provisions of this Agreement shall so far as they are capable of being performed and observed after the Completion Date continue in full force and effect notwithstanding Completion except in respect of those matters then already performed

9.8 No failure to exercise and no delay in exercising on the part of any of the parties hereto any right, power or privilege hereunder shall operate as a waiver thereof nor shall any single or partial exercise of any right, power or privilege preclude any other or further exercise thereof or the exercise of any other right, power or privilege. The rights and remedies provided in this Agreement are cumulative and not exclusive of any rights or remedies otherwise provided by law

9.9 Notwithstanding that any provision of this Agreement may prove to be illegal or unenforceable, the remaining provisions of this Agreement shall continue in full force and effect

9.10 References in this Agreement to clauses and sub-clauses are reference to clauses and sub-clauses of this Agreement

10 Duration

The terms of this Agreement shall remain in full force and effect for so long as but only for so long as any of the Founders continue to hold shares in the Company but in relation to a Shareholder which has transferred all of his shares as permitted by this Agreement and the Company's articles of association for the time being in force they shall thereupon cease to have any further force and effect except as provided in clause 11

11 Termination

The termination of this Agreement howsoever caused and the ceasing by any Shareholder to hold any shares shall be without prejudice to any obligations or rights of any of the parties hereto which have accrued prior to such termination or cesser and shall not affect any provision of this Agreement which is expressly or by implication provided to come into effect on or to continue in effect after such termination or cesser

12 Notices

All notices which are required to be given hereunder shall be in writing and shall be sent to the address of the recipient set out in this Agreement (or in any deed entered into pursuant to clause 5.2) or such other address as the recipient may designate to the Company. Any such notice may be delivered personally or by first class prepaid letter, telex or facsimile transmission and shall be deemed to have been served if by personal delivery when delivered if by first class post 48 hours after posting and if by telex or facsimile transmission when despatched

EXECUTED as a Deed the day and year first before written

THE SCHEDULE

Names of Founders	*Number of Shares*
A	
B	
C	
D	

EXECUTED as a deed by)
in the presence of:)

Witness signature:

Name:

Address:

Occupation:

EXECUTED as a deed by)
in the presence of:)

Witness signature:

Name:

Address:

Occupation:

EXECUTED as a deed by)
in the presence of:)

Witness signature:

Name:

Address:

Occupation:

EXECUTED as a deed by)
in the presence of:)

Witness signature:

Name:

Address:

Occupation:

EXECUTED as a deed by)
LIMITED)
acting by two directors or one)
director and its secretary)

Director

Director/Secretary

10 Simple option agreement over shares

THIS AGREEMENT is made the day of 199

BETWEEN:

1 [ ] LIMITED (Registered in England Number) whose registered office is at [ ] ('the Grantor')

2 [ ] LIMITED (Registered in England Number) whose registered office is at [ ] ('the Grantee')

IT IS HEREBY AGREED as follows:

1 Definitions

In this Agreement the following words and expressions have the following meanings unless inconsistent with the context:

1.1 'Company' means [ ]

1.2 'Option' means the right granted pursuant to clause 2.1

1.3 'Option Period' means the period of [ ] commencing from the date hereof

1.4 'Option Shares' means [ ] Ordinary Shares of 20p each fully paid in the capital of the Company beneficially owned by the Grantor, together with any further shares, stocks or other securities in the Company or in any other Company which are derived from the Option Shares or which are distributed by the Company in respect of the Option Shares

2 Option

2.1 In consideration of the sum of [£1] paid by the Grantee (receipt of which is acknowledged by the Grantor) the Grantor grants to the Grantee at any time during the Option Period the right to purchase the Option Shares for a total purchase price of £[ ] upon the terms and subject to the conditions of this Agreement

2.2 The Option shall be exercisable at any time during the Option Period and only in respect of all (but not some only) of the Option Shares

2.3 The Option may be exercised by the Grantee by notice to the Grantor and the parties shall be bound to complete the sale and purchase of the Option Shares 14 days after the date of service of such notice of exercise

3 Completion

Completion of the sale and purchase shall take place at the offices of the Grantor or at such other place as the parties shall mutually agree not later than 3.00 pm on the relevant day when:

3.1 The Grantor shall deliver to the Grantee:

3.1.1 a duly executed acknowledgement under seal in such form as the Grantee may reasonably request to confirm that the Grantor has no claim to or interest in the Option Shares accompanied by the relative Share Certificates (if held by the Grantor);

3.1.2 such other deeds and documents as may be necessary to transfer to the Grantee the Option Shares with limited title guarantee

3.2 The Grantee shall deliver to the Grantor a Banker's Draft in the sum of £[ ] in respect of the total purchase price

4 Option Shares

All rights attached to the Option Shares shall accrue to the Grantee on the date of service of its notice exercising the Option and, following the exercise of the Option, the Grantor shall account to the Grantee for all dividends or other distributions of the Company (so far as received by the Grantor) declared or paid by reference to a record date which is subsequent to the date of service and shall exercise all voting and other rights at the direction of the Grantee

5 General

5.1 This Agreement shall be binding upon each party's successors and assigns and personal representatives (as the case may be) except as expressly provided above, none of the rights of the parties under this Agreement may be assigned or transferred

5.2 Any notice required to be given by any of the parties under this Agreement may be sent by post to the address of the addressee as set out in this Agreement or to such other address as the addressee may from time to time have notified for the purpose of this clause. Communications sent by post shall be deemed to have been received 48 hours after posting.

SIGNED by)
on behalf of the Grantor)
in the presence of:)

Witness's signature:

Witness name:

Address:

Occupation:

SIGNED by)
on behalf of the Grantee)
in the presence of:)

Witness's signature:

Witness name:

Address:

Occupation:

11 Powers of Attorney over shares

THIS POWER OF ATTORNEY made on 199

by of

('the Appointor') being the registered holder of ordinary shares of £1 each in the capital of Limited ('the Shares')

WITNESSES as follows:

1 The Appointor hereby appoints [ ] ('the Attorney') to be the Appointor's attorney in the Appointor's name and on the Appointor's behalf to attend and vote at general meetings, to nominate proxies, to execute consents to short notice and written resolutions, and to exercise all other rights and powers attached to the Shares

2 This power of attorney is executed by the Appointor to secure the interest of the Attorney in the Shares and shall accordingly be irrevocable

3 The Appointor hereby undertakes:

3.1 to ratify and confirm whatever the Attorney shall lawfully do or cause to be done by virtue of this power of attorney, and

3.2 not to exercise or attempt to exercise any rights attached to the Shares which are exercisable by the Attorney hereunder

4 This power of attorney shall be governed by and construed in accordance with English law

This document is executed as a deed and delivered on the date stated at the beginning of this document

SIGNED as a deed by)
)
in the presence of:)

Witness signature:

Name:

Address:

Occupation:

BY THIS POWER OF ATTORNEY made the day of 199

I of

hereby irrevocably appoint

of

(hereinafter called 'the Attorney') to be my true and lawful attorney with full power and authority in my name and on my behalf to do, sign or execute all acts, documents or deeds as may be necessary or desirable in connection with the sale of the ordinary shares of £1 each ('the Shares') owned by me in Limited ('the Company') and in particular, but without prejudice to the generality of the foregoing, the Attorney shall have power and authority:

(A) to complete and deliver on my behalf all consents and proxies which may be necessary for the purpose of any extraordinary general meeting of the Company and all deeds, documents and other instruments necessary or proper in connection with any share transfer or disposal in respect of the Shares and to give a good receipt and discharge for all consideration payable in respect of their sale or disposal;

(B) to attend and otherwise take part in all meetings held in connection with the Company;

(C) generally to exercise all rights and privileges as holder of the Shares during the continuance of this authority.

I hereby undertake to ratify and confirm any act or documents whatsoever that the Attorney shall do or lawfully cause to be done by virtue of this power of attorney and to indemnify him against all costs and expenses properly incurred by him under it.

This authority of the Attorney under this power of attorney shall cease on the expiry of the four months from today's date.

SIGNED as a deed by)
in the presence of:)

Witness signature:)

Name:)

Address:)

Occupation:)

12 Sample 'majority protection' clauses

MANDATORY TRANSFERS AND COME ALONG CLAUSE

0.1 Mandatory Transfer of 'B' Shares

In the event that any holder of 'B' shares shall (for whatever reason) cease to be employed by the Company then:

0.1.1 such member shall be bound to give a transfer notice in respect of all the shares registered in the name of such member as at the date when such member ceases to be employed by the Company ('the Relevant Date') and once such member has given a transfer notice the provisions of Articles [ ] shall apply mutatis mutandis in respect of such transfer notice;

0.1.2 in the event that such member fails to serve a transfer notice within 14 days from the Relevant Date then any other member shall be entitled to give on behalf of such member a transfer notice at the expiration of such period of 14 days and to specify therein as the price per share the amount to be certified in accordance with Article 6.1.3 and the provisions of Articles [ ] and Article [ ] shall mutatis mutandis apply.

0.2 If any share of any class is transferred pursuant to any of the provisions of these Articles to a member holding shares of a different class, such share shall as on and from the time of registration of the transfer of that share in the register of members of the company be ipso facto redesignated as a share of the same class as those already held by that member.

0.3 Come Along Rights

0.3.1 Notwithstanding Article [ ] should the holder of shares of whatever class who has a controlling interest (as defined in Article [ ]) ('the Proposing Vendor') wish to sell the shares held by such holder in the Company to a bona fide unconnected third party then the Proposing Vendor will notify the other holders and consult with them with a view to the holders agreeing (or otherwise) such sale but if agreement is not reached and the Proposing Vendor still wishes to proceed with that sale then the Proposing Vendor shall be entitled to give notice in writing (a 'sale notice') to the other holders confirming that the Proposing Vendor has received an offer to purchase the share capital of the Company from a bona fide unconnected third party, the identity of such third party and the terms of such offer whereupon the other holders shall be 'obliged to sell their shares to such third party subject to such holders receiving the same or equivalent consideration per share from such sale as the Proposing Vendor receives and the sale of the shares held by such holders being otherwise on the same or equivalent terms as the sale of the shares held by the Proposing Vendor;

0.3.2 Any dispute as to whether the consideration per share or other terms of a sale pursuant to a sale notice under Article [ ] is or are the same or equivalent shall be conclusively determined by the auditors for the time being of the Company acting as experts and not arbitrators;

0.3.3 In the event that a sale notice is given under Article 0.3.1 each of the holders hereby irrevocably appoints the Proposing Vendor to act as his her or their attorney and agent in relation to any sale pursuant to Article 0.3.1 so that the Proposing Vendor shall be entitled to execute deliver complete and do any act deed document or thing to complete such sale provided that their power of attorney shall not be exercisable and to receive the proceeds of such sale on behalf of the relevant holder (so that the receipt of the Proposing Vendor shall be a good discharge to the Purchaser) unless the relevant holder fails to execute deliver complete or do any such act deed document or thing within seven days after notice requiring such holder to do so.

13 Sample preference share rights

[ ] Rights of preference shares

The rights attaching to the preference shares are as follows:

[ ].1 As regards income:

The holders of the preference shares shall be entitled to a fixed cumulative preferential net cash dividend at the rate of [ ]% per annum on the capital for the time being paid up thereon ('the fixed dividend') but shall not be entitled to any further or other right of participation in the profits of the Company

The fixed dividend shall be payable in equal half-yearly instalments on the [30th June] and [31st December] in each year provided that the amount of the payment of the fixed dividend on any of the preference shares in the financial year of the Company in which those preference shares are issued or redeemed shall be the same proportion of [ ]% as the period between the date of such issue or redemption and to the end or beginning of such financial year respectively bears to one whole year

[ ].2 As regards capital:

On a return of capital on liquidation or otherwise the assets of the Company available for distribution among the members shall be applied first in repaying to the holders of the preference shares the amounts paid up on such shares together with a sum equal to any arrears or accruals of the fixed dividend thereon, to be calculated down to the date of the return of capital and to be payable whether or not such dividend has been declared or earned, but the preference shares shall not entitle the holders thereof to any further or other right of participation in the assets of the Company

[ ].3 As regards issue of further preference shares:

The Company shall not be entitled to issue any further shares ranking as regards participation in the profits and assets of the Company either in priority to or pari passu with the preference shares save with the consent or sanction of the holders of the preference shares given in accordance with the provisions of Article [ ]

[ ].4 As regards redemption:

[ ].4.1 The Company shall have the right subject to the provisions of the Act to redeem at par, together with all arrears or accruals of the fixed dividend thereon, calculated down to the date fixed for redemption and to be payable whether or not such dividend has been declared or earned, all or any of the preference shares for the time being outstanding at any time after the first of the following occurs:

[ ].4.4.1.1 [19]; or

[ ].4.4.1.2 the consolidated net profits before taxation of the Company and its subsidiaries (if any) in any financial year (as disclosed by the audited consolidated profit and loss account of the Company and its subsidiaries (if any) for such financial year) have reached or exceeded [£];

upon giving to the holders of the particular shares to be redeemed not less than one month's previous notice in writing. In the case of any partial redemption, the Company shall redeem (so far as practicable) that number of preference shares registered in the name of each holder of preference shares on the date on which the notice to redeem is given which bears the same proportion to the total number of preference shares so registered in the name of that holder on that date as the total number of preference shares then to be redeemed bears to the total number of preference shares in issue on that date

4.4.2 Any notice of redemption shall specify the particular shares to be redeemed, the date fixed for redemption and the place at which the certificates for such shares are to be presented for redemption and upon such date each of the holders of the shares concerned shall be bound to deliver to the Company at such place the certificates for such of the shares concerned as are held by him in order that the same may be cancelled. Upon such delivery the Company shall pay to such holder (or, in the case of joint holders, to the holder whose name stands first in the register in respect of such shares) the amount then due to him in respect of such redemption

4.4.3 As from the date fixed for redemption of any preference share the fixed dividend thereon shall cease to accrue unless, upon the presentation of the certificate relating thereto and a receipt for the redemption moneys then due duly signed and authenticated in such manner as the board of directors of the Company may reasonably require, payment of the redemption moneys is refused

4.4.4 Notwithstanding any other provision of these Articles, each of the preference shares not previously redeemed shall be redeemed on [31st December 19] or so soon thereafter as the Company shall be able to comply with the provisions of the Act as to redemption at par, together with all arrears or accruals of the fixed dividend thereon calculated down to the date of redemption and to be payable whether or not such dividend has been declared or earned, in accordance with the foregoing provisions of this Article [ ] so far as the same are applicable

4.5 As regards voting:

The preference shares shall not entitle the holders thereof to receive notice of or to attend or vote at any general meeting of the Company unless:

4.5.1 at the date of the notice convening the general meeting the fixed dividend on such shares is in arrear; or

4.5.2 the business of the general meeting includes the consideration of a resolution for winding up the Company or for redeeming the share capital of the Company or any resolution altering or abrogating any of the special rights attached to the preference shares;

in which case the holders of the preference shares shall be entitled to receive notice of and to attend and vote at the general meeting and any holder of preference shares shall be entitled to demand a poll at such meeting in which case if a poll is duly demanded the preference shares as a class shall entitle the holder or holders thereof present in person or by proxy or by representative (in the case of a body corporate) to the same number of votes as are capable of being cast by all other members present in person or by proxy or by representative as aforesaid at the general meeting and the chairman of the meeting shall not be entitled to a second or casting vote.

[ ] Modification of class rights

Subject to the Act, all or any of the special rights for the time being attached to any class of shares for the time being issued may from time to time (whether or not the Company is being wound up) be altered or abrogated with the consent in writing of the holders of not less then three-fourths of the issued shares of that class or with the sanction of an extraordinary resolution passed at a separate general meeting of the holders of such shares. To any such separate general meeting all the provisions of the regulations of the Company as to general meetings of the Company shall mutatis mutandis apply, but so that the necessary quorum shall be two persons at least holding or representing by proxy not less than one-third of the issued shares of the class. If such separate meeting shall be adjourned owing to the absence of a quorum and if at the adjourned meeting a quorum shall not be present within half-an-hour from the time appointed for such adjourned meeting the holder or holders of shares of the class concerned who are present in person or by proxy shall constitute a quorum. Every holder of shares of the class shall be entitled on a poll to one vote for every such share held by him and any holder of shares of the class present in person or by proxy may demand a poll.

14 Loan agreement from shareholder to company

THIS AGREEMENT is made the ...... day of ....

PARTIES

(1) *(name)* of *(address)* ('the Lender')
(2) AB having its registered office at *(address)* ('the Company').

OPERATIVE PROVISIONS

1 The Lender shall lend to the Company the sum of £... ('the Loan') for a period expiring on *(date)* ('the Repayment Date').

2 In consideration of the Lender lending the Loan the Company covenants and undertakes to repay the Loan to the Lender on the Repayment Date or on any earlier date on which the Loan may become repayable pursuant to this agreement.

3 No interest shall be paid on the Loan except (without prejudice to the Company's obligation under clause 2 above) if the Company shall fail to repay the Loan in full on the Repayment Date or to make any repayment of the whole or any part of the Loan on any date on which the same may become payable pursuant to this agreement in which event interest shall be paid on the Loan or the balance thereof from time to time outstanding from such date at the rate of 4% above the minimum base rate for the time being of *(name)* Bank plc as well after as before judgment such interest to accrue from day to day to be payable monthly and if not paid to be compounded.

4 The right is reserved to the Company to repay to the Lender the whole or any part of the Loan prior to the Repayment Date upon giving the Lender 7 days' written notice of its intention to make repayment and of the amount so to be repaid and such amount of the Loan shall then become repayable on the date so specified for repayment.

5.1 Notwithstanding anything else contained in this agreement the whole of the Loan or so much of it as for the time being remains outstanding and all interest accrued but unpaid shall immediately become repayable in any of the following events:

5.1.1 if the Company shall be unable to pay its debts within the meaning assigned to that expression by the Insolvency Act 1986, s 123 or if the Company shall certify that it is unable to pay its debts as and when they shall fall due;

5.1.2 if an order be made or resolution be passed for winding up the Company otherwise than for voluntary liquidation for the purpose of reconstruction or amalgamation the terms of which have been previously approved in writing by the Lender;

5.1.3 if a distress or execution be levied or issued against any of the property of the Company and not be satisfied within 21 days;

5.1.4 if the Company shall cease to carry on its business or substantially the whole of its business or threaten to cease to carry on the same;

5.1.5 if a Receiver shall be appointed or any incumbrancer takes possession of the Company's assets or any part of them or if without the prior approval of the Lender a resolution is passed for a reduction of capital of the Company;

5.1.6 if the Company shall commit or permit any breach of any of the stipulations and provisions contained in this agreement and on its part to be observed and performed.

5.2 The Company shall upon the passing of any Special Resolution at any Extraordinary General Meeting of the Company resolving to repay all or any part of the Loan from time to time outstanding (and any interest accrued thereon but unpaid) forthwith repay the same in accordance with such resolution.

6 The Lender shall not be entitled to assign the benefit of this agreement.

SIGNED by the Lender)
in the presence of:)

Witness's signature:

Witness name:

Address:

Occupation:

SIGNED by)
on behalf of the Company)
in the presence of:)

Witness's signature:

Witness name:

Address:

Occupation:

15 Simple debenture

THIS DEBENTURE is made the day of 19

PARTIES

(1) of ('the Lender')

(2) a company registered in England under number whose registered office is at ('the Company')

BACKGROUND

(A) Lender [proposes to advance] [has agreed to advance] to the Company the sum of £ under the terms of a Loan Agreement ('the Loan Agreement') [to be] made between the parties on the date of this Debenture.

(B) It is a condition precedent to any advance being made under the Loan Agreement that the Company creates this Debenture in favour of the Lender.

OPERATIVE PROVISIONS

1 The Company covenants with the Lender that the Company will on demand by the Lender pay to the Lender:

1.1 all monies due to the Lender under the terms of the Loan Agreement;

1.2 on a full indemnity basis all costs, charges and expenses incurred by the Lender in connection with or incidental to the enforcement or attempted enforcement of its rights and powers including collection of monies due under this security;

1.3 interest on amounts due under this clause 1 at such rate as shall be agreed or (in the absence of agreement) at the annual rate of [ ]% above the base rate for the time being of [ ] Bank plc calculated on a day to day basis until payment.

2 In consideration of the Loan Agreement and advances made or to be made under it the Company with full title guarantee to secure the payment by the Company to the Lender of [all monies due to the Lender by the Company including] the sums covenanted to be paid by the Company to the Lender under clause 1 ('the Secured Liabilities') and so that the security hereby created shall be a continuing security

HEREBY CHARGES:

FIRST all (if any) freehold and leasehold property of the Company both present and future and all fixtures (including trade fixtures) fixed plant and machinery from time to time thereon.

SECONDLY all book debts and other debts of the Company including (but without prejudice to the generality of the same) bank balances and claims both present and future including 'choses in action' and other claims that may give rise to debts including negotiable instruments, rights of tracing unpaid vendors liens and rights of reservation of property and proceeds of insurance.

THIRDLY all machinery vehicles chattels and equipment of the Company now being in, upon or about the Company's premises and which are used in or upon any part of the same or are requisite to complete the equipment for the carrying on of the trade or business now or at any times carried on in and upon the said premises or any part thereof together with all such machinery vehicles chattels and things which may at any time hereafter be in upon or about the said premises whether the same be in addition to or be substituted for all or any of the machinery vehicles chattels and things first mentioned in this paragraph.

FOURTHLY the goodwill and the uncalled capital of the Company both present and future including all intellectual property rights of any description to include but not by way of limitation all patent rights, trade and service marks, design rights (whether registered or unregistered).

FIFTHLY the undertaking and all other property, assets and rights of the Company both present and future (save and except the property effectively specifically charged hereunder).

SIXTHLY all work in progress (that is to say all articles produced and the benefit of services rendered pursuant to a contract by the Company with any third party which articles (including articles in respect of which services have been rendered) are in the possession actual or constructive of the Company and in respect of which property therein and/or possession thereof has not been given to the said third party and all stock in trade of the Company.

The security hereby created shall as regards the property first [secondly] and fourthly described be a First Fixed Legal Charge (and as regards all those parts of the property first described now vested in the Company shall constitute a Charge by way of Legal Mortgage thereon) and as to the property thirdly and sixthly described shall be an assignment by way of security and as to the property fifthly described shall be a First Floating Charge but so that the Company shall not without the consent in writing of the Lender create any Mortgage Debenture or Charge upon any of the property fifthly described ranking either in priority to or pari passu with the Charge hereby created except as provided in clause 10. If the property first described or any part thereof shall be compulsorily acquired the property hereby Charged to the Lender shall include injurious affection, loss of goodwill and severance and disturbance payments.

3 The Secured Liabilities shall upon demand made by the Lender pursuant to clause 1 become due and if the Company shall pay the same to the Lender the Lender will after such payment at the request and cost of the Company duly discharge this Security.

4 This Deed shall be a continuing Security for the payment on demand of the Secured Liabilities.

5 The Company shall not have power save with the written consent of the Lender to create any further Mortgage or Charge ranking in priority to or pari passu with this Debenture [save as provided in Clause 10].

6 Section 103 of the Law of Property Act 1925 shall not apply to this security and the amount hereby covenanted to be paid shall be deemed to be due and the statutory power of sale shall as between the Lender and any purchaser be exercisable at any time after the execution of this security.

7 Notwithstanding anything hereinbefore contained the amount due under the Loan Agreement and all other Secured Liabilities shall become payable and the statutory and other powers of sale and appointing of a Receiver shall arise on the date hereof and shall become exercisable by the Lender immediately upon the happening of any one or more of the following events:

7.1 if the Company makes default in the payment of any money properly demanded hereunder;

7.2 if the Company enters into any composition or arrangement with or for the benefit of its Creditors;

7.3 if the Company is made the subject of an Administrative Order or a Winding Up Order or a Resolution is passed for the winding up of the Company or a Receiver is appointed in respect of any of the Company's assets;

7.4 if a distress or execution is levied or issued against any of the property of the Company and is not paid out within seven days;

7.5 if the Company fails to perform and observe any of the covenants, provisions, agreements and declarations contained herein;

7.6 if the Company ceases or threatens to cease to carry on its business or substantially the whole of its business; or

7.7 if the Company is unable to pay its debts.

8 At any time after the occurrence of any of the events referred to in clause 7 the Lender may appoint by writing any person or persons to be a Receiver or Receivers so appointed and appoint another or others in his or their place and a Receiver or Receivers shall have the following powers:

8.1 to take possession of collect and get in any property hereby charged or assigned and for that purpose to take any proceedings in the name of the Company or otherwise as may seem expedient;

8.2 to carry on manage or concur in carrying on and managing the business of the Company or any part thereof and for any of those purposes to raise or borrow any money that may be required upon the security of the whole or any part of the property hereby charged;

8.3 forthwith and without the restriction imposed by s 103 of the Law of Property Act 1925 to sell or concur in selling and to let or concur in letting and to surrender or concur in surrendering any accept surrenders of leases or tenancies of all or any of the property hereby charged and to carry such sale letting surrender or accepting surrenders into effect by conveying leasing or surrendering or accepting surrenders in the name and on behalf of the Company or other the estate owner and such sale letting surrender or accepting surrenders may be for cash debentures or other obligations shares stocks or other valuable consideration and may be payable in a lump sum or by instalments spread over such period as the Lender shall think fit;

8.4 to sever and sell separately from the premises containing them plant machinery and other fixtures without the consent of the Company being obtained thereto;

8.5 to make any arrangement or compromise which he or they shall think expedient;

8.6 to make and effect all repairs renewals and any improvements of the Company's plant machinery and effects and to maintain or renew all insurances;

8.7 to appoint managers agents officers servants and workmen for any of the aforesaid purposes at such salaries and for such periods as he or they may determine;

8.8 to acquire property and to apply assets for the purpose of such acquisition for any purpose which in the opinion of the Receiver is conducive to the most beneficial ultimate realisation of assets hereby charged;

8.9 to do all such other reasonable acts and things as may be considered to be incidental or conducive to any of the matters or powers aforesaid and which he or they lawfully may or can do as agents or agent of the Company.

ALL money received by such Receiver or Receivers shall be applied first in payment of his or their reasonable remuneration and the costs of realisation secondly in providing for the matters specified in the first three paragraphs of sub-s (8) of s 109 of the Law of Property Act 1925 and for the purposes aforesaid and thirdly in or towards satisfaction of the Secured Liabilities and all the foregoing provisions shall take effect as and by way of variation and extension of the provisions of ss 99 to 109 inclusive of the said Act which provisions so varied and extended shall be regarded as incorporated herein. Any Receiver or Receivers so appointed shall be deemed to be the Agent or Agents of the Company and the Company shall be solely responsible for his or their remuneration (the amount of the said remuneration is to be in the discretion of the Receiver but subject to the consent of the Lender).

The foregoing powers of appointment of a Receiver or Receivers shall be in addition to and not to the prejudice of all statutory and other powers (whether of sale appointment of Receiver or otherwise) of the Lender under the Law of Property Act 1925 (and so that such statutory powers of sale shall be exercisable without regard to s 103 of that Act) or otherwise and so that such powers shall be and remain exercisable by the Lender in respect of any property hereby charged and of which no appointment of a Receiver by the Lender shall from time to time be subsisting and that notwithstanding that an appointment under the powers of this clause shall have subsisted and been withdrawn in respect of that property or shall be subsisting in respect of any other property hereby charged.

9 The company hereby irrevocably appoints any Receiver or Receiver appointed as aforesaid jointly and also severally to be its Attorney for it in its name and on its behalf and as its act and Deed or otherwise to sign seal and deliver and execute and otherwise perfect any such Legal or other Mortgage as aforesaid or (without executing any such Mortgage) any Deed, Assurance or Act which may be required or may be deemed proper on any sale Lease or disposition by such Receiver or Receivers as aforesaid of the said properties or any part thereof under any power of sale leasing or other disposition applicable thereto.

[10 This Security shall rank pari passu in all respects with a debenture of even date given by the Company to]

EXECUTED as a Deed by)
)

acting by a director and the secretary or)
by two directors)

Director

Director/Secretary

SIGNED as a Deed by the said)
in the presence of:)

16 3i Investment agreement and articles

CONTENTS

DISCLAIMER: Neither 3i Group plc nor 3i plc provides personal investment advice. Individuals should seek independent advice as to whether a particular transaction is suitable for them having regard to their own personal and financial circumstances.

Section 1: PARTIES AND INVESTMENT SUMMARY

Parties

(1) *(name of new company)* ('the Company') *(address of registered office)* registered number: ......
(2) *(names of directors)* ('the Directors')
(3) **3i Group plc**

Investment summary

Our investment will consist of:

£1,550,000	redeemable preference shares
£100,000	'A' ordinary shares representing 40% of the equity share capital of the Company
£1,650,000	total investment

Section 2: SHARE RIGHTS

Part 1: Share capital

Immediately after Completion the Company's issued share capital will be:

	Ordinary shares of £1 each	'A' ordinary shares of £1 each	Preference shares of £0.01 each
Directors	150,000	Nil	Nil
3i	Nil	100,000	1,550,000

Part 2: Share rights summary

The following is a summary of the share rights which will be written into the Company's articles of association.

1 Dividends

The Company will pay the dividends set out below (which are expressed net of tax) in the following order of priority:

1.1 preference shares fixed dividend per share

amount	% of the subscription price each year
accrual	cumulative from the date of subscription
payment	half-yearly on 31 March and 30 September
first payment	31 March 1997

1.2 'A' ordinary shares fixed dividend per share amount

amount	% of the subscription price each year accrual
accrual	cumulative from the date of subscription payment
payment	half-yearly on 31 March and 30 September first payment
first payment	31 March 1997

1.3 'A' ordinary shares participating dividend as a class amount

amount	% of Group Profit each year less the 'A' ordinary fixed dividend paid for the same period
accrual	cumulative from the date of subscription
payment	within 14 days of approval of audited accounts by the auditors (but not later than 4 months after the year end).

1.4 'A' ordinary shares compensatory dividend as a class

amount	the amount required to compensate us if Benefits paid to Shareholding Directors exceed £ in any year. This will be calculated by treating the excess Benefits as if they had been paid as dividends on their ordinary shares and giving us a dividend of the same amount per share. The Benefits level of £ will be Index-linked.
payment	at the same time as our participating dividend.

1.5 ordinary shares dividend

amount	the amount per share approved by the members in general meeting not exceeding the amount of the fixed and participating dividend per share paid on the 'A' ordinary shares for the last complete financial period.
payment	as approved by the members in general meeting, but only:

1.5.1 if all preference shares which are then due for redemption have been redeemed;
1.5.2 if all dividends on the preference shares and 'A' ordinary shares are up to date;
1.5.3 if the profits remaining available for distribution after payment of this dividend and all prior dividends will be at least £ ;
1.5.4 if the total of all dividend payments for the year will not be more than 33% of net profit after tax.

1.6 further dividends payable on both 'A' ordinary and ordinary shares (as though they were the same class) with the consent of the 'A' ordinary shareholders.

2 Capital repayment

If the Company's share capital is reduced or the Company is liquidated, the capital available for payment to shareholders will be paid on each share in the following order:

2.1 preference shares: the subscription price paid;
2.2 'A' ordinary shares: the subscription price paid;
2.3 ordinary shares: the subscription price paid on each 'A' ordinary share;
2.4 'A' ordinary and ordinary shares: the surplus (as though the shares were the same class).

If any share has dividend arrears/accruals these must be cleared prior to the return of capital or an equivalent sum added to the amount of capital returned.

3 Redemption of preference shares

3.1 The Company will redeem the preference shares, paying £1 per share and any arrears and accruals of dividend, as follows:

Dates	Number of shares to be redeemed
31 March 1999	310,000
31 March 2000	310,000
31 March 2001	310,000
31 March 2002	310,000
31 March 2003	310,000

3.2 The Company may redeem preference shares earlier, in blocks of not less than 100,000 shares, if the preference shareholders agree.
3.3 The Company will redeem all the preference shares if it floats or if its control passes out of the hands of those who control it immediately after Completion.

4 Class protection

The agreement of the preference shareholders and the 'A' ordinary shareholders will be needed before:

4.1 the Company:
- 4.1.1 changes its memorandum or articles of association;
- 4.1.2 changes class rights (even indirectly);
- 4.1.3 makes bonus issues of shares/loanstock;
- 4.1.4 buys its own shares;
- 4.1.5 redeems its own shares, except by redemption permitted under the articles of association;
- 4.1.6 passes a resolution that it be liquidated; or

4.2 the Company or a subsidiary:
- 4.2.1 changes its authorised or issued share capital;
- 4.2.2 grants an option to subscribe for shares;
- 4.2.3 disposes of all or a substantial part of its business; or
- 4.2.4 acquires or disposes of shares.

5 Share transfer

5.1 A transfer of shares will trigger pre-emption rights in favour of all 'A' ordinary and ordinary shareholders except:
- 5.1.1 a transfer of shares within the 3i group of companies, which can be made without restriction;
- 5.1.2 a transfer of shares to immediate family (ie children and spouses), which can be made without restriction.

5.2 If a member of the management team or any other employee leaves the employment of the Group or ceases to be a director/employee he must immediately offer his shares for sale.

5.3 No share may be transferred if that would give a controlling interest in the Company to:
- 5.3.1 a company controlled by shareholders of the Company;
- 5.3.2 another company or any person not a member immediately after completion, unless the proposed transferee offers to buy:
  - 5.3.2.1 the 'A' ordinary shares at
    - the price per share offered for the other ordinary shares (subject to a minimum of the price we paid) plus
    - a sum equal to the accrued dividends plus
    - the amount of the tax credit on the accrued dividends;
  - 5.3.2.2 the preference shares at
    - £1 per share plus
    - a sum equal to the accrued dividends, plus
    - the amount of the tax credit on the accrued dividends.

6 Voting

6.1 Ordinary shares and 'A' ordinary shares have one vote each.
6.2 Preference shares have no votes.

7 Special director

7.1 The holders of the 'A' ordinary shares may appoint a non-executive director to the Company and its subsidiaries.
7.2 The Company will pay the director's fees. If they cannot agree the level of fees to be paid then 3i will set a reasonable sum.

Section 3: INVESTOR PROTECTION TERMS

1 Borrowing limit

1.1 The Company shall not without our written consent allow Group Borrowings to exceed £ or twice Shareholders Funds whichever is more.

Note: the definition of Group Borrowings includes hire purchase, leasing etc.

2 General restrictions

2.1 The Company may not without our written consent:
- 2.1.1 allow the directors of the Company to invest in any other company or partnership, except for investments not exceeding 1% of any class of security traded on the Stock Exchange;
- 2.1.2 change its accounting reference period;
- 2.1.3 allow the combined Benefits of Shareholding Directors Group Directors to exceed £ a year (Index-linked).

2.2 No company in the Group may without our written consent:
- 2.2.1 expand or develop its business except through itself, the Company or a wholly owned subsidiary of the Company;
- 2.2.2 enter into a service or any other agreement with any director or Connected person, or materially change such an agreement.

3 Disclosure of information

3.1 We may disclose information about the Group to any:
- 3.1.1 lender to the Group;
- 3.1.2 shareholder in the Group.

3.2 We may disclose any information about the Group as required:
 3.2.1 by law;
 3.2.2 by the Stock Exchange and any regulatory authority to which we are subject.

3.3 No party to this agreement may issue a press release about our investment unless its wording is agreed between the Company and us.
3.4 The Company authorises any non-executive director appointed by us to discuss the Company, its business and prospects with us.

4 Policy on exit

4.1 If the Company is floated there will be no restriction on dealing in the shares we hold in it.
4.2 If the Company is sold or floated we will not be required to:
 4.2.1 give any warranty or indemnity (except a warranty as to the title to shares we hold in it); or
 4.2.2 appoint any party (including a sponsor of the Company) to act as our agent.

5 Environmental obligations

In connection with the environment all companies in the Group will:
5.1 comply with all applicable legislation/regulations;
5.2 maintain all required consents and licences; and
5.3 notify us at once if they lose any such consent or licence.

6 Consumer Credit Act 1974

While we hold at least one third of the voting power in the Company, the Company will notify us immediately:
6.1 of any licence issued under the Consumer Credit Act 1974 to it or any company it controls;
6.2 if such a licence is revoked;
6.3 if the Company acquires or loses control of any company which holds such a licence.

Note: We require this information to allow us to meet our obligations under the Consumer Credit Act 1974.

Section 4: PROVISION OF INFORMATION TO 3I

1 The Company will give us:

1.1 *Annual audited accounts*
within 4 months of the end of each financial year copies of:

1.1.1 audited accounts of every Group company;
1.1.2 audited consolidated Group accounts showing the information needed to calculate the dividends due to us;
1.1.3 any management letters from the Company's auditors;

1.2 *Interim management accounts*
within 30 days of the end of each period, monthly management accounts in a form we reasonably approve;

1.3 *Budgets*
not later than 30 days before the beginning of each financial year, a budget for that financial year giving information for each management accounting period in a form we reasonably approve;

1.4 *Other financial information*
within a reasonable time, any further information about the financial position of the Group which we reasonably request;

1.5 *Board papers*
if we ask for them (and then at the same time as they are given to the board) all
- agendas
- minutes, and
- other documents

circulated for (or following) discussion at a board meeting;

1.6 *Take-over proposals*
immediate written details of any offer, actual or proposed, made to any of the ordinary shareholders of the Company to buy their shares.

2 If the Company does not comply with its obligations in clause 1 of this section, we may appoint accountants to attend the Company's premises, investigate and prepare the documents. The Company must co-operate with the accountants and pay their fees and expenses.

Section 5: WARRANTIES

The warranties in this section are given subject to any matters fairly disclosed in any disclosure letter accepted by us.

PART 1

1 Trading history and forecasts

Each Director severally warrants to us as set out below.

2 Information documents

2.1 The factual information in the report of (name of auditors) dated (date) is true and accurate in all material respects and the opinions and forecasts it contains are reasonable.

2.2 2.2.1 The Company has disclosed to us in writing all key assumptions underlying the profit and cash flow forecasts in the business plan dated *(date)*.

2.2.2 The factual information in the business plan is accurate in all material respects.

2.2.3 The opinions and forecasts in the business plan are made on reasonable grounds after thorough enquiries.

2.2.4 The Directors know nothing which invalidates or potentially invalidates the opinions and forecasts in the business plan.

3 Assets and liabilities

3.1 The Company has not traded.

3.2 It has disclosed to us in writing all
- its assets
- director's service contracts
- actual and contingent liabilities
- its share capital (issued authorised and under option).

4 Accounts

4.1 We have been provided with the latest audited consolidated accounts of the Target Group.

4.2 Those accounts give a true and fair view of the financial position of the Target Group as at their date.

4.3 Since the date to which the accounts were drawn there has been no material adverse change in the financial or trading position of the Target Group.

4.4 There has been disclosed to us in writing all:
- commitments of an unduly onerous nature
- litigation (including litigation known to be threatened)
- unusual or non-recurring items significantly affecting the financial position
- debts known to be bad or doubtful
- dividends paid or proposed
- Directors' Benefits

in relation to the Target Group and which have arisen or been paid since the date of the accounts.

4.5 The Company has disclosed to us:
- any directors' service contracts
- its share capital (authorised, issued, and under option).

5 Intellectual property

The Company and the Target Group own outright all the intellectual property rights they need for their current or proposed businesses.

6 Subsidiaries

The Company has no subsidiaries except *(name of subsidiary)* which at Completion will be wholly owned.

7 Information supplied

7.1 The written information supplied to us by the Company and the Directors in connection with our investment was and remains accurate in all material respects.

7.2 The Directors do not know of anything which makes the written information given to us misleading.

7.3 The Directors know nothing which materially adversely affects the financial or trading prospects of the Company or the Target Group.

8 Pollution

The Directors are not aware that any land occupied by the Target Group contains any pollutant likely to cause significant harm to people or property.

PART 2

1 Directors' personal interests

1.1 Each of the Directors warrants, on his or her own account only, that he/she:

- 1.1.1 has no business interests except for shareholdings in the Company or in companies quoted on the Stock Exchange;
- 1.1.2 has never been:
  - 1.1.2.1 convicted of a criminal offence (except any road traffic offence not punished by a custodial sentence);
  - 1.1.2.2 disqualified from being a company director.

1.2 Each of the Directors warrants, on his or her own account only, that neither he/she nor anyone with whom he/she is Connected have any contract with the Company or the Target Group, nor own any property used by the Company or the Target Group.

1.3 The warranties in parts 1 and 2 of this section shall be deemed to be given immediately before Completion.

Section 5A

The following time and financial limits will apply to claims under the warranties but only if the claim, or the delay in discovering it, does not result from a Director's fraud, wilful misconduct or wilful concealment.

1 Each Director's liability for all claims for breach of the warranties is limited as follows:

Director	*Limit (£)*
(name)	
(name)	
(name)	
(name)	

2 We may not claim for breach of the warranties unless the total amount of all claims exceeds £25,000 but may then claim the whole amount and not just the excess over £25,000.

3 We may not claim against a Director unless we have given him and the Company reasonable details of the claim (on the basis of the facts then known to us) within 6 months of receiving the Target Group's audited consolidated accounts for the year ending or current on *(date)*. All notices of claim will be given at the Company's registered office.

Section 6: FEES

1 The Company will pay us
- 1.1 a negotiation fee of £ on Completion.
- 1.2 our solicitors' fees and expenses in connection with this agreement, payable:
  - 1.2.1 on Completion, or
  - 1.2.2 if, having accepted this offer, the Company later decide not to proceed.
- 1.3 an annual monitoring fee of £ plus VAT, payable quarterly in arrears on 31 March, 30 June, 30 September and 31 December in each year.

2 The monitoring fee will be paid by direct debit or any other method we reasonably request.

Section 7: AVAILABILITY OF FUNDS

Our investment will be made available when the conditions set out below have been satisfied.

Part 1: Conditions for first part of our investment

1 We are to be satisfied:
- 1.1 with the Company's and the Target Group's bank facilities and the terms on which they are available;

1.2 with the Target Group's audited accounts for the year ended 31 December 1995 and management accounts to 31 May 1995;
1.3 with the Company's and the Target Group's financial position, and level of trading, immediately before Completion;
1.4 with the Company's procedures for producing management accounting information;
1.5 with the proposed accounting treatment of goodwill;
1.6 with customer references on the Target Group;
1.7 with a schedule showing the Benefits of the Directors;
1.8 with a direct debit instruction for the monitoring fee;
1.9 with the Directors' replies to our environmental questionnaire.

2 Our solicitor is to be satisfied:
2.1 that the Directors have subscribed £150,000 in cash for 150,000 ordinary shares in the Company;
2.2 with the Company's auditor's or solicitor's certificate confirming the authorised and issued share capital, the identity of the directors and shareholders and their shareholding;
2.3 with the result of a Companies Registry search against the Company and each company in the Target Group immediately before Completion;
2.4 with any disclosures against the warranties;
2.5 with the terms on which the Company occupies its trading premises;
2.6 with the agreement by which the Company will acquire the issued share capital of *(subsidiary)*;
2.7 that the Company has supplied details of any licence issued to it (or to any company it controls) under the Consumer Credit Act 1974;
2.8 with the terms of any director's service contract;
2.9 the Target Group owns outright all the intellectual property rights it needs for its current or proposed businesses;
2.10 with the Company's written authority to pay our investment funds to a third party;
2.11 with the unqualified acceptance of this offer by the Company, and the Directors.

Section 8: DEFINITIONS

The following definitions apply in this agreement.

3i Group plc	3i Group plc (registered number 1142830) whose registered office is at 91 Waterloo Road London SE1 8XP. References in this agreement to 'we'/'us'/'our' are references to 3i Group plc.
Benefits	All salary and all sums included as 'emoluments' by the Companies Act 1985, Schedule 6, paragraph 1(4) (as amended). This definition is the one used by the auditors in preparing the Company's audited accounts. It includes benefits in kind and pension contributions.

Complete, Completion	When we make our first payment to the Company.
Connected	As defined by the Income and Corporation Taxes Act 1988, s 839.
Group	The Company and its subsidiaries (if any) from time to time.
Group Borrowings	The total of: 1 amounts borrowed by the Group; 2 any actual or contingent liability under a guarantee given by a company within the Group; 3 amounts due by the Group under any credit sale, hire purchase, and equipment leasing agreements, insofar as any of these can properly be attributed to capital; but excluding loans, and guarantees, from one company within the Group to another.
Group Profit	The profit of the Group on ordinary activities after tax, calculated on the historical cost accounting basis adjusted by adding back any amortisation of goodwill and Benefits paid to Shareholding Directors in excess of £ each year (Index-linked).
Index-linked	Adjusted annually each 1 January starting on 1 January 1997. The amount of the increase shall be the percentage increase in the retail price index for the preceding 12 months except for the first increase which shall be made by reference to the period from the first day of the month in which Completion takes place to December 1996.
Shareholders' Funds	The total of: 1 the Company's nominal paid up share capital; 2 the amount in the Company's share premium account; and 3 both capital and revenue reserves (consolidated if appropriate); but deducting amounts: 1 arising from writing up the book values of capital assets; 2 attributable to minority interests; and 3 set aside for deferred taxation.
Shareholding Directors	All directors and former directors of the Company or its subsidiaries interested in shares in the Company (other than any director appointed by us) and their Connected persons.
The Stock Exchange	Any of London Stock Exchange Limited, any other recognised investment exchange (as defined in the Financial Services Act 1986, s 207) and their respective share dealing markets.
Target Group	*(name of company)* and its subsidiaries (if any).

Note: A reference to an Act of Parliament is to that Act as amended or re-enacted at the relevant time, but if that would defeat the purpose of the clause which refers to it it is to be treated as a reference to the Act as amended up to the date of this agreement.

Section 9: ACCEPTANCE AND SIGNING

We may revise or withdraw this offer unless you accept it within 7 days of today. We may cancel it if our investment is not completed within 5 weeks of acceptance.

If you wish to accept the offer, please sign the enclosed duplicate and return it to us. The agreement will be legally binding on both of us from the time we receive the signed duplicate.

Offered by us on *(date)*

For 3i Group plc

(signature)

Authorised Signatory

Agreed by the Company and the Directors on: *(date)*

For the Company

(signature)

A director authorised to sign for the Company

The Directors

....
....
....

New articles of association

Note: This Form of new Articles of Association is intended for use in conjunction with Form 7A – Investment Agreement below. Both Forms are representations of forms in current use by 3i Group plc and are reproduced with the permission of **3i Group plc**.

THE COMPANIES ACT 1985

COMPANY LIMITED BY SHARES

NEW ARTICLES OF ASSOCIATION
of
(name of company)

(adopted by special resolution on *(date)*)

PRELIMINARY

1 In these articles:

1.1 'the Act' means the Companies Act 1985 and every statutory modification or re-enactment thereof for the time being in force.

1.2 'Table A' means Table A in the Companies (Tables A–F) Regulations 1985 as amended by the Companies (Tables A–F) (Amendment) Regulations 1985.

1.3 'Relevant Directors' means the directors and former directors of the Company and its subsidiaries where such directors or former directors are interested in shares in the Company and their connected persons (as defined by the Income and Corporation Taxes Act 1988, s 839) but excluding any Special Director (as hereinafter defined).

1.4 The word 'emoluments' shall include all salary and all items set out in paragraph 1(4) of Schedule 6 of the Act.

1.5 Where any amount is stated to be Index Linked it shall be increased on 1 January in each year for the following period of 12 months. The first increase shall take place on 1 January 1997. The amount of the increase shall be the percentage increase (if any) in the retail price index published by the Government for the preceding 12 months except that the first increase shall be made by reference to the period from the first day of the month in which these articles were adopted to 31 December 1996.

2.1 The regulations contained in or incorporated in Table A shall apply to the Company save insofar as they are excluded or varied hereby or are inconsistent herewith and such regulations (save as so excluded varied or inconsistent) and the articles hereinafter contained shall be the regulations of the Company.

2.2 Regulations 54, 73–80 (inclusive), 85, 86, 94–98 (inclusive) and 118 of Table A shall not apply to the Company.

SHARE CAPITAL

3 The share capital of the Company is £265,500 divided into 1,550,000 preference shares of 1p each, 100,000 'A' ordinary shares of £1 each and 150,000 ordinary shares of £1 each.

The rights attaching to the respective classes of shares shall be as follows:

3.1 *Income*

The profits of the Company available for distribution shall be applied as follows:

3.1.1 First in paying to the holders of the preference shares a fixed cumulative preferential net cash dividend (hereinafter in these articles referred to as 'the Preference Dividend') of   pence per annum on each share accruing from the date of subscription for the preference shares and payable half yearly on 31 March and 30 September, the first such payment to be made on 31 March 1997.

3.1.2 Second in paying to the holders of the 'A' ordinary shares a fixed cumulative preferential net cash dividend (hereinafter in these articles referred to as 'the Fixed Dividend') of   pence per annum on each share accruing from the date of subscription for the 'A' ordinary shares and payable half yearly on 31 March and 30 September, the first such payment to be made on 31 March 1997.

3.1.3 Third in paying to the holders of the 'A' ordinary shares as a class in respect of each financial year of the Company a cumulative preferential net cash dividend (hereinafter in these articles referred to as 'the Participating Dividend') of a sum which when added to the total of the Fixed Dividend payable in respect of that year is equal to % of the Net Profit (calculated as hereinafter provided) of the Company and its subsidiaries for the relevant financial year. The Participating Dividend (if any) shall be paid not later than 4 months after the end of each successive accounting reference period of the Company or not later than 14 days after the audit report on the accounts of the Company for such period is signed by the Company's auditors, whichever is earlier.

For the purpose of calculating the Participating Dividend, the expression 'Net Profit' shall mean the profit on ordinary activities before taxation of the Company and its subsidiaries calculated on the historical cost accounting basis and shown in the audited consolidated profit and loss account of the Company and its subsidiaries for the relevant financial year (to the nearest £1) but adjusted by:

3.1.3.1 adding back any amortisation of goodwill;

3.1.3.2 adding back any amount in excess of £ Index Linked in the aggregate charged in respect of emoluments payable to Relevant Directors.

3.1.4 Fourth in paying to the holders of the 'A' ordinary shares in respect of each financial year of the Company a cumulative preferential net cash dividend (hereinafter in these articles referred to as 'the Compensatory Dividend') on each share of an amount equal to the Excess Remuneration (as hereinafter defined) divided by the number of ordinary shares held by Relevant Directors on the last day of the relevant financial year.

For the purpose of calculating the Compensatory Dividend the expression 'Excess Remuneration' shall mean emoluments in excess of £ Index Linked in the aggregate payable in respect of the relevant financial year to Relevant Directors after deducting income tax at the basic rate on such excess sum. The Compensatory Dividend (if any) shall be paid on the due date for payment of the Participating Dividend.

3.1.5 No dividend shall be declared or paid to the holders of ordinary shares in respect of any financial year of the Company unless and until:

3.1.5.1 the Preference Dividend and the Fixed Dividend and the Participating Dividend (if any) have been paid in full in respect of that financial year and in respect of all previous financial years of the Company;

3.1.5.2 any Compensatory Dividend due has been paid in full;

3.1.5.3 all preference shares which have fallen due for redemption have been redeemed

but subject thereto and provided that the aggregate of the total amount of all dividend payments made or proposed to be made in respect of that financial year and the Excess Remuneration (as defined above) does not exceed 33% of the amount of the profits after taxation of the Company and its subsidiaries for such financial year calculated on the historical cost accounting basis as shown in the audited consolidated profit and loss account of the Company and its subsidiaries (to the nearest £1) and provided that the profits of the Company available for distribution following payment of all proposed dividends are not less than £ the profits which the Company may determine to distribute in respect of any financial year shall be applied:

3.1.5.4 first in paying to the holders of the ordinary shares a dividend on each share of an amount up to but not exceeding the aggregate of the Fixed Dividend and the Participating Dividend paid on each 'A' ordinary share for such year;

3.1.5.5 second with the prior written consent of the holders of 75% of the 'A' ordinary shares in distributing the balance of such profits amongst the holders of the 'A' ordinary shares and the ordinary shares (pari passu as if the same constituted one class of share).

3.1.6 Every dividend shall be distributed to the appropriate shareholders pro-rata according to the amounts paid up or credited as paid up on the shares held by them respectively and shall accrue on a daily basis.

3.1.7 Unless the Company has insufficient profits available for distribution and the Company is thereby prohibited from paying dividends by the Act the Preference Dividend and the Fixed Dividend and the Participating Dividend and the Compensatory Dividend shall (notwithstanding regulations 102 to 108 inclusive contained in Table A or any other provision of these articles and in particular notwithstanding that there has not been a recommendation of the directors or resolution of the Company in general meeting) be paid immediately on the due date and if not then paid shall be a debt due by the Company and be payable in priority to any other dividend provided that if due to delays in the preparation of the audited accounts of the Company the Participating Dividend cannot be calculated by the date it is due for payment then there shall be paid forthwith an interim dividend in respect of the Participating Dividend of a sum equal to the last Participating Dividend payable. The next and (if appropriate) any subsequent Participating Dividend shall be adjusted to take account of any overpayment or underpayment in respect of the said interim dividend which becomes apparent when the audited accounts are available.

3.1.8 The Company shall procure that each of its subsidiaries which has profits available for distribution shall from time to time and to the extent that it may lawfully do so declare and pay to the Company such dividends as are necessary to permit lawful and prompt payment by the Company of any redemption moneys due on the preference shares and the Preference Dividend and the Fixed Dividend and the Participating Dividend and the Compensatory Dividend.

3.2 *Capital*

On a return of assets on liquidation or capital reduction or otherwise, the assets of the Company remaining after the payment of its liabilities shall be applied as follows:

3.2.1 first in paying to the holders of the preference shares £1 per share together with a sum equal to any arrears or accruals of the Preference Dividend calculated down to the date of the return of capital;

3.2.2 second in paying to the holders of the 'A' ordinary shares £1 per share together with a sum equal to any arrears or accruals of the dividends on the 'A' ordinary shares calculated down to the date of the return of capital;

3.2.3 third in paying to the holders of ordinary shares £1 per share; and

3.2.4 the balance of such assets shall be distributed amongst the holders of the 'A' ordinary shares and ordinary shares (pari passu as if the same constituted one class of share) in proportion to the amounts paid up or credited as paid up on the 'A' ordinary shares and ordinary shares held by them respectively.

3.3 *Conversion*

The holders of the 'A' ordinary shares may at any time convert the whole of their 'A' ordinary shares into a like number of ordinary shares and the following provisions shall have effect:

3.3.1 the conversion shall be effected by notice in writing given to the Company signed by the holders of 75% of the 'A' ordinary shares and the conversion shall take effect immediately upon the date of delivery of such notice to the Company unless such notice states that conversion is to be effective when any conditions specified in the notice have been fulfilled in which case conversion shall take effect when such conditions have been fulfilled;

3.3.2 forthwith after conversion takes effect the holders of the ordinary shares resulting from the conversion shall send to the Company the certificates in respect of their respective holdings of 'A' ordinary shares and the Company shall issue to such holders respectively certificates for the ordinary shares resulting from the conversion;

3.3.3 the ordinary shares resulting from the conversion shall rank from the date of conversion pari passu in all respects with the other ordinary shares in the capital of the Company;

3.3.4 on the date of conversion the Company shall pay a dividend to the holders of the 'A' ordinary shares of a sum equal to any arrears or accruals of the dividends on the 'A' ordinary shares calculated on a daily basis to the date of conversion and the Participating Dividend shall be calculated pro rata according to the profits of the Company and its subsidiaries for the relevant financial year down to the date of such conversion such profits to be calculated by the Company on a basis reasonably acceptable to the holders of 75% of the 'A' ordinary shares.

3.4 *Redemption*

3.4.1 Subject to the provisions of the Act the preference shares shall be redeemed in the proportions and on the dates set out below:

Redemption date	*Number of shares redeemable*
31 March 1999	310,000
31 March 2000	310,000
31 March 2001	310,000
31 March 2002	310,000
31 March 2003	310,000

and any shares not redeemed upon the due date shall be redeemed forthwith upon redemption becoming permissible under the Act.

3.4.2 Subject to the provisions of the Act the Company may with the prior written consent of the holders of 75 % of the preference shares provided there are no arrears of dividend on the 'A' ordinary shares or preference shares redeem all or (in instalments of not less than 100,000 shares) some of the preference shares in advance of the due date for redemption and in the absence of any contrary agreement between such holders and the Company any partial early redemption shall be deemed to relate to the shares falling due for redemption in inverse order of maturity.

3.4.3 Subject to the provisions of the Act all of the preference shares shall (unless the holders of 75% of the preference shares give notice in writing to the Company to the contrary) be redeemed immediately upon any of the following dates:

3.4.3.1 the date upon which any of the equity share capital of the Company is admitted to the Official List of the Stock Exchange or permission for any of the equity share capital of the Company to be dealt in on any recognised investment exchange (as defined in the Financial Services Act 1986, s 207) becomes effective; or

3.4.3.2 the date upon which a successful offer to purchase 90% or more of the issued equity share capital of the Company (or 90% or more of all such capital including any already held by the offeror) is completed.

3.4.4 On the dates fixed for any redemption the Company shall pay to each registered holder of preference shares the amount payable in respect of such redemption and upon receipt of that amount each such holder shall surrender to the Company the certificate for his shares which are to be redeemed in order that they may be cancelled provided that if any certificate so surrendered includes any shares not redeemable at that time the Company shall issue a fresh certificate for the balance of the shares not redeemable to the holder.

3.4.5 The Company shall pay on each of the preference shares so redeemed the sum of £1 and shall contemporaneously pay any arrears or accruals of the Preference Dividend calculated to the date of redemption and in the absence of any direction to the contrary by the holder of the relevant preference share any moneys paid on redemption of such share shall relate first to the said arrears and accruals of Preference Dividend. The Preference Dividend shall cease to accrue from the date of payment of the redemption moneys.

CLASS RIGHTS

4 Whenever the capital of the Company is divided into different classes of shares the special rights attached to any class may be varied or abrogated either whilst the Company is a going concern or during or in contemplation of a winding up, only with the consent in writing of the holders of 75% of the issued shares of that class. Without prejudice to the generality of this article, the special rights attached to the preference shares and the 'A' ordinary shares shall be deemed to be varied:

4.1 by the grant of any option or other right to subscribe for shares and by any alteration or increase or reduction or subdivision or consolidation of the authorised or issued capital of the Company or of any of its subsidiaries, or any variation of the rights attached to any of the shares for the time being in the capital of the Company or of any of its subsidiaries; or

4.2 by the disposal of the undertaking of the Company or of any of its subsidiaries or any substantial part thereof or by the disposal of any share in the capital of any subsidiary of the Company; or

4.3 by the acquisition of any interest in any share in the capital of any company by the Company or any of its subsidiaries; or

4.4 by the application by way of capitalisation of any sum in or towards paying up any share or loan capital of the Company; or

4.5 by any alteration of the restrictions on the powers of the directors of the Company and its subsidiaries to borrow give guarantees or create charges; or

4.6 by the winding up of the Company; or

4.7 by the redemption of any of the Company's shares (otherwise than pursuant to these articles) or by the entering into of a contract by the Company to purchase any of its shares; or

4.8 by any alteration of the Company's memorandum or articles of association; or

4.9 by any alteration of the Company's accounting reference date; or

4.10 by the calling of a meeting of the Company to effect or approve any matter which would by virtue of this article be a variation of the class rights of the 'A' ordinary and preference shares.

FURTHER ISSUE OF SHARES

5.1 Notwithstanding any other provisions of these articles the directors shall be bound to offer to any member of the 3i Group (as hereinafter defined) for the time being holding shares in the capital of the Company such a proportion of any shares forming part of the equity share capital of the Company which the directors determine to issue as the aggregate nominal value of shares in the equity share capital of the Company for the time being held by such member of the 3i Group bears to the total issued equity share capital of the Company immediately before the issue of the shares. Any shares issued to a member of the 3i Group pursuant to such offer shall be issued upon no less favourable terms and conditions than those issued to any other person and so that such shares shall at the request of 3i be registered in the name or names of any one or more members of the 3i Group.

5.2 For the purposes of these articles the expressions '3i' shall mean 3i Group plc and 'a member of the 3i Group' shall mean 3i Group plc, any subsidiary of 3i Group plc, and any company of which 3i Group plc is a subsidiary.

LIEN

6 The lien conferred by regulation 8 of Table A shall apply to all shares of the Company whether fully paid or not and to all shares registered in the name of any person indebted or under liability to the Company whether he be the sole registered holder thereof or one of several joint holders.

CALLS

7 The liability of any member in default in respect of a call shall be increased by the addition at the end of the first sentence of regulation 18 in Table A of the words 'and all expenses that may have been incurred by the Company by reason of such non-payment'.

TRANSFER OF SHARES

8 The directors shall refuse to register any transfer of shares made in contravention of the provisions of these articles but (subject to Regulation 24 of Table A) shall not otherwise be entitled to refuse to register any transfer of shares. For the purpose of ensuring that a particular transfer of shares is permitted under the provisions of these articles, the directors may request the transferor, or the person named as transferee in any transfer lodged for registration, to furnish the Company with such information and evidence as the directors may reasonably think necessary or relevant. Failing such information or evidence being furnished to the satisfaction of the directors within a period of 28 days after such request the directors shall be entitled to refuse to register the transfer in question.

9.1 Notwithstanding any other provision in these articles any member may at any time transfer (or by will bequeath or otherwise dispose of on death) all or any shares held by him to a Privileged Relation. For the purposes of these articles 'Privileged Relation' in relation to a member means the spouse or widow or widower of the member and the member's children and grandchildren (including step and adopted children and their issue) and step and adopted children of the member's children.

9.2 If any person (an 'Employee Member') ceases to be an employee or director of the Company or its subsidiaries, and does not forthwith become or continue to be an employee or director of any of the Company or its subsidiaries Transfer Notices (as hereinafter defined) shall be deemed to have been served forthwith upon such cessation in respect of:

9.2.1 all shares held by the Employee Member; and

9.2.2 all shares originally held by the Employee Member but held by his Privileged Relations at the time of such cessation.

10.1 Save as otherwise provided in these articles every member who desires to transfer any shares (hereinafter called 'the Vendor') shall give to the Company notice in writing of such desire (hereinafter called a 'Transfer Notice'). Subject as hereinafter mentioned a Transfer Notice shall constitute the Company the Vendor's agent for the sale of the shares specified therein (hereinafter called 'the Sale Shares') in one or more lots at the discretion of the directors to all the holders of 'A' ordinary and ordinary shares in the Company (such shares being hereinafter in this article referred to as 'Equity Shares') other than the Vendor at the Sale Price. The Sale Price shall be the price agreed by the Vendor and the directors or if the Vendor and the directors are unable to agree a price within 28 days of the Transfer Notice being given or being deemed to have been given the price which a chartered accountant (acting as an expert and not as an arbitrator) nominated by agreement between the Vendor and the Company or in default of such agreement by the President for the time being of the Institute of Chartered Accountants in England and Wales shall by writing under his hand certify to be in his opinion a fair value thereof on a going concern basis as between a willing seller and a willing buyer ignoring any reduction in value which may be ascribed to the Sale Shares by virtue of the fact that they represent a minority interest and on the assumption that the Sale Shares are capable of transfer without restriction. The Transfer Notice may (save for shares sold pursuant to a deemed Transfer Notice) contain a provision that unless all the shares comprised therein are sold by the Company pursuant to this article none shall be sold (a 'Total Transfer Condition') and any such provision shall be binding on the Company.

10.2 If a chartered accountant is asked to certify the fair value as aforesaid his certificate shall be delivered to the Company and as soon as the Company receives the certificate it shall furnish a certified copy thereof to the Vendor and save for shares sold pursuant to a deemed Transfer Notice the Vendor shall be entitled by notice in writing given to the Company within ten days of the service upon him of the certified copy to cancel the Company's authority to sell the Sale Shares. The cost of obtaining the certificate shall be borne by the Company unless the Vendor shall give notice of cancellation as aforesaid in which case the Vendor shall bear the cost.

10.3 Upon the price being fixed as aforesaid and provided the Vendor shall not give a valid notice of cancellation the Company shall forthwith offer the Sale Shares to all holders of Equity Shares (other than the Vendor) pro rata as nearly as may be in proportion to the existing numbers of Equity Shares held by such members giving details of the number and the Sale Price of such Sale Shares. The Company shall invite each such member as aforesaid to state in writing within 21 days from the date of the notice whether he is willing to purchase any of the Sale Shares so offered to him and if so the maximum thereof which he is willing to purchase. If at the expiration of the said period of 21 days there are any Sale Shares offered which any of the members hereinbefore mentioned have not so stated their willingness to purchase the Company shall offer such shares to such members as have stated in writing their willingness to purchase all the shares previously offered to them. Such remaining shares shall be offered pro rata as nearly as may be in proportion to existing numbers of Equity Shares then held by such members which offer shall remain open for a further period of 21 days. Offers shall continue to be made on the same terms while any member continues to state in writing his willingness to purchase all the shares offered to him.

10.4 If the Company shall pursuant to the above provisions of this article find a member or members of the Company willing to purchase all or any of the Sale Shares the Vendor shall be bound upon receipt of the Sale Price to transfer the Sale Shares (or such of the same for which the Company shall have found a purchaser or purchasers) to such persons. If the Vendor shall make default in so doing the Company shall if so required by the person or persons willing to purchase such Sale Shares receive and give a good discharge for the purchase money on behalf of the Vendor and shall authorise some person to execute transfers of the Sale Shares in favour of the purchasers and shall enter the names of the purchasers in the Register of Members as the holder of such of the Sale Shares as shall have been transferred to them as aforesaid.

10.5 If the directors shall not have found a member or members of the Company willing to purchase all of the Sale Shares pursuant to the foregoing provisions of this article the Vendor shall at any time within six months after the final offer by the Company to its members be at liberty to sell and transfer such of the Sale Shares as have not been so sold to any person at a price being no less than the Sale Price provided that if the Sale Shares were subject to a Total Transfer Condition such sale must be of all the Sale Shares and not part only.

10.6 The foregoing provisions of this article shall not apply to a transfer if the holders of 75% of the ordinary shares and the holders of 75% of the 'A' ordinary shares so direct in writing and the directors shall be obliged to register any such transfer.

11 Notwithstanding any other provisions of these articles a transfer of any shares in the Company held by any member of the 3i Group may be made between the member in the 3i Group holding such shares and any other member in the 3i Group without restriction as to price or otherwise and any such transfer shall be registered by the directors.

LIMITATION ON TRANSFER OF CONTROL

12.1 No sale or transfer of the legal or beneficial interest in any shares in the Company may be made or validly registered without the consent in writing of the holders of 75% of the 'A' ordinary shares if as a result of such sale or transfer and registration thereof a Controlling Interest (as hereinafter defined) would be obtained in the Company:

12.1.1 by a company (other than a company to which the immediately following sub-article applies) or by a person or persons (other than a company) who are not Original Members (as hereinafter defined) unless the proposed transferee or transferees or his or their nominees are independent third parties acting in good faith and has or have offered to purchase all the 'A' ordinary shares at the Specified Price (as hereinafter defined) and (if not redeemed) all the preference shares at a price per share of at least £1 plus a sum equal to any arrears or accruals of the Preference Dividend grossed up at the rate of corporation tax then in force calculated down to the date of sale or transfer; or

12.1.2 by a company in which one or more of the members of the Company or persons acting in concert (which expression shall have the meaning ascribed to it in the July 1993 edition of the City Code on Takeovers and Mergers) with any member of the Company has or as a result of such sale or transfer will have a Controlling Interest.

12.2 For the purpose of this article:

12.2.1 the expression 'a Controlling Interest' shall mean an interest in shares (as defined in Sch 13, Part I and s 324 of the Act) in a company conferring in the aggregate 50% or more of the total voting rights conferred by all the issued shares in that company;

12.2.2 the expression 'Original Members' shall mean persons who were members of the Company on the date of the adoption of these articles and the Privileged Relations of such members;

12.2.3 the expressions 'transfer' and 'transferee' shall include respectively the renunciation of a renounceable letter of allotment and the renouncee under any such letter of allotment; and

12.2.4 the expression 'the Specified Price' shall mean at the option of the holders of 75% of the 'A' ordinary shares either:

12.2.4.1 a price per share of £1; or

12.2.4.2 the consideration (in cash or otherwise) per share equal to that offered or paid or payable by the proposed transferee or transferees or his or their nominees for any other shares in the Company plus the relevant proportion of any other consideration (in cash or otherwise) received or receivable by the holders of such other shares which having regard to the substance of the transaction as a whole can reasonably be regarded as an addition to the price paid or payable for such other shares provided that if any part of the price per share is payable otherwise than by cash the holders of the 'A' ordinary shares may at their option elect to take a price per share of such cash sum as may be agreed by them having regard to the substance of the transaction as a whole;

12.2.4.3 plus in either case a sum equal to any arrears or accruals of the dividends on such share grossed up at the rate of corporation tax then in force calculated down to the date of sale or transfer and in the event of disagreement the calculation of the Specified Price shall be referred to an umpire (acting as an expert and not as an arbitrator) nominated by the parties concerned (or in the event of disagreement as to nomination, appointed by the President for the time being of the Institute of Chartered Accountants in England and Wales) whose decision shall be final and binding.

12.3 All other regulations of the Company relating to the transfer of shares and the right to registration of transfers shall be read subject to the provisions of this article.

VOTING

13.1 Subject to any special rights or restrictions as to voting attached to any shares by or in accordance with these articles, on a show of hands every member who (being an individual) is present in person or (being a corporation) is present by a representative not being himself a member, shall have one vote, and on a poll every member who is present in person or by proxy or (being a corporation) is present by a representative or by proxy shall (except as hereinafter provided) have one vote for every £1 in nominal amount of shares in the capital of the Company of which he is the holder.

13.2 The holders of the preference shares shall be entitled to receive notice of all general meetings but shall not by reason of such holding be entitled to attend or vote thereat.

APPOINTMENT OF DIRECTORS

14 The directors may appoint a person who is willing to act to be a director, either to fill a vacancy or as an additional director. In addition, the holders of shares representing more than half of the shares which carry the right to attend and vote at general meetings of the Company may by notice to the Company together appoint a person who is willing to act to be a director either to fill a vacancy or as an additional director.

PROCEEDINGS OF DIRECTORS

15 Notice of every meeting of the directors shall be given to each director at any address supplied by him to the Company for that purpose whether or not he be present in the United Kingdom provided that any director may waive notice of any meeting either prospectively or retrospectively and if he shall do so it shall be no objection to the validity of such meeting that notice was not given to him.

16.1 Subject to the provisions of the Act and provided that he has disclosed to the directors the nature and extent of any material interest of his, a director notwithstanding his office:

16.1.1 may be a party to or otherwise interested in any transaction or arrangement with the Company or in which the Company is in any way interested;

16.1.2 may be a director or other officer of or employed by or be a party to any transaction or arrangement with or otherwise interested in any body corporate promoted by the Company or in which the Company is in any way interested;

16.1.3 may (and any firm or company of which he is a partner or member or director may) act in a professional capacity for the Company or any body corporate in which the Company is in any way interested;

16.1.4 shall not by reason of his office be accountable to the Company for any benefit which he derives from such office service or employment or from any such transaction or arrangement or from any interest in any such body corporate and no such transaction or arrangement shall be liable to be avoided on the ground of any such interest or benefit; and

16.1.5 shall be entitled to vote and be counted in the quorum on any matter concerning the foregoing paragraphs of this article.

16.2 For the purposes of this article:

16.2.1 a general notice to the directors that a director is to be regarded as having an interest of the nature and extent specified in the notice in any transaction or arrangement in which a specified person or class of persons is interested shall be deemed to be a disclosure that the director has an interest in any such transaction of the nature and extent so specified;

16.2.2 an interest of which a director has no knowledge and of which it is unreasonable to expect him to have knowledge shall not be treated as an interest of his; and

16.2.3 an interest of a person who is for any purpose of the Act (excluding any statutory modification not in force when these articles were adopted) connected with a director shall be treated as an interest of the director and in relation to an alternate director an interest of his appointor shall be treated as an interest of the alternate director without prejudice to any interest which the alternate director has otherwise.

SPECIAL DIRECTOR

17 Notwithstanding any other provisions of these articles 3i shall be entitled to appoint as a director of the Company any person (herein referred to as the 'Special Director') approved by the directors (whose approval shall not be unreasonably withheld) and to remove from office any person so appointed and (subject to such approval) to appoint another person in his place. The remuneration and reasonable expenses to be paid to the Special Director shall be payable by the Company and shall be such sum as may be agreed between him and the Company or failing agreement such reasonable sum as shall be fixed by 3i. Upon request by 3i the Company shall also procure that the Special Director be appointed a director to any subsidiary of the Company.

INDEMNITY

18 Subject to the provisions of the Act but without prejudice to any indemnity to which a director may otherwise be entitled, every director or other officer or auditor of the Company shall be indemnified out of the assets of the Company against all costs, charges, losses, expenses and liabilities incurred by him in the execution of his duties or in relation thereto including any liability incurred by him in defending any proceedings, whether civil or criminal, in which judgment is given in his favour or in which he is acquitted or the proceedings are otherwise disposed of without any finding or admission of any material breach of duty on his part or in connection with any application in which relief is granted to him by the court from liability for negligence, default, breach of duty or breach of trust in relation to the affairs of the Company.

17 TRADING TERMS PACKAGE

17a Standard conditions of sale

1 Definitions

1.1 'Buyer' means the person who buys or agrees to buy the goods from the Seller.

1.2 'Conditions' means the terms and conditions of sale set out in this document and any special terms and conditions agreed in writing by the Seller.

1.3 'Delivery Date' means the date specified by the Seller when the goods are to be delivered.

1.4 'Goods' means the articles which the Buyer agrees to buy from the Seller.

1.5 'Price' means the price for the Goods excluding carriage, packing, insurance and VAT.

1.6 'Seller' means [*(name and address of seller) or (where it is intended to indorse these conditions on the back of an order form)* the person whose name and address appears in the box marked 'Seller' overleaf].

2 Conditions applicable

2.1 These Conditions shall apply to all contracts for the sale of Goods by the Seller to the Buyer to the exclusion of all other terms and conditions including any terms or conditions which the Buyer may purport to apply under any purchase order confirmation of order or similar document.

2.2 All orders for Goods shall be deemed to be an offer by the Buyer to purchase Goods pursuant to these Conditions.

2.3 Acceptance of delivery of the Goods shall be deemed conclusive evidence of the Buyer's acceptance of these Conditions.

2.4 Any variation to these Conditions (including any special terms and conditions agreed between the parties) shall be inapplicable unless agreed in writing by the Seller.

3 The Price and payment

3.1 The Price shall be [the Seller's quoted price or the price set out overleaf]. The Price is exclusive of VAT which shall be due at the rate ruling on the date of the Seller's invoice.

3.2 Payment of the Price and VAT shall be due within [30] days of the date of the date of the invoice. [Time for payment shall be of the essence.]

3.3 Interest on overdue invoices shall accrue from the date when payment becomes due from day to day until the date of payment at a rate of [2]% above *(name)* Bank plc's base rate from time to time in force and shall accrue at such a rate after as well as before any judgment.

4 The Goods

The quantity and description of the Goods shall be as set out in the Seller's quotation.

5 Warranties and liability

The Seller warrants that the Goods will at the time of delivery correspond to the description given by the Seller. [Except where the Buyer is dealing as a consumer (as defined in the Unfair Contract Terms Act 1977, s 12) all other warranties, conditions or terms relating to fitness for purpose, merchantability or condition of the Goods and whether implied by statute or common law or otherwise are excluded.]

6 Delivery of the Goods

Delivery of the Goods shall be made to the Buyer's address on the Delivery Date. The Buyer shall make all arrangements necessary to take delivery of the Goods whenever they are tendered for delivery.

7 Acceptance of the Goods

7.1 The Buyer shall be deemed to have accepted Goods [24 hours] after delivery to the Buyer.

7.2 After acceptance the Buyer shall not be entitled to reject Goods which are not in accordance with the contract.

8 Title and risk

8.1 Title shall pass on delivery of the Goods.

8.2 Risk shall pass on delivery of the Goods.

9 Remedies of Buyer

9.1 Where the Buyer rejects any Goods then the Buyer shall have no further rights whatever in respect of the supply to the Buyer of such

Goods or the failure by the Seller to supply Goods which conform to the contract of sale.

9.2 Where the Buyer accepts or has been deemed to have accepted any Goods then the Seller shall have no liability whatever to the Buyer in respect of those Goods.

9.3 The Seller shall not be liable to the Buyer for late delivery or short delivery of the Goods.

10 Proper law of contract

This contract is subject to the law of England and Wales.

Conditions of purchase

0.1 The Conditions shall apply to all contracts for the purchase of Goods by the Buyer from the Seller to the exclusion of all other terms and conditions including any terms or conditions which the Seller may purport to apply under any sales offer or similar document.

0.2 Despatch or delivery of the Goods by the Seller to the Buyer shall be deemed conclusive evidence of the Seller's acceptance of these Conditions.

0.3 Any variation of these Conditions (including any special terms and conditions agreed between the parties) shall be inapplicable unless agreed in writing by the Buyer.

Price and payment: alternative provisions

A: PRICE TO BE ASCERTAINED BY REFERENCE TO SELLER'S PRICE LIST AT TIME OF DELIVERY

The Price of the Goods shall be the price stipulated in the Seller's published price list current at the date of delivery of the Goods. The Price is exclusive of VAT which shall be due at the rate ruling on the date of VAT invoice.

B: PRICE TO BE AS QUOTED BY SELLER

The Price of the Goods shall be the Seller's quoted price which shall be binding upon the Seller provided that the Buyer shall accept the Seller's quotation within [30] days. The Price is exclusive of VAT which shall be due at the rate ruling on the date of VAT invoice.

C: PRICE MAY BE ADJUSTED BEFORE DELIVERY IN ACCORDANCE WITH A FORMULA

The Price of the Goods shall be the Seller's quoted price which shall be binding on the Seller provided that the Buyer shall accept the Seller's quotation within [30] days. The Seller may by giving notice to the Buyer at any time up to [7] days before delivery increase the Price of the Goods to reflect any increase in the cost to the Seller which is due to factors occurring after the making of the contract of sale which are beyond the reasonable control of the Seller (including, without limitation, foreign exchange fluctuations, taxes and duties and the cost of labour, materials and other manufacturing costs). Provided that the Buyer may cancel this contract within [7] days of any such notice from the Seller. The Price is exclusive of VAT which shall be due at the rate ruling on the date of VAT invoice.

D: PROVISION FOR THE PRICE TO BE FIXED BY THE VALUATION OF A THIRD PARTY

The Price of the Goods shall be the current market value fixed by [*(name of valuer)* [FRICS] or a valuer appointed by *(name of appointor)*] (acting as expert and not as arbitrator) within (number) days [before or after] delivery of the Goods. In the event of such valuation failing for any reason to be made the contract for sale shall be considered to have been made for a reasonable price. The Price is exclusive of VAT which shall be due at the rate ruling on the date of VAT invoice.

E: PAYMENT TO BE MADE BEFORE DELIVERY IS DUE

The Seller shall not be bound to deliver the Goods until the Buyer has paid for them. Payment shall be due before the Delivery Date and time for payment shall be of the essence. The Price is exclusive of VAT which shall be due at the rate ruling on the date of VAT invoice.

F: PAYMENT 'NET 30 DAYS'

Payment of the Price and VAT shall be due on the last working day of the month following the end of the month in which the Goods are delivered. Time for payment shall be of the essence. The Price is exclusive of VAT which shall be due at the rate ruling on the date of VAT invoice.

G: PROMPT PAYMENT DISCOUNT

Provided that no other payments are due from the Buyer to the Seller the Buyer shall be entitled to deduct a prompt payment discount of [9]% of the Price for payment made [in accordance with these conditions or within [7] days of the Seller's invoice].

H: ADDITIONAL REMEDIES FOR LATE PAYMENT

0.1 If the Buyer fails to make any payment on the due date then without prejudice to any of the Seller's other rights the Seller may:
0.1:1 suspend or cancel deliveries of any articles due to the Buyer; and/or

0.1:2 appropriate any payment made by the Buyer to such of the Goods (or Goods supplied under any other contract with the Buyer) as the Seller may in its sole discretion think fit.

I: BUYER'S RIGHT OF SET-OFF

The Buyer may set off against the Price (including any applicable VAT payable) amounts due from the Seller whether under the applicable contract of sale or otherwise.

J: SUPPLEMENTARY PROVISIONS REGARDING PRICES

0.1 Price are the Seller's ex works prices and where the Seller agrees to arrange for the Goods to be sent to the Buyer the Buyer shall be responsible for the costs of loading carriage and unloading.

0.2 The cost of pallets and returnable packing will be due from the Buyer in addition to the Price but will be credited to the Buyer provided that they are returned to the Seller in good condition before the due payment date.

K: PAYMENT BY CONFIRMED LETTER OF CREDIT

The Buyer shall within [21] days open an irrevocable letter of credit with a bank to be confirmed in favour of *(name of seller's bank)* plc payable [30] days at sight against production of a commercial invoice for the Goods and a clean on board bill of lading for the Goods.

Nature, quantity and quality of goods: additional and alternative provisions

A: SALE BY DESCRIPTION – SELLER'S CLAUSE

0.1 The Goods shall be [manufactured and] supplied in accordance with the description contained in the Seller's specification and manufactured in accordance [with all applicable British Standards which relate specifically to the Goods or with British Standard *(number)*].

0.2 The Seller may from time to time make changes in the specification of the Goods which are required to comply with any applicable safety or statutory requirements or which do not materially affect the quality or fitness for purpose of the Goods.

B: SALE BY SAMPLE: SHORT FORM

The contract is a contract for sale by sample.

C: SALE BY SAMPLE: LONG FORM

0.1 This contract of sale is a contract for sale by sample.

0.2 The bulk of the Goods will correspond with the sample in quality provided that the Seller shall have no liability to the Buyer unless more than [5]% of the Goods do not so correspond.

0.3 The Buyer shall be deemed to have had a reasonable opportunity of comparing the bulk of any consignment of goods with the sample after [2] days from delivery have expired.

0.4 Upon the Buyer having been deemed to have had a reasonable opportunity of comparing the bulk of any consignment with the sample the Buyer will also be deemed to have notice of any defect rendering the Goods not in accordance with the contract and to have accepted all the Goods so delivered.

D: ALLOWABLE DISCREPANCIES IN QUANTITY

0.1 The Buyer shall take delivery of the Goods tendered notwithstanding that the quantity so delivered shall be either greater or less than the quantity purchased provided that:

- 0.1:1 such discrepancy in quantity shall not exceed [5]%
- 0.1:2 the Price shall be adjusted pro rata to the discrepancy.

E: SELLER'S CLAUSE EXCLUDING IMPLIED CONDITIONS ABOUT QUALITY OR FITNESS

All implied terms, conditions and warranties relating to the quality and/or fitness for purpose of the Goods or any of the Goods are excluded.

F: SELLER'S CLAUSE EXCLUDING IMPLIED CONDITIONS AND EXPRESS REPRESENTATIONS ABOUT QUALITY OR FITNESS

All terms, conditions and warranties (whether implied or made expressly) whether by the Seller or its servants or agents or otherwise (other than those express warranties set out in the current edition of the Seller's specification) relating to the quality and/or fitness for purpose of the Goods or any of the Goods are excluded.

G: BUYER'S CLAUSE INCORPORATING EXPRESS REPRESENTATIONS MADE PRIOR TO THE CONTRACT

All representations, statements or warranties made or given by the Seller, its servants and agents (whether orally in writing or in any of the Seller's brochures catalogues and advertisements) regarding the quality and fitness for purpose of the Goods or any of the Goods shall be deemed to be express conditions of the contract of sale.

H: BUYER'S CLAUSE INCORPORATING BRITISH STANDARDS INTO THE CONTRACT AS EXPRESS CONDITIONS

The Seller shall ensure that all the Goods shall be manufactured, stored, tested and packed in accordance with [all British Standards applicable to them or British Standard (number)] and that all the Goods are of merchantable quality and [fit for purpose or fit for the purposes for which the Buyer intends to use such Goods].

I: TESTING AND INSPECTION DURING MANUFACTURE – BUYER'S CLAUSE

0.1 The Seller shall comply with the specification and all applicable British Standards and legal requirements concerning the design, manufacture, processing, storage and testing of the Goods.

0.2 The Seller shall permit the Buyer to inspect and test the Goods during their manufacture and processing.

0.3 If the Buyer is not reasonably satisfied that the Goods or their manufacture or processing comply in all material respects with the contract the Seller without extra cost to the Buyer shall take all steps necessary to ensure due compliance.

J: MARKING AND PACKING OF GOODS

The Goods shall be marked in accordance with [the Buyer's instructions or the specifications] and all lawful requirements and properly packed and secured for delivery to the Buyer in an undamaged condition.

K: INTELLECTUAL PROPERTY – SELLER'S CLAUSE

The specification[s] and design[s] of the Goods (including the copyright, design right or other intellectual property in them shall as between the parties be the property of the Seller. Where any designs or specifications have been supplied by the Buyer for manufacture by or to the order of the Seller then the Buyer warrants that the use of those designs or specifications for the manufacture, processing, assembly or supply of the Goods shall not infringe the rights of any third party.

L: INTELLECTUAL PROPERTY – BUYER'S CLAUSE

Where any specification[s] and design[s] of the Goods or any of the Goods have been provided by the Buyer the copyright, design right or other intellectual property in them shall remain the property of the Buyer.

M: TESTING OF GOODS PRIOR TO DELIVERY

The Goods shall within [14] days prior to despatch be tried by the Seller in the presence of a representative of the Buyer by working the Goods in the usual manner. If the Goods shall fail to work in accordance with their specification the Seller shall remedy the defects within [7] days after the trial and the Goods shall then be tried again in the manner set out above. Provided that the trial shall fail to disclose any defects then the Goods shall be deemed to conform to the contract and the Buyer shall be bound to accept the Goods.

N: WEIGHING THE GOODS

The Seller shall on dispatch weigh the Goods [in the presence of a representative of the Buyer] and the weights when ascertained shall be recorded by the Seller and notified to the Buyer upon delivery.

Delivery: additional and alternative provisions

A: GOODS IN POSSESSION OF THIRD PARTY

Due delivery of the Goods shall be deemed to have been made when the Seller supplies to the Buyer [the dock warrant or the shipped bill of lading] for the Goods.

B: RESERVATION OF RIGHT OF RESALE

Unless the Buyer shall open an irrevocable letter of credit with *(name)* Bank plc or procure the acceptance by *(name)* Bank plc of a bill of exchange drawn on *(name)* Bank plc for the Price before the day fixed for delivery the Seller shall be at liberty on its own account to deal with sell or otherwise dispose of the Goods.

C: DELIVER BY INSTALMENTS

0.1 The Seller [shall *or* may] deliver the Goods by separate instalments [in accordance with the agreed delivery schedule]. Each separate instalment shall be invoiced and paid for in accordance with the provisions in this contract of sale.

0.2 [The failure of the Seller to deliver or the failure of the Buyer to pay for any one or more of the said instalments of the Goods on the due dates shall not entitle either party to treat this contract as repudiated.

or

The failure of the Buyer to pay for any one or more of the said instalments of the Goods on the due dates shall entitle the Seller (at the sole option of the Seller):

0.2:1 without notice to suspend further deliveries of the Goods pending payment by the Buyer; and/or

0.2:2 to treat this contract as repudiated by the Buyer.]

D: IMPORT OR EXPORT LICENCES AND OTHER FORMALITIES

0.1 The Seller shall promptly obtain all necessary export licences, clearances and other consents necessary for the supply of the Goods.

or

The Buyer shall promptly obtain all necessary import licences, clearances and other consents necessary for the purchase of the Goods. The Seller shall promptly upon request supply all documents reasonably required by the Buyer for this purpose.

E: SELLER'S CLAUSE EXCLUDING LIABILITY FOR DELAY IN DELIVERY

0.1 The Seller shall not be liable for any loss or damage whatever due to failure by the Seller to deliver the Goods (or any of them) promptly or at all.

0.2 Notwithstanding that the Seller may have delayed or failed to deliver the Goods (or any of them) promptly the Buyer shall be bound to accept delivery and to pay for the Goods in full provided that delivery shall be tendered at any time within [3] months of the Delivery Date.

F: BUYER'S CLAUSE MAKING TIME FOR DELIVERY OF THE ESSENCE OF THE CONTRACT

0.1 The Delivery Date is of the essence of this contract.

0.2 If the Seller fails to deliver all of the Goods in accordance with the contract on the Delivery Date then without prejudice to the Buyer's rights for the breach of contract:

0.2:1 The Buyer may terminate the contract. In this event without prejudice to the Buyer's other remedies the Seller shall promptly collect any Goods which have been delivered.

0.2:2 Where delivery of a quantity of the Goods which correspond to the contract which is less than the agreed quantity has been tendered and the Buyer has not exercised its rights of termination under clause [0.2:1] the Buyer may accept the Goods which correspond to the contract and recover for the Seller's breach in respect of the failure to deliver the remainder of the Goods.

0.2:3 The Buyer may require the Seller promptly to deliver sufficient goods which correspond to the contract to comply with the quantity required.

The Buyer may exercise these rights by [written] notice to the Seller.

G: PROVISION MAKING CLEAR THAT DELIVERY TAKES PLACE AT SELLER'S ADDRESS-SELLER TO HAVE THE OBLIGATION TO ARRANGE FREIGHT TO BUYER

0.1 The Goods shall be delivered to the Buyer at the Seller's address. The risk in the Goods shall pass to the Buyer upon such delivery taking place.

0.2 The Seller shall arrange for carriage of the Goods to the Buyer's address. The costs of carriage and any insurance which the Buyer reasonably directs the Seller to incur shall be reimbursed by the Buyer [without any set-off or other withholding whatever] and shall be due on the date for payment of the Price. The carrier shall be deemed to be the Buyer's agent.

H: DELIVERY PROVISION FOR FREE ON BOARD (FOB) CONTRACT

0.1 The Goods shall be delivered to the Buyer by delivery on board the [Named Vessel] lying at [Named Port] on the Delivery Date. The Seller shall promptly notify the Buyer that the Goods have been delivered aboard. Title to and risk in the Goods shall pass to the Buyer upon such delivery being effected. The Seller shall promptly provide the Buyer with a clean shipped bill of lading in respect of the Goods.

0.2 The Buyer shall reserve the necessary space on board the [Named Vessel] and give the Seller due notice of the loading berth and any revised delivery dates to the [Named Vessel]. The Buyer shall bear any additional costs caused due to the failure of the [Named Vessel] to be available to load the Goods on the Delivery Date.

0.3 No claim for damaged Goods for shortages or for non-delivery will be accepted by the Seller unless written notice of such damage or shortage is received by the Seller within [28] days of receipt of the Goods by the Buyer, or within [28] days of the defect being discovered where the defect could not reasonably have been discovered earlier, or (in the case of non-delivery) [28] days from the date on which the Goods could in the normal course of events have been expected to be received by the Buyer.

I: DELIVERY PROVISION FOR COST INSURANCE FREIGHT (CIF) CONTRACT

0.1 The Goods shall be delivered to the Buyer at [Named Port] on or before the Delivery Date. The Seller shall procure a contract of carriage and insure the Goods from dispatch until delivery on terms current in the trade for the benefit of the Buyer. The Goods shall be at the risk of the Buyer as they are loaded on board. The Seller shall promptly tender to the Buyer a clean shipped bill of lading, the insurance policy and an invoice in respect of the Goods.

0.2 The Buyer shall accept the documents tendered by the Seller if they correspond to this contract and take delivery of the Goods at [Named Port] and bear all other costs and charges arising out of shipment of the Goods to [Named Port].

J: BUYER'S CLAUSE RELATING TO DAMAGE OR LOSS IN TRANSIT

The Seller upon receiving notice to that effect from the Buyer shall repair or replace free of charge Goods damaged or lost in transit and due delivery of the Goods shall not be deemed to have taken place until replacement or repaired Goods have been delivered by the Seller to the Buyer. The Buyer reserves the right to hold such damaged Goods at the Seller's risk or to return them at the risk and expense of the Seller.

Acceptance: additional and alternative provisions

A: BUYER'S PROVISIONS FOR SALE ON APPROVAL

0.1 The Buyer shall not be deemed to have accepted any part of the Goods until after the Buyer has (or the Buyer's sub-buyers have) actually inspected the Goods and ascertained that they are in accordance with the contract. The Buyer may reject Goods which are not in accordance with the contract until a reasonable time after such inspection.

0.2 The Buyer may by notice to the Seller prior to acceptance reject any Goods which are not in accordance with the contract. The Buyer may set off against any payment due to the Seller (whether under this contract or otherwise) the Price of such Goods. Unless within a reasonable time of receipt of notice of rejection the Seller collects such Goods the Buyer may dispose of them as the Buyer shall think fit (provided that if the Buyer sells such Goods the Buyer shall account to the Seller for the net proceeds of such sale).

B: BUYER'S PROVISIONS REGARDING RIGHT TO REJECT GOODS AFTER ACCEPTANCE

The Seller agrees to permit the Buyer to return any of the Goods which are not in accordance with the contract at any time up to [6] months after delivery notwithstanding that the Goods may have already been accepted by the Buyer.

C: SELLER'S PROVISION REQUIRING BUYER TO RETURN REJECTED GOODS OR PAY FOR THEM

If the Buyer properly rejects any of the Goods which are not in accordance with the contract the Buyer shall nonetheless pay the full Price for such Goods unless the Buyer promptly gives notice of rejection to the Seller and at the Buyer's cost returns such Goods to the Seller before the date when payment of the Price is due.

D: SELLER'S PROVISIONS REGARDING RETURN OF GOODS WHICH CONFORM TO THE CONTRACT

0.1 No Goods delivered to the Buyer which are in accordance with the contract will be accepted for return without the prior written approval of the Seller [in accordance with the Seller's returns authorisation procedure and] on terms to be determined at the absolute discretion of the Seller.

0.2 If the Seller agrees to accept any such Goods for return the Buyer shall be liable to pay a handling charge of [10%] of the invoice price. Such Goods must be returned by the Buyer carriage-paid to the Seller in their original shipping carton.

0.3 Goods returned without the prior written approval of the Seller may at the Seller's absolute discretion be returned to the Buyer or stored at the Buyer's cost without prejudice to any rights or remedies the Seller may have.

Remedies in sale contract: additional and alternative provisions

A: GENERAL EXCLUSION OF SELLER'S LIABILITY FOR INDIRECT LOSS

The Seller shall be under no liability whatever to the Buyer for any indirect loss and/or expense (including loss of profit) suffered by the Buyer arising out of a breach by the Seller of this contract.

B: GENERAL LIMITATION OF SELLER'S LIABILITY

In the event of any breach of this contract by the Seller the remedies of the Buyer shall be limited to damages. Under no circumstances shall the liability of the Seller exceed the Price of the Goods.

Remedies in purchase contract: additional and alternative provisions

A: BUYER'S INDEMNITY AGAINST CLAIMS BY SUB-BUYERS

The Seller shall indemnify the Buyer against all claims by the customers of the Buyer and their sub-buyers arising out of any breach whatever by the Seller of this contract of sale [due to want to merchantable quality or lack of fitness for purpose of the Goods or any of the Goods].

B: OBLIGATION ON SELLER TO REPAIR OR MAKE REPLACEMENT OF DEFECTIVE GOODS EVEN AFTER THEY HAVE BEEN SUB-SOLD OR INSTALLED IN OTHER ASSEMBLIES

Without prejudice to the other rights of the Buyer for breach by the Seller where any of the Goods supplied to the Buyer are not in accordance with the contract the Seller shall at the option of the Buyer forthwith upon notice being given either repair or replace such Goods. If it is necessary to open up or dismantle any other works or assemblies to permit such repair or replacement then the Seller shall bear the cost of such opening up or dismantling and of re-assembly and making good after repairs, replacements and testing of such goods have been completed to the Buyer's reasonable satisfaction.

C: SELLER'S CLAUSE RELATING TO CLAIMS FOR DEFECTS, DAMAGE, LOSS OR NON-DELIVERY

0.1 The Buyer shall inspect the Goods on delivery and shall within [3] days of delivery notify the Seller of any alleged defect, shortage in quantity, damage or failure to comply with description or sample. The Buyer shall afford the Seller an opportunity to inspect the Goods within a reasonable time following delivery and before any use is made of them. If the Buyer shall fail to comply with these provisions the Goods shall be conclusively presumed to be in accordance with the contract and free from any defect or damage which would be apparent on a reasonable examination of the Goods and the Buyer shall be deemed to have accepted the Goods.

0.2 The Buyer shall notify the Seller of any non-delivery of a whole consignment of complete cartons within [14] days of the date of dispatch (as stated on the invoice). Notwithstanding the receipt by the Seller of any such notice a clear signature on a carrier's delivery advice sheet shall be deemed to signify receipt of the quantity of cartons indicated on the advice sheet.

0.3 If the Goods are not in accordance with the contract for any reason the Buyer's sole remedy shall be limited to the Seller making good any shortage by replacing such Goods or, if the Seller shall elect, by refunding a proportionate part of the Price.

0.4 The Seller's liability to the Buyer, whether for any breach of contract or otherwise, shall not in any event exceed the Price and the Seller shall be under no liability for any direct loss and/or expense or indirect loss and/or expense suffered by the Buyer or liability to third parties incurred by the Buyer.

0.5 All warranties and conditions whether implied by statute or otherwise are excluded from this contract Provided that nothing in this contract shall restrict or exclude liability for death or personal injury caused by the negligence of the Seller1 or affect the statutory rights of a buyer dealing as consumer.

Choice of law, jurisdiction and arbitration: additional and alternative provisions

A: THE LAW OF ENGLAND AND WALES TO APPLY AND THE COURTS OF ENGLAND AND WALES TO HAVE EXCLUSIVE JURISDICTION

0.1 This contract is subject to the law of England and Wales.

[0.2 All disputes arising out of this contract shall be subject to the [exclusive] jurisdiction of the courts of England and Wales.

or

The parties submit to the [exclusive] jurisdiction of the courts of England and Wales and irrevocably agree that proceedings issued out of the said courts may without prejudice to the rules of service of such courts be served on them by delivering such proceedings in an envelope addressed to the party to be served at the address for such party set out in this contract.]

B: ARBITRATION CLAUSE – SIMPLE FORM

0.1 This contract is subject to the law of England and Wales.

0.2 If any dispute or difference shall arise between the parties as to the meaning of this contract or any matter or thing arising out of [or connected with] this contract then it shall be referred to the determination of an arbitrator to be appointed by agreement of the parties or (in default of agreement within [21] days of the service upon one party of a written request to concur in such appointment) by the [President] for the time being of the [Chartered Institute of Arbitrators].

Passing of property and risk: additional and alternative provisions

A: SELLER'S RETENTION OF PROPERTY CLAUSE

0.1 The Goods shall be at the Buyer's risk as from delivery.

0.2 In spite of delivery having been made property in the Goods shall not pass from the Seller until:

0.2:1 the Buyer shall have paid the Price plus VAT in full; and

0.2:2 no other sums whatever shall be due from the Buyer to the Seller.

0.3 Until property in the Goods passes to the Buyer in accordance with clause [0.2] the Buyer shall hold the Goods and each of them on a fiduciary basis as bailee for the Seller. The Buyer shall store the Goods (at no cost to the Seller) separately from all other goods in its possession and marked in such a way that they are clearly identified as the Seller's property.

0.4 Notwithstanding that the Goods (or any of them) remain the property of the Seller the Buyer may sell or use the Goods in the ordinary course of the Buyer's business at full market value for the account of the Seller. Any such sale or dealing shall be a sale or use of the Seller's property by the Buyer on the Buyer's own behalf and the Buyer shall deal as principal when making such sales or dealings. Until property in the Goods passes from the Seller the entire proceeds of sale or otherwise of the Goods shall be held in trust for the Seller and shall not be mixed with other money or paid into any overdrawn bank account and shall be at all material times identified as the Seller's money.

0.5 The Seller shall be entitled to recover the Price (plus VAT) notwithstanding that property in any of the Goods has not passed from the Seller.

0.6 Until such time as property in the Goods passes from the Seller the Buyer shall upon request deliver up such of the Goods as have not ceased to be in existence or resold to the Seller. If the Buyer fails to do so the Seller may enter upon any premises owned occupied or controlled by the Buyer where the Goods are situated and repossess the Goods. On the making of such request the rights of the Buyer under clause [0.4] shall cease.

0.7 The Buyer shall not pledge or in any way charge by way of security for any indebtedness any of the Goods which are the property of the Seller. Without prejudice to the other rights of the Seller, if the Buyer does so all sums whatever owing by the Buyer to the Seller shall forthwith become due and payable.

0.8 The Buyer shall insure and keep insured the Goods to the full Price against 'all risks' to the reasonable satisfaction of the Seller until the date that property in the Goods passes from the Seller, and shall whenever requested by the Seller produce a copy of the policy of insurance. Without prejudice to the other rights of the Seller, if the Buyer fails to do so all sums whatever owing by the Buyer to the Seller shall forthwith become due and payable.

0.9 The Buyer shall promptly deliver the prescribed particulars of this contract to the Registrar in accordance with the Companies Act 1985 Part XII as amended. Without prejudice to the other rights of the

Seller, if the Buyer fails to do so all sums whatever owing by the Buyer to the Seller shall forthwith become due and payable.

Miscellaneous clauses for conditions of sale or purchase

A: CLAUSES REGARDING THE PROVISION BY ONE PARTY OF DRAWINGS, SPECIFICATIONS AND TOOLING TO FACILITATE PERFORMANCE OF THE CONTRACT

0.1 All specifications, patterns, drawings, photographs, samples and information provided by the Buyer to the Seller shall remain the exclusive property of the Buyer and shall not be disclosed by the Seller to any third party without the Buyer's written consent.

0.2 All moulds, tools, dies, fixtures, plant or other equipment provided by the Buyer to the Seller shall remain the exclusive property of the Buyer and shall be maintained in good order and condition while in the Seller's possession or control and shall be insured by the Seller in the name of the Buyer on an 'all risks' basis for their full replacement cost.

0.3 The Seller shall not use the Buyer's property referred to in clauses [0.1] and [0.2] above nor allow it to be used for any purpose other than the supply of Goods in accordance with the contract.

0.4 The Buyer shall clearly mark the Buyer's property so that it is clearly identified and identifiable as belonging to the Buyer and the Seller shall not deface, obliterate or remove such identifying marks. The Seller shall permit the Buyer to enter the premises where the Buyer's property is kept to inspect and/or take possession of the Buyer's property.

B: CLAUSES RELATING TO THE SUPPLY OF GOODS WHICH BEAR THE TRADE MARK OF THE SELLER

0.1 All goods sold in retail packaging may be resold by the Buyer only in the packaging supplied by the Seller and in no case may any trade mark other than those applied by the Seller be marked on or applied in relation to the Goods.

0.2 No right or licence is granted under this contract of sale to the Buyer under any patent, trade mark, copyright, registered design or other intellectual property right except the right to use or resell the Goods.

C: NOTICES

Any notice required to be served pursuant to this contract of sale shall be in writing and served by first class post or by hand on the Seller at *(Seller's address)* or such other address as the Seller may from time to time notify to the Buyer and on the Buyer at the Buyer's registered office or principal place of business.

D: INSOLVENCY OR OTHER DEFAULT OF BUYER

If the Buyer fails to make payment for the Goods in accordance with this contract of sale or commits any other breach of this contract of sale or if any distress or execution shall be levied upon any of the Buyer's goods or if the Buyer offers to make any arrangement with its creditors or commits an act of bankruptcy or if any petition in bankruptcy is presented against the Buyer or the Buyer is unable to pay its debts as they fall due or if being a limited company any resolution or petition to wind up the Buyer (other than for the purpose of amalgamation or reconstruction without insolvency) shall be passed or presented or if a receiver administrator administrative receiver or manager shall be appointed over the whole or any part of the Buyer's business or assets or if the Buyer shall suffer any analogous proceedings under foreign law all sums outstanding in respect of the Goods shall become payable immediately. The Seller may in its absolute discretion and without prejudice to any other rights which it may have:

0.1 suspend all future deliveries of Goods to the Buyer and/or terminate the contract without liability upon its part; and/or

0.2 exercise any of its rights pursuant to clause *(number of clause relating to the seller's retention of title)*.

E: SET-OFF AND COUNTERCLAIM: SELLER'S CLAUSE

The Buyer may not withhold payment of any invoice or other amount due to the Seller by reason of any right of set-off or counterclaim which the Buyer may have or allege to have or for any reason whatever.

F: SET-OFF AND COUNTERCLAIM: BUYER'S CLAUSE

The Buyer may set off against any sums due to the Seller whether under this contract of sale or otherwise any lawful set-off or counterclaim to which the Buyer may at any time be entitled.

G: BACK ORDERS: SELLER'S CLAUSE

The Seller shall be entitled to a general lien on all goods of the Buyer in the Seller's possession (including goods of the Buyer which have been paid for) for the unpaid price of all goods sold to the Buyer by the Seller under this or any other contract.

H: GENERAL CLAUSES FOR INCLUSION IN SUPPLY AGREEMENTS AND LONGER SALE AND PURCHASE CONTRACTS

0.1 Headings

All headings are for ease of reference only and shall not affect the construction of this contract.

0.2 Severance

Any provision of this contract which is or may be void or unenforceable shall to the extent of such invalidity or unenforceability be deemed severable and shall not affect any other provision of this contract.

0.3 Waiver

No waiver or forbearance by the [Seller *or* Buyer] (whether express or implied) in enforcing any of its rights under this contract shall prejudice its right to do so in the future.

0.4 Sub-contracting

[The Seller may licence or sub-contract all or any part of its rights and obligations under this contract without the Buyer's consent.

or

The Seller shall not assign sub-contract licence or otherwise dispose of any part of its rights or obligations under this contract without the prior written consent of the Buyer.]

I: FORCE MAJEURE CLAUSE

Neither party shall be liable for any default due to any act of God, war, strike, lockout, industrial action, fire, flood, drought, tempest or other event beyond the reasonable control of either party.

J: SELLER'S CANCELLATION CLAUSE

The Seller may cancel this contract at any time before the Goods are delivered by giving written notice. On giving such notice the Seller shall promptly repay to the Buyer any sums paid in respect of the Price. The Seller shall not be liable for any loss or damage whatever arising from such cancellation

K: BUYER'S CANCELLATION CLAUSE

The Buyer may cancel this contract at any time before all of the Goods are delivered by giving written notice. On giving such written notice:

0.1 the Seller shall cease to be bound to deliver and the Buyer shall cease to be bound to receive delivery of any further goods;

0.2 the Buyer shall cease to be bound to pay that part of the Price which relates to goods which have not been delivered;

0.3 the Buyer shall not be liable for any loss or damage whatever arising from such cancellation.

17b Credit account – application form

PLEASE ANSWER FULLY THE FOLLOWING:

If further space is required please use attached supplemental sheet

If you have any queries regarding any of the particulars requested please contact:

....

1 STATUS OF APPLICANT

(Please tick **ONE** box below)

Is The Applicant a

☐ LIMITED COMPANY

☐ PARTNERSHIP

☐ SOLE TRADER

OTHER
(please specify) ....

2 TO BE COMPLETED BY LIMITED COMPANIES

FULL NAME OF THE COMPANY:

OTHER NAMES WITH WHICH THE COMPANY HAS BEEN REGISTERED SINCE INCORPORATION:...

....

....

COMPANY REGISTRATION No*:...

REGISTERED OFFICE:...

....

FULL NAMES OF DIRECTORS:...

....

....

....

FULL NAME OF COMPANY SECRETARY:...

DETAILS OF ANY PERSONS OTHER THAN THE ABOVE WHO HAVE HELD OFFICE AS DIRECTOR OR SECRETARY WITHIN THE LAST [3] YEARS: (Please state why such person(s) ceased to hold office)

....

....

....

* This information will appear on the Company's Certificate of Incorporation and Certificate of Incorporation on Change of Name (if applicable)

3 TO BE COMPLETED BY SOLE TRADERS AND PARTNERSHIPS

Please supply the FULL NAME, HOME ADDRESS and TELEPHONE NUMBER of The Principal (SOLE TRADER) or EVERY PARTNER** in the Firm (PARTNERSHIPS)

NAME:..

HOME ADDRESS:..

....

Tel No...

NAME:..

HOME ADDRESS:..

....

Tel No...

NAME:..

HOME ADDRESS:..

....

Tel No...

IN ADDITION IN EACH CASE PLEASE GIVE PREVIOUS ADDRESS IF RESIDENT FOR LESS THAN TWO YEARS

DETAILS OF ANY PERSONS OTHER THAN THE ABOVE WHO HAVE BEEN PARTNERS IN THE FIRM WITHIN THE LAST [3] YEARS: (Please state why such person(s) ceased to be partners)

....

....

....

** Please include details of any 'silent partners'

4 ALL APPLICANTS TO COMPLETE

FULL TRADING NAME OF BUSINESS:...

BUSINESS ADDRESS:...

....

....

BUSINESS TELEPHONE NO:..

HOW LONG HAS THE APPLICANT TRADED UNDER THIS NAME:

....

ANY PREVIOUS TRADING NAMES USED IN THE LAST [3] YEARS:

....

....

....

DESCRIPTION OF BUSINESS:..

BANK DETAILS

BANK:...

BRANCH ADDRESS:...

BANK SORT CODE:..

BANK ACCOUNT NUMBER:..

NAME AND ADDRESS OF TWO TRADE REFERENCES (not associated companies):

REFERENCE 1:

NAME:...

ADDRESS:...

....

TEL NO:..

REFERENCE 2:

NAME:...

ADDRESS:...

....

TEL NO:..

ANTICIPATED CREDIT LIMIT REQUIRED

5 ALL APPLICANTS TO COMPLETE

[In respect of each of the individuals named in answer to the above questions please supply full details of:
any criminal convictions for an offence involving fraud or dishonesty:

....

....

any involvement in any capacity in any business which failed due to insolvency:

....

....

Please give full details of any other relevant facts which may affect your credit worthiness:

....

....

....]

We/I hereby apply for a Credit Account and agree to pay accounts within [30] days of the date of the relevant invoice.

[We/I have given full, true and accurate answers to the above and have made full disclosure of any factors that might affect the credit status of the Applicant. [*(where the Applicant is a limited company)* **I understand that this warranty shall be given both by the Applicant and by us/me personally]]**

We/I agree to operate our/my account in accordance with your Company's Conditions of Sale and agree that all transactions are entered into on the basis of these Conditions to the exclusion of all others. I understand that the current Conditions of Sale which have been supplied to me may be varied from time to time by the Company.

Signature of Applicants...

....

NAME IN BLOCK CAPITALS:...

POSITION IN COMPANY/FIRM:..

DATE:..

(using the headed notepaper of the supplier:)

Dear

Thank you for your recent application to open a credit account. May we draw your attention to our Conditions of Sale contained in the enclosed application form.

Subject to receipt and approval of your duly completed application form, acknowledging acceptance of our terms of trading, we will be pleased to commence operation of your credit account.

Yours faithfully

[director] for and on behalf of ....

18 Simple form of personal guarantee

THIS IS AN IMPORTANT DOCUMENT. SIGN ONLY IF YOU WANT TO BE LEGALLY BOUND. YOU ARE RECOMMENDED TO TAKE INDEPENDENT LEGAL ADVICE BEFORE SIGNING.

PERSONAL GUARANTEE

Parties

'the Creditor': Limited a corporation under the laws of registered under number having its registered office at

'the Debtor': a corporation registered under the laws of having its principal place of business at

'the Guarantor': of

and

of

Operative Provisions

1 In consideration of the Creditor agreeing to allow credit to supply goods from time to time to the Debtor at the request of the Guarantor the Guarantor hereby guarantees as a continuing guarantee the due payment on demand of all monies (including interest) at any time due and owing to the Creditor by the Debtor ('the Guaranteed Liabilities')

2 The Guarantor hereby agrees to pay the Creditor interest on amounts demanded under clause 1 from demand hereunder until payment in full at the rate of 2% per annum above the base rate for the time being of [ ]Bank Plc accruing on a daily basis together with all legal and other costs and expenses (on a full indemnity basis) arising out of or in connection with the recovery by the Creditor of the Guaranteed Liabilities under this guarantee

3 The Guarantor's liability hereunder will be a primary liability and is additional to and independent of any other security or guarantee held by the Creditor and the Creditor will not be required before claiming payment from the Guarantor to seek to enforce any other right or security or to avail itself of any legal remedies which it may have against the Debtor or any other person

4 The Guarantor's liabilities hereunder will not in any way be released, discharged, diminished or affected by:

4.1 the granting of time or indulgence to or the effecting of any compromise with or agreement not to sue the Debtor whether made with or without the Guarantor's assent or knowledge

4.2 any failure by the Creditor to give the Guarantor notice of any default by the Debtor or of any action taken by the Creditor

4.3 any variation made in the Creditor's arrangements or agreements with the Debtor whether or not the same are made with or without the Guarantor's assent or knowledge

4.4 any breach by the Creditor of any of its arrangements or agreements with the Debtor

4.5 anything which would not have released, discharged, diminished or affected the Guarantor's liability if the Guarantor had been a principal debtor, this being without prejudice to any other provision hereof

5 Any settlement or discharge between the Guarantor and the Creditor shall be conditional upon no security or payment to the Creditor by the Debtor or any other person being avoided or reduced by virtue of any provisions or enactments relating to bankruptcy or liquidation (or similar status in the Debtors' country of residence) for the time being in force and the Creditor shall be entitled to recover the value or amount of any such security or payment from the Guarantor subsequently as if such settlement or discharge had not occurred

6 This Guarantee shall be determinable as to future transactions by the Guarantor serving on the Creditor one month's notice in writing to that effect

7 Any notice or demand hereunder will be deemed to be well served if given personally or left at or sent by registered post or recorded delivery to the party on whom it is intended to be served at its registered office or at its last known address and shall be deemed to have been served 48 hours after the date of posting

8 Where there is more than one person comprised in the expression 'the Guarantor' covenants, undertakings, agreements and obligations undertaken by the Guarantor shall be given by such persons jointly and severally

9 This guarantee shall be governed in all respects in accordance with English law and the parties submit to the non-exclusive jurisdiction of the English courts

This guarantee has been executed as a deed on 199

SIGNED as a Deed by the said)
in the presence of:)

Witness signature:

Witness name:

Address:

Occupation:

SIGNED as a Deed by the said)
in the presence of:)

Witness signature:

Witness name:

Address:

Occupation:

19 Sample business stationery

Butterworths

Halsbury House 35 Chancery Lane London WC2A 1EL
Tel: 0171 400 2500 Fax: 0171 400 2842 DX London, Chancery Lane 1023

YOUR REF:
OUR REF:

DIRECT LINE:
DIRECT FAX:

SAMPLE

Butterworths is a division of Reed Elsevier (UK) Limited
Registered office 25 Victoria Street London SW1H 0EX Registered in England number 2746621

A member of the Reed Elsevier plc group

REED ELSEVIER

Direct line

Direct fax

SAMPLE

Reed Elsevier plc 25 Victoria Street London SW1H 0EX
Telephone +44 (0) 171 222 8420

Registered Office as above. Registered in England number 2746616

Index